# REVOLUTIONS, SYSTEMS, AND THEORIES

# THEORY AND DECISION LIBRARY

AN INTERNATIONAL SERIES

IN THE PHILOSOPHY AND METHODOLOGY OF THE

SOCIAL AND BEHAVIORAL SCIENCES

*Editors:*

GERALD EBERLEIN, *University of Technology, Munich*

WERNER LEINFELLNER, *University of Nebraska*

*Editorial Advisory Board:*

VOLUME 19

# REVOLUTIONS, SYSTEMS, AND THEORIES

## Essays in Political Philosophy

*Edited by*

H. J. JOHNSON, J. J. LEACH, *and* R. G. MUEHLMANN

*University of Western Ontario, Ontario, Canada*

D. REIDEL PUBLISHING COMPANY

DORDRECHT : HOLLAND / BOSTON : U.S.A.

LONDON : ENGLAND

Library of Congress Cataloging in Publication Data

Main entry under title:

Revolutions, systems, and theories.
    (Theory and decision library ; 19)
    Consists of 13 papers, 8 of which were originally presented at the
7th University of Western Ontario Philosophy Colloquium held Oct.
29–31, 1971.
    Includes bibliographical references and index.
    1.   Revolutions—Congresses.   2.   Political ethics—
Congresses.   I.   Johnson, Harold Joseph, 1919–      II.   Leach,
James J.   III.   Muehlmann, R. G.   IV.   University of Western
Ontario Philosophy Colloquium, 7th, 1971.
JC491.R493     321′.09    78–10889
ISBN 90–277–0939–4

# TABLE OF CONTENTS

# PREFACE

In spite of the seeming heterogeneity of topics in its title — *Revolutions, Systems, and Theories* — this volume purports to be something more than a random collection of *Essays in Political Philosophy*. The Colloquium of the Philosophy Department of the University of Western Ontario (29–31 October, 1971) at which initial versions of the first eight papers were delivered was entitled 'Political Theory'; and while the organizers anticipated and indeed welcomed topicality in the issues accorded priority and in the empirical evidence invoked, they were also hoping for a reasonably comprehensive exploration of some of the central issues of political philosophy. For this reason it was quickly decided that in such a field a philosophical focus on clarification of ordering concepts required the supplement — and test — of researches into more particular subject matters by social scientists. Thus, to speak in general terms (where the specializations and their taxonomies multiply fissiparously!), contributors include political scientists, economists and sociologists (Barnard, Easton, Tullock, Rapoport) as well as philosophers (Scriven, Morgenbesser, Braybrooke, Taylor), and juxtaposed as proponents and commentators to generate exchanges across disciplinary frontiers. While the five additional invited papers are all by professional philosophers, they extend the original Colloquium either by continuing controversy on its fundamental issues (e.g., Rubinoff, Nielsen, Roy) or by their continued explorations in what are acknowledged to be boundary areas (e.g., Schick, Wartofsky).

The greatest topical emphasis is that on revolution. Revolutions and their alarums have not been rare since World War II, ranging from palace coups, through anti-colonialist struggles of national liberation, to fundamental alterations by political means of entire socio-economic systems as in China and Cuba. At the same time concern over the disparity of living standards in the 'developed' and 'underdeveloped' worlds, anxieties about run-away depletion of resources and pollution of environment, high levels of unemployment combined with spiraling rates of inflation, *etc., etc.,* have created enormous dissatisfactions with 'the system' so that to many its rapid, radical, and possibly riotous transformation has come to seem a decidedly live option. But consideration of that live option likewise progressively draws in the perennial *aporiae* of political philosophy: the willingness to overthrow government

vii

implies the rejection of its legitimacy; the rival claims to legitimacy of governmental and anti-governmental activities of course involve the *raison d'être* of the political state; and — to sum up, and at the same time return to the words of our title — *revolutions* are made and resisted within *systems* (in at least some elastic meanings of the term), and systems are understood and evaluated in *theories*. So the challenge to government has dialectical advantages in concentrating attention towards the basic issues of political philosophy.

That umbrella claim to have touched the main bases, however, perhaps needs some verification by a survey of the articles themselves. Such a survey may also help a selective reader decide where he wants to begin.

Michael Scriven and Frederick Barnard discuss criteria for evaluating the desirability of revolution. Scriven interrupts his progressive and generally deflationary refinements to a formula of relevant variables with the problems of the 'happy slave' indifferent to the improved quality of life revolution might bring him, and concludes to the need for an education that fosters 'revolution in every sphere' but also 'the capacity to cope with it'. Barnard, citing 'the sheer heterogeneity of variables' finds Scriven's formulae premature in the absence of definitions and particularly such as would distinguish revolutions from 'incremental reformism' and 'Utopian vision'.

Broadening the discussion from revolution in particular to politics in general, David Easton and Sidney Morgenbesser debate the 'systems' approach. Easton defends its appropriateness to complex wholes characterized by goal-directed conduct and its responsiveness, as an admittedly abstract model, to the more immediately urgent demands of political life. Morgenbesser has difficulties with an approach that is explicitly 'behavioural' without being 'behaviouristic' and concludes that in the concentration on wholes and the acts they undergo, individuals as 'parts' of political life have all but dropped from sight.

Gordon Tullock and David Braybrooke return to the effort to develop formulae that would spot the variables determining individuals' participation in or resistance to revolutionary activity. Tullock finds that actual agents in revolutionary situations are likely to have perspectives quite different, more egoistic and usually more realistic as well, than those of external observers like historians and journalists on whom we habitually depend for evaluations and who tend to inflate the public benefit aspects. Braybrooke, citing especially the cases of Che Guevara and Alexander and Vladimir Ulianov (Lenin) finds it necessary to extend the formulae with a 'conscience' factor, an 'Other-Regarding No-Sucker Principle'.

The applicability of ethical standards to judgments of politics is the topic

of the exchange among Anatol Rapoport, Charles Taylor, and Lionel Rubinoff
(who was the interested but necessarily mainly silent Chairman of this ses-
sion). Rapoport uses the conception of ethics as 'incentives or restraints' on
conduct applied by 'approval or disapproval' of individuals and groups (rather
than 'imposed by authorities') to comment on politics as a profession (in
Western society strongly influenced by the model of the competitive entrepreneur), as a theory of legitimacy in the distribution of power (a legitimacy
paradoxically challenged in Western society not by exploited workers, but
*e.g.* by relatively affluent intelligentsia), and as a process of decision and
policy making (where the opposed attitudes of committed ideologists and
uncommitted positivists both tend — unfortunately — to discount ethical
evaluation). Taylor finds this an overly abstract characterization of ethics that
thereby misses real middle generality problems such as the unavoidable and
painful disparity between ethical ideals and political realities, a disparity dis-
guised by the qualitative homogenizations of utilitarians (for whom a sufficiently attractive end will justify any means) and terrorist-idealists (for whom
present realities are so obstructive of the ideal that any violence against them
is a contribution). Rubinoff suspects that the restriction of the concept of
rationality by social science to the efficiency of means tends to substitute
whatever the means can successfully produce for the ends that might have
been chosen by a rational consideration of man's moral nature and meta-
physical status in the world.

Frederic Schick is interested in extending the concept of the political
state as a system for translating individual preferences into collective policies
by more responsively taking account of our many preferences dependent on
the fulfillment of certain conditions, but he realistically balances off greater
sensitivity to preference profiles with 'effectiveness' in settling on policies
broadly acceptable in meeting our most unconditional needs.

Marx Wartofsky worries about the discipline of political philosophy and its
relation to politics itself, for on the one hand even in the relativity insulated
setting of the university the subject matter of philosophical theorizing is significantly determined by the larger political world (as the emphasis on revolution in this collection itself might illustrate), but on the other that responsiveness to the practical may foster for political theorists the 'mystification' that
in resolving conceptual difficulties, they are themselves performing the essential tasks of politics.

Finally in the exchange between Kai Nielsen and Jean Roy we return to
the choice between revolution and its alternatives, and more specifically to
how such choice might determine or be determined by definitions of terms

such as 'revolution', 'reform' or 'social transformation'. Nielsen finds a continuum in the radicality of political change so that there is neither an essential dividing line between reform and revolution nor, considering the rival persuasions of Popper and Marcuse, a general non-contextual rule as to which ought to be chosen. Roy feels that the conceptual insistence on what appears to be an empirically empty class, that of non-violent revolutions, skews the analysis: in any revolutions yet to come to Western society he seeks some assurance that certain values of liberal democracy will be regarded as permanent acquisitions of political evolution.

If that is not the ocean, it is at least a thorough immersion.

H. J. JOHNSON
J. J. LEACH
R. G. MUEHLMANN

# ACKNOWLEDGEMENTS

As always in projects of even this magnitude, those whose names appear on title pages are indebted to a great many whose names do not. And especially after sensitization by a subject matter like *Political Theory*, acknowledgement of such essential debts to institutions and persons should be made explicit. The editors gratefully acknowledge:

Professors Yvon Blanchard of Faculté de Philosophie, l'Université de Montréal and T. M. Lennon, Department of Philosophy at University of Western Ontario for assistance in translating Professor Roy's commentary from French. They can be thanked for many improved renderings, but not blamed for my final editorial decisions.

Professor David Braybrooke for undertaking to standardize the symbolism in the papers of Scriven, Tullock and Braybrooke.

Professor Kai Nielsen and Universitets Forlaget, Oslo, publishers of *Inquiry*, for permission to reprint the article 'On the Choice between Reform and Revolution'.

The secretaries of the Department of Philosophy, University of Western Ontario (and to those who showed the good sense of hiring them), especially Mrs. Fran Aird, Mrs. Alice Smith, and Mrs. Eleanor Sever.

And Canada.

H.J.J.

MICHAEL SCRIVEN

# THE EVALUATION OF REVOLUTIONS

1. The naive person, contemplating social reforms, thinks that they are justified if the end-state, $E$, is better than the initial state $I$, i.e., if

$$E > I.$$

2. A more reflective person realizes[1] that the inequality must include reference to the cost of the reform, $C_R$, and action will only be justified if

$$E > I + C_R.$$

A consequence of this is that small reforms of large societies are usually unjustifiable because $C_R$ is so large. Another lemma is that small, flexible, societies can reap the benefits of improvements that are 'inaccessible' to larger ones.

3. It might be argued against the consequences of (2) just mentioned that even a small reform will *eventually* accumulate enough credit to pay off any $C_R$. Realism requires another refinement of the basic formula. There is a well-known tendency for reforms to become rigidities, for reformers to become repressors, and thus for revolution to create new costs — in short, the gains are not to be counted on as constants. The two states, $I$ and $E$, must be regarded as variable over time. Treating the cost of reform as one-shot, we get;

$$\int_{t_1}^{\infty} E(t) \ dt > \int_{t_0}^{\infty} I(t) \ dt + C_R,$$

where reform occurs over the period $(t_1 - t_0)$.

A common pattern in revolution is the take-over by a new group which nationalizes some large industries — thereby giving the economy a significant shot in the arm — makes some useful changes such as land-reform, and then starts going down hill. Here, we may suppose, the ultimate end-state approximates the initial state and the crucial balance is between the blood in the streets and a few years' bread.

Thus a realistic form of the formula can reasonably cut off the calculations after a relatively modest period, say by $t_2$:

1

H. J. Johnson, J. J. Leach, and R. G. Muehlmann (eds.), Revolutions, Systems, and Theories, 1–9. All Rights Reserved.

$$\int_{t_1}^{t_2} E(t)\ dt > \int_{t_0}^{t_2} I(t)\ dt + C_R,$$

where, to be more exact, it is supposed that

$$C_R = \int_{t_0}^{t_1} C_R(t)\ dt, \quad t_2 - t_1 \gg t_1 - t_0.$$

Notice that if the peculiar stringencies of the revolution continue for long (as they often do, with suspension of all civil rights, etc.) $C_R$ may begin to creep up on the prospective gains, since $t_2$ — the date of deterioration to a pre-revolutionary overall quality of life — is often not a very distant date.

4. Unfortunately, the view from the plaza doesn't coincide with that from the balcony. The short years of benefit for the people may not outweigh the loss of lives and liberties. But they may be quite long enough to transfer a few millions over to those numbered accounts in Switzerland, and *that* big prize fuels many fiascos. A have-not's evaluation of the benefits to the people, of a revolution that will certainly give him power and wealth, are unlikely to be objective. Nor are those who have the power now, and would lose it, any better candidates for judge. The hope lies in an informed populace, with a strong tradition of assassination of their betrayers. It is remotely possible that the statistically significant correlation between shoddy revolutions and universities without intellectual freedom may reflect the inhibitory influence of good higher education on cheap coups d'état rather than the bad effects of politicized campuses.

The same formula applies for revolutionary leaders with purely selfish interests — but the calculations are based on pay-off for the subgroup seizing power rather than for the people.

Recognition of the regressive tendencies in reform movements, then, eliminates the argument that *every* significant gain in $E$ will be worth a high $C_R$ since one will *eventually* recoup any finite $C_R$ over the $\int_{t_0}^{\infty}$.

But there is a far more serious problem about the evaluation of revolutions, or the need for them than any we have so far considered, and the stage is now almost set for introducing it. We need one more refinement.

5. Reforms, and particularly revolutions, are often accompanied by a 'change of consciousness'. Indeed, they are sometimes impossible without such a change, at least on the part of the revolutionaries. For there are times when a

repressive regime can guarantee that rational calculations of risk, relative to the ordinary citizen's utility-distribution, make the attempt to revolt a very poor option. Only if he undergoes a radical transformation of his basic attitudes can the formula give a different answer. Madness will do that, and so will three classical traumas; falling in love, religious conversion, and revolutionary inspiration.

It is necessary to insert probabilities into the formula to represent these choice situations adequately.

The would-be revolutionary chooses between acting and inaction. If he acts, he may or may not succeed, with probability $p$. If he tries and fails, he (or his group, or the country) will be likely, with conditional probability $p'$, to pay a special price $C'$ (we drop the subscripts on $C$, and let $E$ and $I$ represent the more exact integrals.) So the expectations of gain from acting are

$$p(E-C) - (1-p)(I-p'C')$$

and he should act if this outweighs the expectations from inaction, $I$. (We can assume that success will definitely have the cost $C$, so we do not modify that with a further probability.) Notice that the crucial question for the revolutionary is not whether $p>1-p$ (i.e., $p>\frac{1}{2}$), or $E>I$, or even $p(E-C)>(1-p)(I-p'C')$, but whether the difference is greater than $I$ itself, which is typically a significant positive quantity. (This conclusion, if correct, is about the first non-obvious one the formalism has generated). The establishment, or the counter-revolutionary, can make the prospect of revolution unattractive by *increasing* the size of the elements, $I$, $C$, $C'$, $p'$ or *decreasing* the size of $E$ and $p$, all corresponding to fairly obvious courses of action, with one possible exception. It might appear that a government cannot control $E$. But it can, or it can act in a way that has the same effect.

6. A change of consciousness is a re-evaluation of the welfare currency we presuppose in talking about $I(t)$ and $E(t)$, and it is of great importance to both revolutionaries and the establishment. It appears to have three effects of particular significance for our present purposes. It can harness the forces of martyrdom for the revolution, it can make a revolution obligatory without any change in the 'objective' situation, and it can make a revolution appear successful when it was 'objectively' a disaster.

These possibilities are separable from one referred to in the last section, which concerns the exploitation of the gap between $E$ (or $I$) and the *perception* of $E$ (or $I$) by the populace (etc.). A government that ruthlessly controls the educational system and the media can cut off visions of possible utopias

(*E*), details of significant improvements elsewhere (*E* & *C*), and knowledge of the machinery of revolution (*p'*, *C'*). And it can feed in adulatory material about its own country (*I*), and the efficacy of its own police (*p*). The combination must have a massive effect on the intuitive perception of the rationality of revolution. Such services can be individualized in the process originally referred to as brain-washing.

7. Corruption of perceptions by limiting or distorting the information-intake is significantly different from changing consciousness, however. When a woman or a Cherokee or a Japanese-American comes to realize the nature and extent of the oppression that has affected them, they are coming to perceive reality correctly, not incorrectly. They are, typically, involved in the *reversal*, the *undoing*, the *dissolution* of a corrupted perception. In the light of these new perceptions, however, certain features of their environment now appear abrasive, even unbearable, that were previously not only tolerated, but appreciated — for example, in the case of women, being 'looked after', being 'spared from financial worries'. As they now see the world, it is worth a struggle to change it. As they were, it was not. But the struggle may be long and hard, it may not be successful, the intervening period will be one during which the abrasiveness persists, and failure will provide a second poison in the air around. Would it not be better to restrain one's consciousness, at least to let others do the fighting? Many of the sisters and brothers that do not join these movements have a powerful intuitive awareness of this point, to the sorrow and often despair of the activists.

WHO IS RIGHT?

8. The two most venerable ancestors of this issue are the paradoxes of (a) the happy slave (b) the rational justification of morality.

(a) Isn't a happy slave better off than a discontented slave-owner? If not, how can you prove it to him? (And if you can't, how valuable is the point?) If he is, why should he undertake a perilous and unhappy struggle to change the system?

(b) A rational justification of morality cannot begin by assuming the merits of the moral life, for that would be circular. On the other hand, it cannot proceed by showing that the moral life is nothing more than prudence for the rational but selfish man, for that would be a *reductio ad absurdum* (i.e., if morality reduces to that, it isn't morality; a defining feature of morality being that it calls for transcendence of selfishness).

9. If the slave is already highly moral, i.e., values justice, etc., then the basic formula will give low $I$, high $E$, and may make revolt mandatory. But — one would suppose — it would also mean being unhappy at the injustice around one. So the fact that the slave is happy shows he's not too hung up on justice. Or — a most important alternative — that he can segregate his disaffection, smiling by day and digging at night.

I can only think of two other lines of argument to the non-moral slave. One is to focus on the appropriate comparison, which is with himself given freedom, not with his unhappy master who has freedom. We may suppose that the slave has performed better in overcoming life's handicaps than his master and this may well continue to be so if he gains freedom and a wage. It is likely that we can at least prove $E - I \gg 0$, and begin to look at other parameters. $C'$, of course, is going to be a hurdle since it often means death.

The only other line of argument is that leading to adoption of the moral attitude itself, from which point considerations of justice may — we cannot say must — lead on to revolt.

10. The rational justification of morality is only paradoxical as long as one assumes that attitudes of the selfish listener are themselves beyond evaluation or beyond alteration. Morality is indeed more than enlightened self-interest — in one sense. The argument for it, however, consists in showing that enlightened self-interest must lead to valuing others. (That is, enlightened *purely* selfish interest cannot be an optimal long-run strategy.) It is an argument for changing, not the selfish man's *behavior* — still evaluated with respect to the currency of selfish interest — but his currency.

Virtue is its own reward only for a virtuous man. That reward can be reaped by a selfish man if he can bring himself to value virtue. Of course, by so doing he will cease to be a selfish man. But he has not ceased to be rational, and he began by being selfish. So we can, in principle, produce a rational argument that converts a selfish man to morality. Since it would also apply to the considerations of a moral man who was considering changing *his* basic values, it establishes the superiority of morality, without paradox. Of course, the whole argument involves several other components designed to show that the gains from a currency shift are enough to swing the balance. Only one of these is considered at all here — details of the rest are given in *Primary Philosophy* (McGraw Hill, 1966).

11. Thus one route for the apostle of revolution seeking converts is to appeal to or increase the purely moral sensitivities of his listeners. (Lenin's fifth rule

for revolutionaries was precisely this.) But this may be a discouraging route
and it is all too attractive to exploit jealousy, envy, the desire for mere power
or labile hostility. The cost of *that* pathway is the counter-revolution. Often
the idealist is used as a front to carry the masses and then is slaughtered in a
palace revolution by the masters of intrigue — the Lenin/Trotsky model.
(After all, Lenin had four *other* rules.) And there is also a more moral pathway to the counter-revolution, as we shall see.

The crucial attitude-shift in revolutionary dynamics is thus double-edged.
In almost every case, the commitment (the change of consciousness) that is
the means of success undercuts it later. There *are* cases where the revolutionary is *only* motivated by selfish considerations. But this is often not enough.
Now those prepared for martyrdom have devalued their own lives by comparison with achieving the end-state they see as right and just; and once having done this, they have lower tolerance for deviations from that end-state
even (or perhaps especially) when authored by erstwhile allies. This applies
to the entirely moral revolutionary as well as the somewhat committed power-
seeker. But the former is at least open to acceptance of an equitable solution,
which has a better chance of general acceptance than any other. In a wide
range of situations, that is the optimal solution, i.e., the one most likely to be
achieved and be stable. There are fewer, but of course some, cases where the
power-seeker will settle and the moralist will not.

12. If the revolutionary, in addition to his relative de-emphasis of self-preser-
vation (whether or not for partly selfish reasons) can also achieve a value shift
towards the necessity for the acceptance of compromise within a basically
improved framework, then the revolutionary organization has some chance of
survival after success. But the change of consciousness (values) that is most
useful for successful revolution may only be hatred of the oppressors, i.e.,
those who are the powerful and ruthless; and that transfers immediately to
the revolutionary government if they act unjustly (in the eyes of this individual).

Those who let slip the dogs of civil war take a highly irreversible step. The
cost, *win or lose*, will be high for a long time, since the new attitudes are
usually only oriented towards change, not a better stability.

And thus those whose unresponsiveness to just demands precipitates the
conversion of protesters into revolutionary martyrs — what other way to
justice if the establishment will not reform unless forced to do so? — are
doubly guilty. Not only are they unjust, but they are unjust in a context
where the penalty for all from continued injustice may well be gross social

disruption. Every exploitation, indeed every petty corruption becomes loaded with its contribution towards a final reaction by the camel of the people for some more of whom this sordid story will prove to be the last straw.

13. The only moderately interesting theory of revolution which attributes them to the frustration of rising expectations, is critically involved with this re-evaluation process. But its emphasis is mainly on economic expectations. No less is it true of political or moral ones. If you teach people about principles (of their democracy), you create an expectation which you can then ignore only at increasing peril.

14. The extension of the paradox of the happy slave to revolutionary contexts might be called the paradox of artificial progress. If we raise the consciousness of the oppressed to the point where a revolution becomes a reasonable procedure for enough of them to pull it off, and if the costs are high, the pay-off may only outweigh the costs if measured in the new currency. "The people as whole", we may conclude, "would have been better off under the old regime". This is the 'those trouble-makers' line – and it can't be laughed off if the welfare of the people is really of interest, and not just grasping the reins of power, vicariously or otherwise.

It can not be handled satisfactorily by merely asserting that the new regime is more just or more democratic. Freedom of speech comes far below freedom to eat, even though the Bolsheviks used that point to justify horrors.

15. One must instead go back to the foundations upon which the argument for the revolution should be based, and on which the moral considerations are ultimately founded. At what level can this be done? If the 'slaves' were enjoying life to some extent, would not an increase in their *expectancy* of life be of value to them, even if they are not aware that this has occurred? Yes, but surely this would be an 'objective' improvement, even if not a conscious one. The problem is with changes of which they are conscious but which are not objective.[2] To starve free is a poor substitute for eating well as a slave, is it not? *Only if* you do not believe in the *power* of equality. The argument for a just society is an argument that it is more powerful and more flexible from being just – and that means it's more likely to survive in the long run. It's worth a little hunger now to be sure you eat *something* later.

16. The evangelical Christian who argues that the outsider cannot possibly appreciate the Christian life is suggesting a change of consciousness, too –

what he calls the "leap of faith". Today one hears the same call coming from proselytizers for the Eastern faiths. One may concede in advance that one might find happiness by burying one's reason in the joys of holy communion. But the objective correlative is missing; one's reason is a barometer of future storms and its messages are not just sad but sometimes sound. One can break the barometer and enjoy the euphoria only so long as the hurricane stays away.

17. Thus one might see an analogy between the arguments for a just war, that say morality has a place even in the holocaust, and the epistemological or methodological counterparts which persuade us that reason must be retained even when assessing changes in the passions to which it is a slave. Rationality provides one of the pricks against which the revolutionary wishes to kick. It is not surprising that anti-rational movements have so much support today. But the pricks of reason he has to accommodate, for they represent the only unchangeable element in reality.

There is a sense of 'reason' that means or implies moderation. I do not refer to that sense. There is thought to be a sense which equates it with the values and prejudices of the academy today. Such an identification is absurd. There is indeed a sense in which the full life must go beyond reason. But I speak only of a stricter sense when I say that revolution within reason is the only kind from which justice can come. It may be violent; it may reject most of our most precious values; it may be foreign to the processes that logicians have studied. But if it has any sense to it, it retains reason. Reason is the sense of reality, the enemy of nonsense, the content of sense.

18. It follows that education for revolution is possible. For the framework of sensible thought can be taught − and the many structures that have so far been built upon it can be exhibited and analyzed for the wisdom we can acquire from them − not worshipped as we have supposed too often in our curricula. Education for survival is indeed education for revolution. The problem is objectivity in judging the effects and probabilities in the revolutionary formula, the problem of exploring new styles of life or modes of consciousness (as well as old). The problems of *devising* new solutions and inventions are problems around which we need to concentrate our efforts and our programs. We need to foster revolution in every sphere, and the capacity to cope with it. It is not a tradition-*oriented* task − but in a sense it is a traditional one, within the tradition (at least) of Socrates. One interpretation of Mao's contribution to revolutionary thought would have it that *his* lesson is the

necessity for perpetual revolution.[3] Not many in the academy are equipped for this mental Maoism – they are more inclined to view with alarm. But they *can* be replaced and they *will* retire and we *may* have that much time.

19. If we do have that much time and we do undergo the change of consciousness that I see as necessary for survival, the change towards openness to new forms, the change towards distinguishing the substance of reason from the happenings of our time, what will be the effect on the revolutionary outside the establishment? For many observers, this outcome will be seen as cooptation. For many revolutionaries, it will be seen as frustration. These reactions confuse form with function; the function of a revolutionary is to get things changed with no holds barred. That the form involves a massive transfer of power or the shape of institutions seems to me irrelevant, common but not necessary.

*University of California, Berkeley*

## NOTES

[1] I recall Kurt Baier making this point to me in 1951.

[2] The most interesting discussion I have ever had on revolution convinced me that no conclusive case can be made for 'objective' gains by the people in the major revolutionary paradigms, especially the French and Russian ones. Reasonable extrapolation of industrialization trends and analogies makes the outcome quite dubious.

[3] *The Economist* 1–14–67, quoted by Dennis Goulet in 'The Troubled Conscience of the Revolutionary', *The Center Magazine*.

FREDERICK M. BARNARD

# THE EVALUATION OF REVOLUTIONS

## A Comment on Michael Scriven's Paper

Revolutions are real enough occurrences; this both the 'naive person' and the 'more reflective person' (Scriven's terms) might readily agree upon. But there are all kinds of revolutions. People speak of scientific revolutions, of cultural revolutions, of industrial revolutions, of social revolutions, as well as of political revolutions. And, naive or reflective, a person may well be at a loss for an answer if pressed to determine what these 'revolutions' conceivably have in common. Presumably, however, *this* problem need not be surmounted, since the context in which Professor Scriven's paper was presented was that of political theory. I advisedly say 'presumably' since it is not always clear whether his paper is indeed chiefly concerned with the evaluation of *political* revolutions. There are a number of occasions when he talks of 'social reforms' and 'revolutions' as if these were interchangeable terms. Here and there he also appears to suggest that, somehow, the gaining of political power is not really what political revolutions are about. And, as to violence, he is at best ambivalent. Consequently, neither the naive person, nor the more reflective person is in a position at times to know *what* precisely is being evaluated.

I

Admittedly 'revolution', even confined to the political area, is a slippery concept. Any definition is bound to be a stipulative one. Nonetheless, the stipulation of at least some criteria in terms of which one might approach the problem of identifying what is being evaluated could help to lessen confusion. In this direction a few distinctions would certainly be instructive. Would it not, for example, he helpful to be told to whom the 'we' refers when *we* are said to be evaluating an event identified (let us assume) as a revolution? Does it refer to participants or observers, to those who lead as distinct from those who follow, to participants or observers assessing a revolution prospectively, or retrospectively? How much clearer are we on any of these distinctions by merely being informed that "the view from the plaza doesn't coincide with that of the balcony"? (Section 4) Similarly, the transfer of "a few millions over to those numbered accounts in Switzerland" (*ibid.*) does not disclose to the naive or the more reflective person if this was the main purpose of the

11

H. J. Johnson, J. J. Leach, and R. G. Muehlmann (eds.), Revolutions, Systems, and Theories, 11–19. All Rights Reserved.

revolution or one of its (intended or unintended) by-products. Surely, one ought to attempt to distinguish – at least in principle – between *sequences*, i.e., those occurrences that follow a revolution over time, and *consequences*, i.e., those occurrences that were clearly caused by a revolution.

Though certain demands for social change may indeed decisively mobilize men into revolutionary action, it does by no means follow that social reforms of a variety of sorts, say, penal reforms, sanitary improvements, economic or educational changes, require a revolution for their implementation. Yet by treating social reform and political revolution as if they were pretty much the same thing (Section 5), Scriven gives rise to the misconception that the cost of the former is easily comparable with the cost of the latter. This, obviously, cannot be the case if by 'revolution' we understand – at least in the political realm – the (frequently violent) *replacement* of an existing regime, because in order to evaluate its cost we would have to take into account *both* the destructive aspects of the negation of the status quo and the constructive aspects of creating the alternative order. I am not suggesting, of course, that the question concerning the cost of these two-fold processes can easily be resolved. I am merely suggesting that computing the cost of a revolution is quite a different question from that pertaining to social reforms *per se*, where the assumption of destruction (partial or total) is scarcely warranted. But if the very basis of comparison in evaluating the cost of change in each case is seriously in doubt, is it very meaningful to urge existing power holders to measure the cost of embarking on social reforms against the cost involved in a revolution? Moreover, apart from the problem of a "currency shift" (Section 10) which clearly raises imponderables of an almost intractable kind, one cannot ignore the not-uncommon experience that revolutionaries prove themselves to be utterly incapable of bringing about any reforms, in view of the considerable gap between the skills needed to seize the reins of power and the skills needed for the constructive application of power. If this is so, it *fundamentally* questions the applicability of cost-benefit analysis to the evaluation of political revolutions, as distinct from the applicability of the notion of "calculation" to revolutionary strategy about which more will be said below.

II

Professor Scriven uses the symbol '$E$' to denote the 'ultimate end-state' of revolutions, but he does not tell us from what historical vantage point such an *ultimate* end-state is to be evaluated. Even if we assume that he possibly means the intended or anticipated end-state, we are still faced with the problem of what calculus we are to apply. Surely, any calculation can only accommodate probabilities, i.e., consequences that, with the knowledge available, can reasonably be expected to occur. This means that we are forced to exclude an indefinite range of 'improbabilities' from our reckoning. Yet, since improbabilities are merely such because they are not expected, we might well rule out what in point of fact could decisively determine the 'end-state', for nothing is less uncommon than the totally unexpected. If I am correct in what I am saying, only an inordinate faith in the operation of self-fulfilling prophecies can underpin an evaluation of anticipated end-states. Perhaps Prof. Scriven wholly agrees with me here, but this is not evident — at least to me — from his formulae.

However, by focusing on costs as well as ends, Prof. Scriven points up an important consideration, the consideration of *responsibility*. Revolutionaries, whatever their ends, have political responsibilities like any other contenders for political power. Moral concerns apart, they have to weigh the pay-off or consequences of the strategy which they employ in the promotion of their political ends. This being so is not, however, the same as saying that they have a choice "between acting and inaction." (Section 5) A revolutionary is, by definition, committed to action. His choice, therefore, merely lies between different paths of action, and it is here that calculation as to the most effective matching of means to ends looms prominently in the strategy of revolutionary elites. The range of options will, to be sure, also hinge on factors which lie outside ideological and organizational parameters set by the elites. Revolutions occur in given socio-historical settings, and thus the situation itself, in particular the responses of existing authorities, will drastically affect the revolutionaries' choice of tactics, especially the resort to violence. Wherever a regime is in disarray this will undoubtedly favour revolutionary designs (of seizing power) and where chaos does not exist it may well be worth creating. Nonetheless, a revolutionary elite's ability to blend ideological and organizational requirements in such a way that they succeed in effectively shaping events rather than being overtaken by them may appreciably decide the outcome in a situation of 'crisis'. Even then, the seizure of governmental power is only the beginning of a revolution and, by itself, a fragile indicator of the revolutionary regime's political viability and its capacity to transform ideological slogans into operational policies.

But whatever the eventual fortunes of a revolutionary *regime*, no revolutionary *struggle* is politically meaningful if its ends do not entail the acquisition of governmental power. To talk, therefore, of "entirely moral revolutionaries" (Section 11), that is, of revolutionaries who merely cherish moral ends without any concern for their political realization, is to commit a category mistake of the first order. To employ such a phrase is to becloud political reality. For an *entirely* moral revolutionary is of necessity a political fiction, an actor in the purely theatrical sense. A revolutionary who does not seek political power will not know what to do with it if it is presented to him on a silver platter. This was evident enough in 1968, during the student riots in Paris — in spite of the virtual break-down of governmental power — and I suspect much the same would hold for student riots in West Germany or North America. No less misleading, though perhaps even more politically naive, is Scriven's nebulous plea for an "education for revolution" (Section 18). But then I cannot really pretend to understand what he is talking about when he urges "revolution in every sphere, and the capacity to cope with it" (*ibid.*). Maybe he is no longer thinking about political revolutions at all.

## III

Violence is of course a crucial variable in the evaluation of political revolutions. Though the attempt to define precisely the concept of violence may prove futile, this does not justify the superficial treatment it receives in Scriven's paper. One would like to know, for example, if he regards violence as the sole variable, or, if so or not, whether he views it as a dependent or independent variable. One would also like to know in what sense he envisions the applicability of 'rationality' and 'morality' to violence. This would not only help to shed light on his conception of violence, it would also sharpen one's grasp of the categories of rationality and morality in the context in which he uses them and, indeed, purports to join them.

Some distinctions are once again clearly called for. Let us suppose that violence (however defined) is so firmly embedded in a given revolutionary ideology that it is thought of not merely as a strategic option but as an intrinsic value commitment, departure from which would spell the demise of the movement, or, conversely, as in the case of non-violent resistance, that violence is ruled out at all costs. Whether or not these opposite value commitments are attributable to the prevailing socio-political culture of a given society does not concern us here. What does concern us is the applicability of the notions of rationality or irrationality to either value commitment as evaluational criteria. As I see it, there is no *intrinsic* meaning assignable to 'rationality' or 'irrationality' in such ultimate value commitments. Whatever meaning is assigned to these categories will be extrinsic; it will, that is, derive not from the actor's own value position but from that of an external observer in accordance with *his* 'currency' of values. Prof. Scriven does not set forth any objective criteria of rationality as an ultimate value (in the sense that Max Weber speaks of *Wertrationalität*), but judging from what he does say towards the end of his paper one might surmise that he assumes them to exist. Unfortunately, his remarks on this point are so vague that one can surmise almost anything.

Next we would wish to know what, if any, objective criteria of rationality could be applied when violence is used merely as an instrumentality. Presumably in such an event, it is the effectiveness of violence as a means of furthering revolutionary ends (Weber's *Zweckrationalität*) that is likely to serve as a basis of evaluation. Presumably, too, this is feasible only *ex post facto*. Yet even then the degree of objectivity attainable seems limited; disagreements about the most effective means are not as a rule purely factual or 'technical'; and in the absence of demonstrable proof about the inexorable linkage of means and ends, whatever consensus emerges as to the rationality of violence as a means will invariably hinge on variables other than violence that impinge on revolutionary strategy. Be that as it may, the *content* of rationality, understood in the instrumental sense, begs all sorts of possible questions and is almost as elusive as that of rationality conceived as an ultimate value.

Thirdly, if violence and non-violence, conceived as instrumentalities or ultimate values, do not by themselves disclose the evaluational significance of such other variables as concern for legality, moral legitimacy, publicity, popular support, ideological principles, or organizational structure, it would seem to follow that there is no reason to suppose that violence is indicative of the intensity of moral righteousness felt or voiced by revolutionaries, or of their mass following, or their ideological aspirations. To concede, therefore, that some or all of these variables may at times be found closely inter-related is not the same as to say that they are thus *inherently* related. In principle, but also in practice, they appear to constitute independent rather than dependent variables.

Finally, the notion of morality is not one whit less problematical in the evaluation of revolutions than the notion of rationality. In a purely formal (and tautological) sense all revolutionary designs are 'moral' in so far as they involve categorical claims to rightness, just as they are also 'rational' in so far as their normative justifications constitute *reasons*. More bread, freedom, justice, stability, unity, national independence, law and order, abortions on demand, or whatever, may be advanced by revolutionaries as ends amelioratively superior to the status quo in the terminology of ethical or prudential 'oughts'. But once again the moral evaluation of such revolutionary claims poses the question of *what* precisely is being evaluated, *when*, and *by whom*. Is it revolutionary rhetoric or practice, before or after the seizure of power, from what historical vantage point, and from what perspective, that of the participant or of the hypothetical observer?

Prof. Scriven does not seem bothered with such considerations. Instead he strings together a set of statements which apparently are designed to demonstrate the possibility of deriving from 'rational argument' objective evaluative criteria for the assessment of moral gains (if any) resulting from revolutionary action. (Section 10) He sees the crucial problem in the conversion of a rational but 'selfish' man into a rational but 'virtuous' man. Rightly enough, he postulates a 'currency shift' as the *sine qua non* for the emergence of a 'moral attitude', but he fails to show by what 'rational' process this is to be brought about. In other words, what constitutes the very core of the problem − the change in the 'currency' of value in terms of which 'gains' are to be measured − remains a completely unknown, if not unknowable, variable, a veritable *deus ex machina*, which simply cannot be accounted for. As a result we are not only left in the dark about the 'currency' in terms of which costs and benefits are equated in the original formula, but we are also no wiser about the 'currency shift' introduced into the 'refined' formula. One scarcely resolves a question by begging it further.

## IV

I shall not dwell at any length on what may be termed a 'revolutionary condition', but it does seem somewhat loose to identify it simply with a situation in which 'enough of them' (those who consider themselves oppressed) think they can "pull it off" (Section 14). For, clearly, whatever the 'objective conditions' are that make a revolution probable, if not inevitable (or, in Scriven's words, "a reasonable procedure"), they are not necessarily or chiefly a question of numbers. But perhaps this is not what Prof. Scriven means and hence there is no point in pursuing this question further. But I might in this connection return to the problem of evaluating revolutionary 'gains'.

Whether rendered more likely after a period of rising expectations and a subsequent period in which they are frustrated, or, as Tocqueville believed, during periods of amelioration, or, as Marx held, after an escalation of misery and social degradation, or, as Burke maintained, when they become a necessity that is not chosen but chooses, revolutions are scarcely going to benefit all the people; the gains (irrespective of the costs) will hardly be total. Even to speak of partial gains makes sense only − as I have argued earlier − in terms of the evaluator's own hierarchy of values. Burke, for example, computing the gains of the French Revolution, was in no doubt that "France has bought undignified calamities at a higher price than any nation has purchased the most unequivocal blessings! France has bought poverty by crime! France has not sacrificed her virtue to her interest; but she has abandoned her interest, that she might prostitute her virtue." (*Reflections on the Revolution in France*, Todd, ed., New York, 1962, p. 43.) Another contemporary, the German thinker Johann Gottfried Herder, by contrast, hailed the French Revolution as "the most important historical event since the Reformation." (*Works*, Suphan, ed., Berlin, 1877–1913, vol. XVIII, p. 314.)

Now, if it is doubtful if any single revolution can be evaluated in terms of anything approaching a common currency of values, how much more problematical must we view an undertaking that attempts the evaluation of revolutions in general? Clearly, every revolution occurs in its peculiar historical setting. The sheer heterogeneity of variables that enter into diverse political revolutions renders common explanatory or evaluational hypotheses exceedingly unlikely. Nonetheless, it may be argued, and I think quite properly, that there is one characteristic common to all political revolutions, namely the propensity (on the part of some or of many) to disobey, challenge, or resist a given political authority. To probe into the reasons for such propensities is surely no less warranted than to deliberate why others are disposed to accept, obey or support existing governments. These contrasting types of perceptions and forms of 'consciousness' are therefore of more than peripheral interest in a discussion of revolution. Indeed I am inclined to suggest that they touch the very heart of the matter. Prof. Scriven's insightful observations on the concepts of perception and consciousness, consequently, seem to me of the highest importance. I should like, therefore, in my remaining comments to add a few remarks to his observations.

## V

It is undeniably true that one's perception of given conditions will crucially help to shape one's attitude to the political regime one is living under. Hence to perceive, say, injustice, will undoubtedly constitute a necessary ground for the manifestation of political dissent and resistance. It is less evident, however, that such a perception would constitute also a *sufficient* ground for dissent and resistance. For we cannot blandly assume that those perceiving the existence of injustice will necessarily consider it to have relevance to their own situation, or that their perception will be so intense as to arouse feelings of anger, frustration, or resentment. Even if we grant that some (or even a fair number) do harbour such feelings, it still does not follow that they will find it prudent, or proper, or meaningful, to express their feelings openly by way of protests, or demands, or, when no permissible or effective channels for their expression exist, by acts of defiance and resistance of one form or another. (The motives for their reluctance, diverse and mixed as they invariably will be, do not concern us here particularly; but it would be rash to infer that they need necessarily be less moral — as Scriven seems to imply in his 'happy slave' argument — than of those who do not hesitate to act. Indeed, the reverse might actually be the case. For what may well be involved here is a question of the highest moral significance, the question of *responsibility*. In contrast to the committed revolutionary who, as I argued earlier, cannot escape *acting* one way or the other, the man who merely perceives injustice not only can, but conceivably *ought* to weigh carefully the consequence of acting *versus* non-acting. If I say that he conceivably 'ought' to weigh them, I am indeed saying no less than that to do so is precisely what an 'ethic of responsibility' consists in.)

For dissent to assume a politically significant (overt) complexion requires, therefore, an unbroken continuity from perception to protest. Even then the manifestation of dissent is not tantamount to a total negation of an existing regime. For dissent to escalate into *revolutionary* action, more than perception plus the subsequent unbroken chain of responses (as described above) seems necessary. And I would suggest that the 'more' consists in a switch from 'perception' to 'consciousness'.

Viewed within the context of revolution, the switch from perception to consciousness is not so much, or conceivably not at all, a change in cognition. What is involved is not a change in degree but a change in kind. Consciousness is not simply a sharpened form of perception, that is, a more intense awareness of, say, injustice, or a fiercer sense of resentment over it, nor is it merely a changed *attitude*. As envisaged here, namely as revolutionary consciousness, it is no other than an action-promoting, if not action-compelling, *commitment*. It is a commitment to more or less clearly defined goals. I say advisedly "more or less clearly defined goals", for, unlike Scriven, I do not make the existence of a commitment contingent upon a clearly conceived positive value, such as, say, "justice". (Section 9). As I see it, a commitment to revolutionary goals entails essentially the rejection and destruction of the status quo in pursuit of an alternative order, the actual configuration of which need only (and perhaps in a sense *can* only) be inadequately grasped. Thus understood, a revolutionary commitment must be sharply distinguished (as Marx clearly recognized) from a utopian vision, on the one hand, and from mere reformism, i.e., the incremental tinkering with this or that governmental policy (or lack of policy), on the other. And, as I argued earlier, an integral part of such a commitment is the determination to seize and hold political power, in order to create the alternative order *authoritatively*.

Returning to the concept of perception, I have no quarrel with Scriven's distinction between perception that has been deliberately corrupted by feeding people, be they dedicated communists or liberals, with lies, and perception that is based on authentic information and experience. I doubt, however, whether what I have described as the switch from perception to consciousness will appreciably, or at all, be affected by the nature of its genesis; whether, that is, it has been caused by a 'corruption' of perceptions or by the "reversal, undoing or dissolution" (Section 7) of previously corrupted perceptions. For I am not clear why or how the 'structure' of revolutionary consciousness should be distinguishable in these two cases. On the other hand, I can see the point of speaking of a change in one's sense of commitment as a result of discovering that one's consciousness was induced and maintained by deliberate distortions and lies that were presented as truths. For this is precisely what did happen in Hungary in 1956, in Czechoslovakia in 1967/68, and what might happen in the United States in the seventies. It is of course a moot point if any revolutionary commitment or, for that matter, anti-revolutionary commitment, can most effectively be induced or maintained without some distoriton, if not corruption, of people's perception of reality.

Philosophers are much-misunderstood people. At times I cannot help wondering, though, if philosophers would really enjoy being understood, utterly and completely. Thus, while I have tried not to misunderstand Michael Scriven's paper, I am far from certain that he will not feel misunderstood here and there, and perhaps this is, after all, as it should be.

*University of Western Ontario*

DAVID EASTON

# SYSTEMS ANALYSIS IN POLITICS AND ITS CRITICS

An age may often be defined by the great new ideas that sift into all the varied crevices of thought of a given civilization. Regardless of where these ideas may have their start, whether in the natural or the social sciences or in the humanistic disciplines, it is testimony to their compelling strength that as these ideas are exposed to ever widening areas of knowledge, the older ways of thinking give way to the new. Yet as these new ideas leave their original grounds and move into strange fields seldom do they retain their pristine meaning. Each succeeding host discipline kneads and molds them to its own special purposes. But once again the power of the new ideas may be such that regardless of these shifts in meaning, some part of the original sense is retained. This part succeeds in transforming the way men think about their traditional problems and gives birth to whole generations of new ones. Newtonian mechanics and Darwinian evolution were two such universal solvents of traditional ways of thinking about nature, both physical and social.

In the present day there can be little doubt that a new expansive idea has again emerged and is gaining for itself a similar place in history. This is the apparently simple idea of systems. When I first began to develop a systems approach for political science in the 1950's there was little indication that the idea of system would prove so pervasive and influential. But today there is scarcely an area of thought or, for that matter, of action, that has escaped its effects.

The conveners of this Colloquium have asked me to speak about systems analysis in politics perhaps as illustrative of this great transformation in the thinking of one discipline at least. If so, it might appear that such an assignment would involve demonstrating how some established body of knowledge called 'systems theory' has been applied to the particular subject matter of politics. In fact this is not and could not be the case.

In the first place, even if there were such a corpus of knowledge as systems theory, the mode of analysis that I have been developing in political science for the last two decades, under the rubric of systems analysis, does not pretend to transfer such knowledge from one area to another. Rather, in the light of the contemporary shift of much scientific thinking in the direction of

21

*H. J. Johnson, J. J. Leach, and R. G. Muehlmann (eds.), Revolutions, Systems, and Theories, 21–36. All Rights Reserved.*
*Copyright © 1979 by D. Reidel Publishing Company, Dordrecht, Holland.*

systems, I have sought to fashion a theoretical tool uniquely adapted to the needs of political research.

In the second place, despite frequent talk about systems theory, there is in fact nowhere to be found a recognized body of knowledge of that kind. At most there is a broad and still growing tendency in all areas of science, and even in some of the humanities, to engage in what has been called systems thinking.[1] It can be found in such fields as general systems theory, the theory of open systems, systems engineering, operations research, linear programming, cybernetics or information theory, and the theory of machines. Out of this tangled growth of systems sciences, pure and applied, general systems theory alone has ambitions for bringing about some rational order by weaving the essentials together into a single coherent set of propositions. But this is still only a distant hope. It would make little sense, therefore, to attempt to apply a nonexistent body of theory called 'general systems theory' to existing political phenomena. Furthermore, even though sophisticated theories of information have been devised in the field of physical communications, no social science has as yet successfully superimposed that body of thought, or even substantial portions of it, on social data.

In short, there is as yet no theory in the strict sense that can be conveniently borrowed for application to political science or for that matter to any other social science. Indeed the incoherence of systems thinking as an area of research in most disciplines is such that any effort to import it into political science is as likely to contribute as much to the further development of this mode of analysis as it is to borrow from or lean upon it.

Even though there is little unity, if there is a single characteristic that distinguishes systems thinking, it lies in the way in which it approaches the analysis of complex wholes, especially those that manifest goal directed behavior. Traditionally the models of research emerging from the physical sciences have taught us that understanding comes from first breaking a whole entity down into manageable parts. The relationships between pairs of variables are the foundation stones upon which the edifice of physics as an empirical science has in the past rested. Upon this solid base there was slowly built up knowledge of the whole. The whole was conceived initially as largely a putting together or summing of the parts.

The strength of classical science lay in demonstrating that a whole entity cannot be readily understood as such. Analysis into significant elements for purposes of precise understanding is essential. Biology was a major science outside the physical sphere to question the universality of this approach. Knowledge of how the parts of an organism operated shed too little light on on an understanding of the functioning of the organism as a whole. The whole, in the popular expression, seemed to be more than the sum of its parts. By starting with parts in relative isolation the analytic approach of classical science when applied to more complex entities such as organism, lost much of its power. It did not seem able to take into account easily the extent to which a part of an entity might behave differently insofar as it was part of an organized network of interconnections with other parts of the same entity. Furthermore, the classical pattern of analysis from physics could comfortably ignore the possible consequences for the behavior of such an organized whole as occasioned by its goal seeking behavior. Purposive behavior was either overlooked or denied since it had little apparent place in the physical world.

Systems thinking, especially after World War II, sought to overcome this neglect of complex, organized wholes and of goal directed behavior. Although biology was the first of the natural sciences to begin to question the physical model, information theory subsequently provided one possible means for probing the mechanisms through which organisms and other organized entities are able to regulate their overall behavior. Self-regulation through feedback loops was discovered to be a primary means whereby a specified course of behavior could be sustained.

Regular information feedback about each succeeding state of an entity provides the basis for possible modification of behavior of the whole entity so as to keep it directed to some predetermined end. The thermostatically controlled heating system, the homing missile, the automated manufacturing processes are today all commonplace illustrations of how organized entities may be guided along a preferred path. Information theory has clearly demonstrated that any simplistic summation of knowledge about parts will miss the critical control mechanisms, such as information feedback and steering devices, that bring all the parts into some coherent form of organization for the attainment of built-in goals. The whole indeed behaves like more than the mere sum of the parts.

Peculiarly, although most of the social sciences have eagerly embraced the methods of the natural sciences in the last half century or so, they have not been much troubled by the dangers of overlooking the parts-whole controversy, particularly as it relates to purposive or goal oriented behavior. Unlike the physical sciences, the social sciences have traditionally begun with the whole, whether it be a society, a polity, an economy, or a culture. From Plato and Aristotle through Montesquieu and Marx to the present, social philosophers and scientists have sought out, not fled from these global concepts as initial points of referrence. In recent years Max Weber's *Verstehen* sociology and the Aristotelean tradition in contemporary social science have presented thick walls of resistance against the invasion of or domination by analytic science.

It is true, in the last few decades some social scientists may seem to have been moving rapidly towards the analytic model as it looked before the arrival of information theory. The well-known behavioral revolution in the social sciences seemed to signal the victory of anti-holistic scientific thinking. In almost all the social sciences, excepting perhaps economics, after World War II especially, inordinate attention was devoted to the painstaking accumulation of data and the testing of the relationships between sets of variables relatively isolated from their larger entities. The concentration on such detailed elements did much to arouse the fears of many social scientists that the broader whole would indeed be lost from sight, that the significance of the parts would be unidentifiable, and in the end that research would be in danger of becoming precise and accurate but entirely trivial.

Yet regardless of the complaints to the contrary, any close inspection of the social sciences, and certainly of political science, will reveal that this barefoot empiricism presented no real threat. The reason for this is perhaps an accident of history. The introduction of behavioral science occurred at precisely the moment that the systems sciences in cybernetics and systems engineering also began to flourish.

The fusing of the behavioral revolution with the emergence of systems thinking has had profound implications for political research. It has meant that in political science we could adopt the best of traditional science, its analytic method. This permitted us to decompose our enormously complex political relationships into two and three variable relationships or into aggregative analysis. We could begin to construct a solid base of precisely formulated and validated knowledge. At the same time, however, we could satisfy the ancient and traditional needs of political philosophy for a broader and more comprehensive interpretation of the significance of these otherwise isolated areas of knowledge. Just as the behavioral revolution was taking root in political science, systems thinking offered an opportune way of drawing the newly generated findings together for a broader interpretation. It has been my contention that in political science at least, these two movements — behavioralism and the more theoretically inclined systems thinking — were never separate and independent forces. They emerged almost simultaneously and have brought about a transformation in the discipline that has been both methodological and theoretical.

There is then little new for political science in looking at whole entities, such as societies and polities, and exploring their goals and their relationship to the various parts of the system. What is new is the effort to devise a more coherent and scientifically acceptable theoretical structure within which to interpret first, the relationships among the parts that constitute the whole political system and second, the significance of the goal-seeking behavior characteristic of all political units. Systems analysis as an integral part of the behavioral revolution has been one kind of answer that I first began to formulate in the early 1950's.

System analysis in political science has proceeded in the following way. First, it postulates that we can usefully conceive of any two or more objects as forming a system. Second, such a system may lie somewhere between the limits of a mere aggregate and an indivisible whole. In an aggregation the constituent parts would be independent of each other. To that extent they would be of little interest to a generalizing science. To the degree that the parts do show some interdependence or coupling, they become increasingly significant in understanding the operation of a political system.

Third, the more tightly coupled the units in a system are, the more likely are they to possess the following kind of properties. The position and activity of each part or subsystem will be determined not solely by its relationship to specified other parts in a one-to-one relationship, but by the principles or rules of operation that may apply to the whole system, that is, which may govern the operation of the parts. This is essentially what is meant by the notion of organization of the whole. The position of each part and its activity is a function to some extent of the influence of other parts but also of the way in which the whole is organized. To put this negatively, if the parts were not constituents of an organized whole, they would behave differently and would stand in a different relationship to each other.

Thus, for example, a subsystem uncoupled from the rest of the system would no longer display the same properties. This is as true of a citizen separated from his state as of an arm severed from the body. In the former instance, the citizen loses important rights and obligations once he leaves the network of political relationships usually implied in the notion of the modern state.

By adopting this interpretation of the part-whole relationship, any conflict between the classical method of physics on the one side, and that of systems analysis in social science on the other, disappears. Systems analysis is simply the extension of the natural science model to a rigorous search for an understanding of the operation of organized social units. A social whole is an organized set of objects whose related activities are capable of creating collective outcomes that would be impossible if the constituent elements behaved independently of each other, without more or less co-ordinated rules of behavior. In this sense a political system as a whole unit is certainly different from its parts and more than any mere summation of them. It is a complex organization of parts. The search for an understanding of this organization differentiates systems analysis from the study of variables in semi-isolation.

A fourth property of significance to a systems analysis of political life, already implicit in what has just been said, is the work achieved through the operations of a total system. A political system is not just a set of variables passively acting and reacting on each other and with their environment until some point of equilibrium is approached. The equilibrium model was indeed once prevalent in political research.[2] But it entirely missed an important point. A political system gets work done. Through well known but not well understood conversion processes, a political system transforms what I have called the 'inputs' of demands and support into characteristic 'outputs' of policies and administrative actions. These outputs help to reshape the environment and may have vital consequences for the subsequent behavior of the members of the political system itself. Systems analysis thus represents a dynamic approach. It searches not for the conditions of equilibrium but for the relationships that permit political systems to perform their characteristic work.

Every theoretical formulation derives a certain distinctiveness from the kind of central problem on which it focuses and which serves to lend coherence to its point of view. For systems analysis the main issue is a relatively simple one. How does it happen that any society can sustain some kind of political life? What accounts for the capacity of any kind of political system to persist? Once posed this question leads to the generation of what may be called a 'stress model' of a political system although the use of the term 'model' is an unnecessary scientific arrogation. What I have had to say amounts to no more than a framework of analysis or a set of categories. At the level of general theoretical formulations this is about all that most of the social sciences have proved capable of producing at their present stage of development.

To appreciate the nature of the stress to which political systems are typically subjected we need first to clarify what we mean by our major object of reference, the political system. I have defined it as consisting of all those interactions through which values are authoritatively allocated for a group, such as a society. Unlike the whole entities that constitute physical systems, such as atoms and their constituents, political systems are composed only of political interactions. These are aspects of the total behavior of a person that relate more or less directly to the authoritative allocation of values. These interactions are the units of analysis in this theoretical approach. The primary focus is not on the whole person in all his behavior but only on the individual to the extent that he engages in actions defined as political. For this reason we may say that a political system is an analytic system. We abstract out of the total interactions in which a person engages only those that are political. This creates certain problems for some scholars which time prevents us from exploring.

A system so defined does not operate in a vacuum. It is an open system entering into exchanges with its environment. This environment is exceedingly complex but can be simplified if we view it as consisting of an intra-societal group composed of the economy, culture, social structure and personality systems; and an extra-societal environment consisting of what is generally recognized as the internationnal sphere. The inputs of demand and support and the outputs of authoritative decisions are abbreviated and convenient ways of summarizing the exchanges that take place with these social environments. It is through these exchanges as well as through certain processes internal to a political system that stress may be imposed on a system.

Systems analysis as etched so starkly here takes the form of a stress model for two reasons. When we look at a set of human relationships under tension, some of their most important characteristics are apt to be revealed. More importantly, however, this approach accurately reflects a primary property of political relationships. In every society conflict is in fact generated over who is to make authoritative decisions, the kind of decisions that are to be made, who is to implement them, and how they are to be applied. Yet in one way or another all ongoing societies are able to cope with such stress, at least adequately enough to prevent their political systems from flying apart and becoming completely inoperative. A hidden but demonstrable assumption here is that no society could endure without some provision for arriving at the political resolution of some differences among its members.

The question this approach poses clearly lies at a very general level. It does not inquire into the conditions for the existence of a democratic system, however defined, or the means for the improvement of existing systems, whatever the criteria. Rather it seeks to understand something about the operation of any and all kinds of political systems regardless of whether they are democratic or authoritarian, transitional or traditional, industrialized or peasant, mass or tribal. All political systems rather than a general type of system is the focus of interest. For many social scientists who are accustomed to dealing with special classes of political systems, especially democratic ones, the broader orientation of this systems approach is sometimes difficult to grasp and bear in mind.

What are the typical sources of stress on any and all types of political systems? Stress arises out of the volume and variety of demands put into the system, the nature of the conversion processes, the degree to which outputs or authoritative decisions meet the demands of the politically relevant members of the system, the properties of the feedback loops, and the level of support available to various central objects in all systems. These objects are the political authorities, the regime, and the political community. Most systems engage in typical kinds of responses to cope with the stress occasioned in these ways although the details are far too complex to mention here. But the point to be made is that no amount of research at a subsystem level, say, about voting behavior, party structure, roll calls, pressure groups, public opinion, or recruitment to positions of power can help us to understand how systems do manage to persist under the inescapable stresses and strains of political conflict. Inquiry into parts of the system, however rigorously they may adhere to the canons of scientific method, will be unlikely to pose questions relevant to the operation of the political system as a whole organized entity. Systems analysis provides us with an overview of the political system. More formally, it represents an initial step, hopefully, on the way to the development of an empirically oriented general theory of politics.

The critical question posed by a systems analysis, it will be recalled, is how do political systems manage to persist even in the face of constant threats generated by the normal level of tensions in political life, let alone during less frequent periods of severe strife? It is in response to this question that we are able to probe into certain aspects of the overall organization of political systems that have in the past been overlooked.

Every system displays some means through which it seeks to regulate the inflow of demands and their variety so as to keep them at some manageable level. As a simple illustration, in every society cultural inhibitors specify the kinds of matters which may appropriately be made a subject of political discussion. Some societies exclude religion, others economic planning, and still others the kind of food people may eat or the age at which they may marry. But in no society is the input of political demands entirely a matter of individual discretion. Some cultural constraints prevail. The types of needs and wants which may be injected into the political process are subject to some conventional restrictions. From the point of view the operation of the political system this helps to keep the inflow of political demands down to some manageable proportion and thereby may prevent the occurrence of demand input overload. It may have other important political consequences such as on the use and distribution of power in the system. This is a different although vital matter.

Outputs may be looked upon as another systemic means for regulating potential stress. The level of support for the central objects of the political system — the authorities, the regime and the political community — is in part determined by processes of socialization. As members of a system grow to adulthood, they learn to place varying degress of confidence in these objects of a system. In part, however, the input of support is regulated by the nature of the outputs or authoritative decisions made in any and all systems. Where support drops to a low level it may be bolstered by outputs that use force or the threat of violence; or the outputs may seek to satisfy the expressed demands and anticipated needs of the members of the system. The match between demands and support is clearly a critical regulatory mechanism in all systems even though the equation will vary in every specific system.

The persistence of a political system will depend upon certain other system properties that would not normally be visible to research focusing on sets of relatively isolated variables. For example, in all political systems the input of demands and support is regulated through feedback mechanisms of a complicated kind. Regardless of the specifics in each situation, the authorities in all systems require information about what it is the politically relevant members of the system want done and the degree of support they appear to be extending to the authorities themselves, to the regime, and to the political community. The relevant members of the system similarly require some minimal information about the kinds of outputs being produced and about the relationship of these outputs to their demands. We are dealing here with human perceptions and consciousness, so there is of course wide room for error, distortion, and deliberate misrepresentation. These conditions may contribute to feedback failure which in turn may be an important source of total system failure.

One may cavil with my identification of regulatory mechanisms within a political system — a subject about which I shall have more to say in a moment — or with my interpretation about how they operate. But aside from these and other substantive considerations, the point is that but for a more generalized or holistic approach to the understanding of political life, implicit in the idea of a system of politics, there would be little incentive or opportunity to search for system related means through which members of a society are able to mobilize their resources for the resolution of their political differences.

To this point one might conclude that the regulatory mechanisms briefly illustrated here, but typical of all political systems, are analogous to those of physical communication systems. What we might appear to have is a crude and simplistic effort to transpose the approach of information theory to political phenomena. Given the adequacy of feedback channels, it appears that efforts could be made by members of the system to regulate the inflow of demands and support. Thereby they could assure the conditions under which political decisions in a society could continue to be made. The relevant members would be guaranteeing the persistence of some kind of political system.

If this were the whole story we might well conclude that political systems are simply self-regulating entities comparable in most respects, aside from subject matter, to physical systems. But to stop here would be to disregard other typical responses of political systems for coping with stress, kinds of responses that go well beyond self-regulation as it is known in physical or even biological systems.

In both the latter types of systems, feedback regulation normally operates to keep a system within some predetermined structural limits and goals. In physical systems, for example, even the most sophisticated homing devices can make adjustments in their trajectory only within the range permitted by the built-in structural design and goals. If circumstances, either internal or environmental, call for a revision of this design or the opening of new goals, the homing system must await adjustments external to itself, from the engineers. Within its present limits, a physical system is self-regulating or self-steering, in its efforts to cope with disturbances or stress. But in a basic sense the mechanical system is externally rather than internally controlled.

This conclusion applies with almost equal force to biological systems. Organisms too can maintain themselves in a steady state (a preferred state 'designed' through the process of evolution) to the degree that the existing structure of relationship among the parts permits. Under stress, however, organisms are able to adjust and compensate only within their own 'design' limits. They are unable to re-examine their means for self-regulation, or to modify fundamentally their internal organization and coping mechanisms, or even to change their preferred state. Under certain circumstance – war, for example – the preferred state of the human organism, survival, might be better served if the body were covered by an impenetrable hide, even more resistant than that of the rhinoceros. Adjustment in the human organism might take place in this direction through the long process of evolution, and in a sense this process could be interpreted as a very long run regulatory device. But it is slow, unpredictable, and as yet, not very manageable.

Political systems, on the other hand, have at their disposal far larger and more flexible repertoires for coping with stress. They illustrate the fundamental distinction between social systems and all other types of systems. Like many physical and biological systems, political systems, of course are able to take steps to regulate their behavior within existing structural and purposive limits. This is being done on a daily basis in every political system as it adjusts its policies to meet changing circumstances. But political systems are also able to establish entirely new goals for themselves and to revise their internal organization fundamentally so as to be able to achieve old ends or newly created ones. Every true change in regime or in the political community represents a fundamental alteration of structure and goals. Political systems are also able to reach out into their environment and modify it as well in a fundamental way, in a search to alleviate the stress on the system. Current governmental efforts to create the conditions of a stable, productive economy is an obvious example. In short, political systems are not only self-regulating within predefined limits; they are also self-transforming, goal-creating systems.

For example, if the inflow of demands has been so restricted by the particular regime that pressures of frustration are built up in the system, one way of coping with this could be for the authorities to increase and open up channels of access to the decision centers. In many systems, however, this avenue might not be available realistically, as in systems with authoritarian regimes. Typically such regimes cope with the stress of unwanted variety and numbers of demands by outright suppression. As politically involved persons we will feel strongly about such restrictions on freedom. Yet, from a general theoretical point of view, we can get a better understanding of how political systems in general operate if we interpret this response also as a form of self-regulation, for an authoritarian system, as it seeks to perpetuate itself.

At the same time, however, this very act of self-regulation in the traditional cybernetic sense may give rise to an alternative, more dynamic means for coping with the stress. Suppression may help to generate crucial oppositional forces that strive to change the goals, rules and structure of the system and to achieve a revolution in the regime. Revolution may be the decisive historical culmination of a process of self-transformation of a political system, a creative, goal-oriented act of which no physical or biological system is capable as it strives to cope with inputs from its environment.

From the longer perspectives of general political theory this kind of response by members of a political system might also result in permitting a particular society to sustain some kind of processes for making and implementing authoritative decisions. Historically not all societies have endured; more have probably perished than have survived, regardless for the moment of the level of survival or moral value attached to it. The question posed by systems analysis is whether many of the societies that have disappeared may have done so *not* because of their inadequate technology, or their failure to control disease, and the like but because of the incapacity of the members of the society to solve their political problems.

Clearly, political systems are armed with powerful means for responding to stress. These means range from pure adaptation, to reconstruction of internal organization and purposes, to modifications and manipulation of the environment. It is equally clear that stress is not a negative concept or one that carries any moral overtone. Positive and creative acts of change by a political system are no less probable, in the abstract, than negative and defensive ones. It is this broader range of response alternatives that serves as one fundamental difference of theoretical significance between physical and social systems. No simple transfer of theorizing about physical or biological systems is likely to be able to take this distinction into account.

This is but a skeletal outline of a systems type analysis of political life. Although various aspects of it have been adopted in the discipline and numerous efforts applying it for specific research purposes can be cited, the more interesting considerations are the doubts that have been expressed about its utility. Time permits but an introduction to them.

These challenges are of several kinds. The first one I shall only mention. But for each of the other major types of criticisms I shall offer one illustration of general interest.

First, there are those within political science who in principle deny the possibility of discovering generalizations with predictive power about human behavior. They therefore look askance at any effort to move towards an empirically oriented theory about political systems. I shall not attempt to take up this challenge. Both the arguments and responses are so well known through frequent if not excessive repetition as to form almost a catechism for a dispute.

Second, there are also those, however, who have accepted the essentials of the behavioral revolution in political science but who have serious misgivings about general theory. They reject any effort to develop such a theory of politics at this stage in the history of our discipline. To them the task seems both premature and perhaps ultimately impossible. Indeed they point to my writings as an example of how far short of a theory any current effort must fall, arguing that I offer no lawlike generalizations with predictive power but only a set of categories. Systems analysis, it is said, constitutes a political taxonomy, not a general theory.

My response is simple. They are correct. I have nowhere argued that systems analysis provides a general theory of politics after the pattern, say, of economics or physical theory. Indeed I have explicitly shared and expressed the judgment of my critics well before they themselves first aired it.

This is not to say that generalizations are absent from my writings. It is virtually impossible to speak about human behavior without implying or explicitly making lawlike statements. But these are not central to the analysis. I have argued instead that insofar as political science accepts a commitment to the discovery of verifiable generalizations about political behavior, the major and most feasible current task is to establish a coherent and logically consistent set of categories for purposes of analysis. These will help research into politics by identifying the critical variables, justifying their utility by clearly specified criteria, and thereby providing significant guidelines for ongoing research. A logically related set of concepts can be expected to lend some degree of coherence to a discipline that historically has found great difficulty in creating a strong sense of identity for itself as a separate discipline.

The alternative to even a framework of analysis is continued blind groping in research according to intuitive criteria of significance or the selection of tasks as they are dictated by the urgent issues of the day. I shall return to the matter of a purely problem oriented discipline in a moment. Although there is something to be said for outright, theoretically uninformed empiricism in a fresh field of endeavor, in political science, with some two thousand years of inquiry behind us, there does seem somewhat less justification. Systems analysis represents an effort to formulate a set of consistent and useable categories as an initial step, hopefully, towards the construction of a body of generalizations out of which theory in the full blown sense may some day emerge. We may deplore the current lack of such a theory. But the fact is that, aside from economics, no social science has reached the stage where it has been able to offer more than very low level kinds of verified or verifiable generalization. And in economics there is serious question about the predictive power of the logical theory that does exist.

In addition to those who would argue against the possibility of any science of man and those who see general theory as an academic fantasy, there are others who fall into a third category of criticism. These accept the application of the methods of science to human behavior. They are even willing to tolerate the thought that some day empirically oriented general theory may be achieved in political science. But they have doubts about systems analysis as a step in that direction.

Among these critics, strangely, there appears only the occasional serious challenge to holistic thinking as represented in a systems approach. Even in these instances the objections are seldom directly to the holistic approach; they are normally aimed at some specific aspect of systems analysis as I have formulated it. I shall deal with only one of these criticisms, namely, the argument that this mode of analysis lacks substantive relevance. In this decade I would consider this to be a damaging criticism of an approach, although not necessarily decisive for all purposes.

Even if we were to grant the utility of systems analysis as a theoretical framework, this argument runs, as with all pure science it is far too remote from the practical issues of the day to offer an attractive alternative to direct research on urgent social problems. Political research needs to concentrate on a direct understanding of the political causes and consequences of war, poverty, ethnic intolerance, urban blight, and generational alienation. Demands, support, conversion processes, outputs, feedback, coping with stress, and the like seem to mask the real issues of the day, the power struggle among groups for command of the resources in society.

This criticism appears to ring true but only if one permits himself to be distracted by the formal nature of the approach and fails to read into the necessarily generalized language the underlying specific human issues to which they must refer. For example, the inputs of demands as a concept exposes the very bedrock on which many major contemporary issues are founded. Demands deal with what people do in fact want, how they seek to go about getting it politically, the extent to which they are able to satisfy their wants, the relationship of these wants to their objectively determined needs, and the awareness by people of their right to have wants and express them as demands. At a still lower level of specificity, such demands may reveal themselves as aspects of the political activity of ethnic and linguistic groups, of social classes, of economic interest groups, and the like. Or these demands may be put into a system by a clan or lineage segment in a tribal society, or even by the authorities themselves in a peasant society where political quiescence is the accepted norm. In fact, beginning with the general problem of persistence, in this one area of demands alone we have a field of research to which far too little attention has been devoted by political science. We have too little accurate knowledge of needs, wants and politically formulated demands and of the impact that political outputs have upon them. And yet these demands constitute the raw materials out of which political conflict is created.

Another example of the substantive significance of a systems approach, relates to the identification of outputs as one major mechanism for regulating the level of support. The notion of outputs as a relatively simple way of interpreting the product of political processes has gained considerable acceptance and it has left its imprint on the whole policy analysis movement of the present day.[3] Systems analysis has carefully discriminated outputs, or authoritative decisions, from outcomes, or the secondary and tertiary consequences of these decisions. It has also posed the question as to whether the outcomes of outputs do in fact meet the demands to which they may have been a response or whether they only serve as symbolic gestures to appease political pressures. The growing policy analysis movement today has adopted as one of its central tasks the assessment of the consequences of policies. This represents the first serious effort to devise an effective way of determining the nature of the consequences of actions by authorities. In this area alone the implications of systems analysis have been far more practical than we might have had a right to expect from so generalized a theoretical approach.

In spite of this natural bridge between the theoretical concepts and the practical world as illustrated in these instances, the critics do have a point. But it is one rather different from the complaint about non-relevance, and I have made this point elsewhere.[4] It has to do with the place of pure science in a world in crisis.

In every science there is a constant tension between the pure and the applied, those who are searching for the solid foundations of knowledge and those who are eager to apply at once whatever knowledge is available. During the 1950's and 1960's, while systems analysis was being formulated and elaborated, even though there were transparently critical social issues, it did seem that there was sufficient time for some of the resources of political science to be devoted to the long run needs of knowledge. Towards the end of the sixties, the insane war in Vietnam, the justifiable impatience of a new generation with the procrastination of those in power, and the decreasing willingness of large numbers to tolerate unnecessary poverty and ethnic and linguistic discrimination quickly shortened the time scale available for science.

These new circumstances have indeed moved the social sciences into what I have characterized elsewhere as the post-behavioral revolution.[5] It is distinguished by the fact that a decreasing share of our human and economic resources are now available for the long run purposes of pure science. Instead these resources are being diverted to direct inquiry into critical issue areas in the hope that through a combination of new and accurate data, informed intuition, and the small available backlog of fundamental science, more helpful judgments can be made about ways of solving our critical immediate problems.

In the tensions between pure and problem oriented science, the pendulum has now swung towards the latter. This shift has seemed to me necessary and appropriate. It is clear that if major steps are not taken quickly to begin to deal effectively with short run critical issues, there may be no long run for which theoretical science can prepare itself. This judgment does not imply that pure science needs to be abandoned in the social sciences entirely but only that even the small share of attention that it has ever commanded may temporarily need to be decreased somewhat further. This, it has seemed to me, is the significance of the post-behavioral transformations currently under way in most of the major social sciences.

Systems analysis, it is true, was formulated in the hope that it would take a significant step towards the generation of empirically oriented theory at a general level. The illustrations I have just advanced permit me to argue, however, that its concepts and structure are not so distant from political realities as to lack immediate utility and social pertinence. Indeed systems analysis represents a kind of theoretical orientation that effectively bonds theory to practice.

In conclusion, systems analysis derives its distinctive character from an effort to link the many parts of a political system more meaningfully to the operation of the whole. It seeks to achieve this goal through a model that focuses on the stress to which any and all systems are typically subjected. In formulating a set of categories useful for probing such questions at a general level, systems analysis nonetheless manages to remain in close touch with the practical realities of political life.

*Queen's University and University of Chicago*

## NOTES

[1]  F. E. Emery (ed.), *Systems Thinking*, Penguin Books, London, 1969.
[2]  See D. Easton, *The Political System*, Knopf, New York, 1971, 2nd edition.
[3]  See A. Ranney (ed.), *Political Science and Public Policy*, Markham, Chicago, 1969; T. R. Dye, *Politics, Economics and the Public: Policy Outcomes in the American States*, Rand McNally, Chicago, 1966; and I. Sharkansky (ed.), *Policy Analysis in Political Science*, Markham, Chicago, 1970.
[4]  D. Easton, 'The New Revolution in Political Science' *American Political Science Review* 63 (1969), 1051–1061, Presidential Address to American Political Science Association 65th Annual Meeting, September 2–6, 1969, New York City.
[5]  *Op. cit.*

# A NOTE ON MR. EASTON'S REVOLUTIONS

The new message speaks stridently of scientific revolution and discontinuous scientific change, drowning out the older Burkean one that scientific growth is slow, cumulative, and cooperative. Mr. Easton's paper may be viewed as an interesting attempt to harmonize the old and the new, one that defends two political scientific revolutions – the systems approach and the behaviouralistic one which apparently resulted from interdisciplinary cooperation and stimulation in, among other things, attacking the powers that were entrenched when they began. Needless to say, the paper blesses the current entrenchment of these systems, and is prepared to do battle against their detractors.

At any rate, Mr. Easton is not a Che Guevera of the intellectual world, and hence I may take leave to begin by raising an old-fashioned question: What does he mean by behaviouralism? I am not sure of the answer, but I think it is evident that he does not use 'behaviouralism' interchangeably with 'behaviourism'. He contenances mental entities, and the explanations he offers contain mentalistic terms in an essential way. 'Behaviouralism' without 'behaviourism' is a strange doctrine, somewhat akin to Christianity without Christ, but not perhaps a mysterious one. It may be that 'behaviouralism' is the name of a negative doctrine, one which allows the political scientist to attempt to explain and to predict, but forbids him to assess, evaluate, criticise, or justify political actions and the behaviour of political systems; forbids the tough-minded political scientist to follow the ways of his high-minded but soft-headed political-philosophical predecessor. Perhaps, but if so Mr. Easton is not a behaviouralist; he raises and attempts to answer questions not only about the behaviour of political systems but also questions about what the political systems could have done or ought to have done, and hence allows the political scientist to offer and to defend value judgments, at least in one obvious sense of that term. If we adhere by Mr. Easton's practice, and hence use him as a paradigm case of a behaviouralist, then the previous specification is not to be respected, and as a result the intended contrast between the new tough-minded empiricist-behaviourist and his benighted predecessor seems to be going. Going, but not perhaps gone. Allowing ourselves the distinction between value judgments in general and moral ones in particular a new negative version of behaviouralism is at hand: A behaviouralist does not allow

H. J. Johnson, J. J. Leach, and R. G. Muehlmann (eds.), Revolutions, Systems, and Theories, 37–45. All Rights Reserved.

himself the luxury of passing *moral* judgments on political actions and political systems. Once again Mr. Easton's practice counts against the specification or counts in favour of the thesis that he is not a behaviouralist, for it is clear, or at any rate it seems to be clear, that he allows himself to pass moral judgments on some of our political actions and practices and on our failure to act as well. But it could be said that he does so *qua* citizen and not *qua* political scientist, and the specification of behaviouralism above did not intend to preclude the political scientist *qua* citizen, only the political scientist *qua* scientist, from making moral judgments. Fair enough, provided it is understood that the behaviouralist *qua* political scientist is debarred from making moral judgments only because his theories either don't express such moral judgments or propositions or can't be used directly to support them; otherwise, what is the cash value of the phrase '*qua* political scientist'? And hence, the political scientist cannot use such *theories qua* citizen either. Mr. Easton, however, asserts or implies strongly that the statements we make when we attempt to deal with political problems to solve them can or should be viewed as instances of the application of pure theory. Does he imply that when we describe or evaluate or assess a political system we can do so without using moral terms, and hence that his theories do not contain moral ones, or the reverse? Neither alternative seems correct, and at any rate I am not sure how his judgments about the Vietnam War are related to his general theoretical commitments, or the way that they can be viewed as an application of some of them; and I presume – or rather, hope – that his judgments are moral ones.

The bulk of Mr. Easton's paper is devoted to a defense not of behaviouralism but of systems analysis, or more pointedly to a defense either of the necessity or the wisdom of a systems approach in political science. Our friendly reader may anticipate our friendly greeting: What then is he defending when he is defending the systems analysis? Many things, of course, some of which seem safe and sane enough. Thus I think there is little amiss with his arguments in favour of the indepensability of law and theory in political science, and little to object to in his all but too brief critique of 'barefoot empiricism'. But though some of his theses are safe and sane enough, some of them, at least to my mind, seem to be of dubious merit and to lead to dark corners.

Note first, that there is an ambiguity in his argument about the necessity of appeal to law and theory. He assumes – and I will not question the assumption – that it is the aim of the political scientist to explain and to predict phenomena, and to do so by law (i.e., that all his explanatory and predictive arguments contain well-confirmed, lawlike statements). But he thinks that the defense of that assumption is tantamount to a defense of the view that it is the task of the political scientist to find one general theory, or alternatively one small set of lawlike sentences, to which he can appeal for all his explanatory and predictive purposes. But the second assumption or thesis is obviously different from the first, and though one may grant the first, one may object to the second. This is not a trivial point because I think that his acceptance of the second thesis is essential to Mr. Easton's entire approach to political science and to his quest for general theory. Why that quest? After all, we cut up the world in all sorts of ways, and there is no reason to think that a way in which we cut it up — and which mirrors our interests and actions — is of great theoretical significance. The distinction between games and non-human games is an important one, but it is of doubtful theoretical relevance; few would or should try to manufacture and confirm one general theory which can be used to explain and predict the outcome of all games. Some people win simply because they trained well; others because their opponent suddenly had a heart attack; still others because the game was thrown. Again and more seriously, when we try to understand why Fischer, for example, has been successful in chess, we try to specify certain mental traits or mental abilities that he had and that his opponents, including Spassky perhaps, did not have, or did not have to the same degree. But if we try to generalize, and say that all people who are sports winners possess these kinds of mental activities or abilities, we are headed to oblivion. And, come to think of it, why restrict ourselves to sports winners, why not all winners?

Incidentally, I take it that this was the point of issue, at least with some members of the tradition, that Mr. Easton alludes to and dismisses, I think, somewhat too quickly and dogmatically by simply saying that they began with the whole. After all, Montesquieu and Marx, for example, do not simply talk about complex entities or complex political systems as complex political systems and let it go at that. They also try to discover and specify the interconnections between political systems and other factors, and among those other factors the parts of which those political systems were composed. Still, they did not look for a general political theory of the kind we are now attempting to discuss. Marx, for example, thought that the political generalizations that we can make about political systems, or more directly about the state under capitalistic situations or capitalistic economic conditions, may not be applicable elsewhere, or to be more direct, may be disconfirmed if tested by reference to other situations, and he may be right. Notice, that in all of this, I am not disputing the point that there may be general social scientific laws that we may discover, and which may be of relevance for all domains of social enquiry; there may very well be such laws, I'm merely contesting the view that specific disciplines have specific laws. Obviously there are general laws of mechanics, thermodynamics, etc. that the geologist and the meteorologist use, but no one would argue that whether forecasters must try to discover a special kind of law; or that geologists must discover one general theory of geology when they are concerned to deal with geological – or should we now say lunar? – phenomena. An obvious reminder: Mr. Easton's claim that in order to discuss political phenomena or political decisions one needs a special vocabulary is here not being denied. Obviously, we may need a special vocabulary in order to discuss the weather or games.

Still, we may say nothing ventured, nothing gained, and we have little to lose by trying to think up system laws of the type suggested by Mr. Easton. I recall his position: Mr. Easton is not now prepared to offer us a theory but merely to sketch one, ready to affirm that all the laws of political science will ultimately be system laws in the sense that all the laws will be laws stating the interconnections between parts of a political system, will describe how a political system acts to meet certain goals, will specify how political systems change over time either by adapting themselves to stresses and demands or by positing new ones. These are the kinds of laws that he thinks the political scientist will ultimately get. But why? The answer that is suggested in the paper is that the predicates of the lawlike sentences just adumbrated, are predicates that are true of a political system. But this answer will not lead us very far. Water is wet, but the laws that we appeal to for interesting explanations of water do not appeal to wet things; and similarly, though political systems may be of the type described by Mr. Easton, it may be the case that the general laws which we will have to find in order to offer any interesting explanations of political phenomena will be a different sort. The general laws may turn out to be general social-psychological ones, from which the laws – if any – of our political systems are to be derived only after definitions of 'political system' by reference to the terms that appear in the social-psychological laws are available. Or to revert back to the previously defended thesis, it may be that we will have to explain different political acts of different political systems or agents by reference to different laws.

Mr. Easton does not consider this possibility and it may very well be that he does not think it is a serious one; at any rate, he thinks that he has another rock upon which to build. He notices that the quest for system laws has been very successful in other disciplines, and he appeals to the successful quest for system-laws in other disciplines to support his quest for system laws in political science. Unfortunately, Mr. Easton provides us with some data which leads us to doubt the solidity of the ground upon which he wants to place his rock. He reminds us that many social scientists have mistakenly argued from the success of mechanics and physics to the conclusion that the laws of social science should in some relevant sense be mechanistic; and that others have been misled to the success of evolutionary theory to seek evolutionary laws in the social sciences. Given that we have been misled in this way in the past, why should we now think that this quasi-inductive argument to which Mr. Easton has appealed is in any way a reliable one? Notice further, that if one is prone to argue along the lines just indicated — that is, to accept the quasi-inductive argument — one would I think have the better of the case if he argued not from the success of systems analysis, but from the success or relativity theory and quantum mechanics, and try to look for laws in political science which in some suitable way resemble the laws found there. After all, the major action was there; and off-hand we might side with the many behaviourists who were convinced that the success of operational definitions in the physical sciences dictated their strategy of restricting themselves to operational definitions only. Off-hand, until one notices the limitations of these quasi-inductive arguments, limitations which I think are properly conveyed in an amusing anecdote which is perhaps apocryphally attributed to Einstein: There is a story to the effect that Einstein at a conference in the late '20s, criticized a man who was defending operational definitions in the physical sciences, that is he criticized a scientist who was defending the thesis that all the definitions in the physical sciences must be operational ones. At the end of the meeting, Einstein was approached and confronted by someone who raised the following question: "But Einstein, why you? After all, you're the man who introduced operational definitions in physics, you are in many ways the father of operational definitions, why shouldn't we now follow your lead? And why shouldn't we now restrict ourselves to operational definitions only?" The story has it that Einstein looked at the man and said: "Shhh, one must not repeat a good joke too often."

Note finally, that on occasion Mr. Easton does not use the phrase 'system law' along the lines I have suggested. He refers to empirical gas laws as 'system laws', but obviously that reference must give us pause: the terms 'pressure' and 'volume' do not name names of parts of gases, in any interesting sense of the term 'parts'. But if, on independent grounds, we argue that Boyle's and kindred laws are system laws then I think that Mr. Easton's position could reduce itself to the thesis that all laws of science are in point of fact system laws, and hence that there was no twentieth century science systems revolution in the first place.

To this point I have not tried to challenge Mr. Easton's assertions about political systems and their behaviour, and I will not in what follows attempt to overthrow them. Indeed, in a rough and ready way I think I know what they mean, and I think that in a rough and ready way I agree with some of them, them, if properly interpreted. But only in a rough and ready way; on some important non-trivial details I think I fail to follow him.

We can raise at least two questions about scientific theses: questions about their truth or credibility and questions about their value, their scientific value for scientific purposes. As I understand him, Mr. Easton asserts the important thesis – which he does not develop – that it is the function of a political system authoritatively to reallocate values. Granting its truth for the moment, what may we say about its scientific value? What role does such a statement play within political scientific inquiry? I think no greater role than the role played by such statements as 'All men seek happiness', 'All men pursue values', or 'All men need reward'. The trouble with such statements is that they cannot, given current knowledge, be conjoined with statements that enable us to specify and to account for the differences as well as the similarities, of the cases that they cover. To take the simple case of 'All mean seek happiness,' the trouble is that we have no theories which enable us to specify in advance and to explain why some men seek happiness by pursuit of the hunt, and others by the pursuit of the Talmud. Indeed, we cannot have such theories, unless we think that all doors are open when we say that men do what they do because they are conditioned to do what they do; or they do what they do because the culture of which they are a part does what it does, namely encultures them. Marxists, of course, have here an advantage over Mr. Easton: they could claim that their theory enables them to specify which values are allocated or protected in society $x$, and which in society $y$. But Mr. Easton, of course, is no ally of Marxism, and has no alternative relevant theory of his own.

I must also admit to scepticism about the credibility or truth of statements of the form: the function of the political system is $x$. My grounds are partly empirical and partly conceptual. I doubt that the evidence allows us to claim that all political systems uniquely perform one function, or even that any single one does that. Our political system both allocates and creates values, and so does our economic system, and others as well. Note finally, that the rules governing the connections between the expressions: 'The role of part of the political system' and 'The role of the political system', are not clear. Should we say on Mr. Easton's view that if $x$, (example given, a Congress or a revolutionary group) which is part of the political system performs role $z$, or fulfills function $z$ prime, then the political system $y$, of which $x$ is a part, is a $z$, or a $z$-er, or a $z$ primer? And if we do, do we get the result that the political system behaves in bizarre and mysterious ways? It both allocates values with authority and denies the authority the right to allocate the values in the first place. Needless to say I have no objections to the thesis that among other things the political system does or parts of the political system do authoritatively reallocate values. It is trivial that many acts of Congress and the courts have as a consequence the reallocation of values; but it is not trivial, indeed it is false, to conclude that every act of Congress is one that authoritatively reallocates values. The reasons are obvious, many of the things that Congress does are unconstitutional, and many things that the courts do are corrupt; not every act done by an authority is authoritative or done with relevant political authority. And not every authoritative act which is performed by an authority authoritatively reallocates values. The political system is not simply a market mechanism for the reallocations of antecedently available values. Many acts of Congress and many laws are enabling laws: they enable men, or specify the conditions under which men may legally go into business, form corporations, declare themselves bankrupt, and − I hope this not redundant − get married. At best we may say that it is a function of the legal or political system to make legally possible some acts which reallocate values. For acts of Congress are not necessary for the reallocation of values: we don't have to wait for Congress before we start distributing kisses, even authoritatively.

In previous paragraphs I have attempted to criticize Mr. Easton's thesis giving diverse types of examples; I have referred to certain acts or types of acts, to political groups, to laws, to procedures, which may be countenanced as possibilities and which have many possible realizations. It may be claimed that I tacitly applied the terms 'political system' and 'parts of a political system' to diverse types of entities, entities that belong to diverse ontological types. I have been. I have allowed myself to do so because I think that Mr. Easton does so. Officially, however, he denies that that is the case, and he simply asserts that a political system is composed of acts, that the basic units are acts, and that all complex systems must be understood simply as composed of acts − or if one wishes, complex systems are complexes of acts or events. But obviously this could not be his intent: acts or events come and go, acts don't change, and it is evident that we do not want to talk about acts having goals, rights, and being in a position of authority. I think, but certainly I'm not certain, that Mr. Easter may have been misled by three *prima facie* plausible theses that he may accept. I think that he began by accepting (a) All causal explanations in political science refer to events. (2) To apply a political predicate to an individual or a group we must abstract from many factors and attend only to the actions performed by individual human beings. (3) It is a mistake to view the political system of a community as a complex entity made up of discontinuous parts, each one of them being a single human being; it is a mistake for no other reason than the obvious one that the complex individual — the political system — thus specified would have to be falsely viewed as identical with the religious system of that community. And having accepted these three theses, he was tempted to conclude — somewhat hastily — that the only entities countenanced by the political scientist are acts, and that all complex entities are composed of acts. Fortunately, it is not part of my job to try to deal with the complex issues that arise when we try to specify what we mean when we refer to a political system; it may very well be that we will have to treat political systems as relational structures. At all events if we want to find out whether someone was married we have to find out whether he did certain things, whether he took out a marriage license; but if we want to talk about the family system we are talking about people and the interaction between the people and it would be silly to conclude that when we talk about the family system we are only talking about the acts and events which we use as evidence for the fact that people are actually members of a system.

Traditionally political scientists, or at least some of them, attempted to define or explicate such predicates as 'is a state', 'is a legal system', 'the political system'; and to specify the nature of the entities to which these predicates apply. Mr. Easton often appears to be critical of this approach but as my remarks indicate he is not *that* critical, he too wants to explicate such terms and also attempts to deal with ontological issues, to my mind in a somewhat unclarifying manner. There is perhaps another way of interpreting Mr. Easton: the process way. The latter Mr. Easton is not concerned with ontological issues, at least not primarily; he is more concerned with political life as a process, and is concerned to depict the variety of ways in which those in and out of power act and interact and think up mechanisms which — among other things — have the role of reallocating values. There is an air of the American and the pragmatist about the latter Mr. Easton and to my mind he is to be applauded for all that. But he is not, I think, pragmatic enough, at least not pragmatic in the way James and John Dewey were, or were at their best. He frequently talks as if we can understand the political process in the following way: There are certain people in power and there are certain people out of power, and the people out of power have certain kinds of demands and these demands are made upon the people in power. And then the people in power try to see how they can — at least in part — meet these demands, or set up new goals to see if these demands can be met, or possible change the political system to fulfill these demands. And possibly if they can't — either out of stupidity or lack of imagination — face the alternative of the disappearance of the political system because of the stress upon it as a result of all of these demands. This is an obviously crude formulation of the complicated picture that Mr. Easton wants to present, but I think it depicts some of its main features. And if I am right, it is the kind of a picture that James and Dewey would have found unsatisfactory. Among other things, it does not provide us with a clear picture of the self, and seems to lead to the view that the expressions 'agent $x$ made demands upon political system $z$', is not conceptually connected with such statements as 'agent $x$ has beliefs about the legitimacy of $z$, and of the legitimacy of demands'. And it also fails to specify the various ways in which we are transformed as we are engaged in political action. I myself would opt for the refinement of the traditional thesis — which does not seem to be favored by Mr. Easton — that the self is formed as a result of involvement in political activity, at least the selves of some of us are formed in actually coming to conclusions as to what kind of political system we in point of fact want. And indeed if that is the case, then I think that we must say that the task of the political scientist is not simply to see how a particular political system meets certain kinds of demands of apolitical agents; but how, over time, human beings define and redefine themselves as they come to conclude what they think is politically acceptable or politically justified. And a political scientist can only come to evaluate specific outcomes if he pays attention not merely to the formal nature of the political system and the psychological demands of agents, but pays attention both to the moral convictions and the political ideals that individual human agents have, including hopefully, those in power.

*Columbia University*

GORDON TULLOCK

# THE ECONOMICS OF REVOLUTION

*Table of Symbols*

| Symbol | Definition |
|---|---|
| $B_{(i,\ d)}$ | Payoff to participation in revolt on side of existing government. |
| $D_i$ | Private reward to individual for participation in putting down revolt if government wins. |
| $\Delta p_i$ | Change in probability of revolutionary success resulting from individual participation in revolution.' |
| $G_i$ | Public good generated by successful revolution. |
| $G_{(i,\ in)}$ | Total payoff to inaction. |
| $G_{(i,\ r)}$ | Total payoff to subject if he joins revolution. |
| $J_i$ | Injury suffered in action. |
| $p$ | Likelihood of revolutionary victory assuming subject is neutral. |
| $p'$ | Likelihood of injury through participation in revolution (for or against). |
| $P_i$ | Private penalty imposed on individual for participation in revolution if revolt fails. |
| $R_i$ | Private reward to individual for his participation in revolution if revolution wins. |
| $S_{(i,\ d)}$ | Private cost imposed on defenders of government if revolt succeeds. |
| $T_i$ | Entertainment value of participation. |
| $V_{(i,\ r)}$ | Opportunity cost (benefit) to individual from participation rather than remaining neutral. |

1. Although I have not read the other papers in this conference at the moment of writing, I feel fairly confident that mine will turn out to be radically different from all of them. My reason for this opinion is not that I propose to use a little high school algebra in my paper, but more substantive.[1] It is the purpose of this paper to introduce this conference to a new and radically different theory of revolutions. This theory begins by inquiring why individuals would enter into revolutions, and uses some tools of economic analysis to conclude that almost all existing discussion of revolutions has been misleading.

I should like to begin by raising a question which, so far as I know, has not been discussed by philosophers, although it is very important in the modern economic investigation of governmental processes. Why is it necessary to coerce people into paying taxes? Assuming that government generates a

47

*H. J. Johnson, J. J. Leach, and R. G. Muehlmann (eds.), Revolutions, Systems, and Theories, 47–60. All Rights Reserved.*
*Copyright © 1979 by D. Reidel Publishing Company, Dordrecht, Holland.*

benefit — and I think most people will agree that it does — why are people not willing to pay for it voluntarily? So far as I know, no government has ever successfully depended on the citizens' sense of duty, obligation, or willingness to make voluntary payments. Coercion is always the principal method relied upon to obtain tax revenue. This is as true in democracies as in dictatorships, in primitive as in developed societies.

The economic answer to this problem is usually attributed to Paul Samuelson, although he did not claim originality in his famous article, and had a number of important predecessors including Pigou.[2] Consider the position of an individual citizen if he had the right to refrain from paying taxes without being threatened with confiscation and imprisonment. If he failed to pay his taxes there would be less police protection, less military protection from foreigners, less roads, and less of many other things. In each case, however, the reduction would be extremely small.

He would still receive services from other people's payments, but even if he thought these were inadequate, making his own payment would make very little difference. Almost all of the money that he would put in voluntarily would be spent on providing services to other people. He could anticipate something on the order of 1/200 millionth of the payoff from each dollar he contributed would return to him. Under the circumstances, he would not make the payments and indeed no government has ever depended upon the sense of duty or moral obligation of its citizens for its financial support. In a democracy, in a sense, we all voluntarily agree to coerce each other through the tax collecting apparatus in order to avoid this problem. Without the apparatus of coercion, the government would be unable to obtain goods and services to carry out its functions.

2. Revolutions raise the same problem. Let us consider, for a start, a very simple situation. Ruritania is governed by a vicious, corrupt, oppressive, and inefficient government. A group of pure-hearted revolutionaries are currently attempting to overthrow the government, and we know with absolute certainty that if they are successful they will establish a good, clean, beneficial, and efficient government. What should an individual Ruritanian do about this matter? He has three alternatives: he can join the revolutionaries, he can join the forces of repression, or he can remain inactive.[3] Let us compute the payoff to him of these three types of action.[1] Equation (1) shows the payoff to inaction. This simply indicates that the payoff is

$$(1) \qquad G(i,\ in) = G_i \cdot p$$

the benefit which he would receive from an improved government times the likelihood that the revolution will be successful.[4] Note that this payoff is essentially a public good. He will, of course, himself benefit from the improved government and he may well benefit from his feeling that his fellow citizens are well-off. But in this case, he will receive no special, private reward.

The payoff for participating in the revolution on the side of the revolutionaries is shown by Equation (2).

$$(2) \qquad G_{(i, \ r)} = G_i\,(p + \Delta p_i) + R_i\,(p + \Delta p_i)$$
$$- P_i\,[1 - (p + \Delta p_i)] - J_i \cdot p' + T_i,$$

$$(2a) \qquad G_{(i, \ r)} = G_i \cdot p + G_i \cdot \Delta p_i + R_i \cdot p + R_i \cdot \Delta p_i - P_i +$$
$$P_i \cdot p + P_i \cdot \Delta p_i - J_i \cdot p' + T_i.$$

This differs from Equation (1) in two respects. First, the individual's participation on the side of the revolutionaries increases the likelihood of revolutionary victory to some extent, presumably to a very small extent in most cases. Second, the individual now has a chance of reward, perhaps in the form of government office, if the revolution is successful and a chance of being penalized by the government if the revolution fails. Finally, he runs an additional risk of being injured or killed.

Note, however, that generally speaking the individual's entry into the revolution will actually change the likelihood of revolutionary success very little. Indeed, the value of $\Delta P_i$ is approximately zero.

Assuming this is so, then Equation (2) simplifies to the approximation (3).

$$(3) \qquad G_{(i, \ r)} \cong G_i \cdot p + R_i \cdot p - P_i \cdot (1 - p) - J_i \cdot p' + T_i.$$

Approximate Equation (3), however, shows the total payoff for participation in the revolution. The individual should be interested in the net, i.e., the participation in the revolution minus the payoff he would receive if he were inactive. This is shown by Equation (4).[5]

$$(4) \qquad V_{(i, \ r)} \cong R_i \cdot p - P_i \cdot (1 - p) - J_i \cdot p' + T_i.$$

It will be noted that the public good aspect of the revolution drops out of this equation. The reason, of course, is that we are assuming that the individual's participation in the revolution makes a very small (in fact approximately zero) difference in the likelihood of success of the revolution.

If this approximate line of reasoning seems dubious, we may go back to Equation (2a), rearrange the terms a little bit, and get Equation (5) which is an exact rather than an approximate expression.

(5)     $V_{(i,\ r)} = (R_i + P_i) \cdot p + (G_i + R_i + P_i) \cdot \Delta p_i$
$- P_i - J_i \cdot p' + T_i.$

Once again, it is obvious that unless $\Delta p_i$ is large (say at least 10% of $p$), Equation (4) is a very good approximation. What we have been saying is, once again, that the revolution itself is a public good. Individuals, we have known since Samuelson's basic article, are likely to underinvest in production of public goods.

Let us now, however, turn to the opposite possibility – entering the revolution on the side of the government. Equation (6) shows the payoff for this activity.

(6)     $B_{(i,\ d)} = G_i (p - \Delta p_i) + D_i [1 - (p - \Delta p_i)]$
$- S_{(i,\ d)} (p - \Delta p_i) - J_i \cdot p' + T_i.$

Note that the individual's intervention by lowering the probability of revolutionary victory lowers the probability that he will receive the public good. Once again, assuming that the individual's participation has very little effect, i.e., $L_i$ is approximately equal to zero, we find Equation (7) which corresponds to Equation (3), i.e., it is the net return from participating on the side of reaction.

(7)     $B_{(i,\ d)} \cong D_i \cdot (1 - p) - S_{(i,\ d)} \cdot p - J_i \cdot p' + T_i.$

The equivalents of Equations (5) and (6) could also be produced easily.

$D_i$, the private reward for participation in putting down the revolt if the government wins, may be taken to include some of the incentives which the government might offer to people otherwise sympathetic with the revolutionary cause, perhaps even participants on the revolutionary side, to betray the revolution. Other things being equal, everybody who appreciates the public good offered by the revolution would be a sympathizer. Nevertheless, if the government offers private rewards for information or other forms of betrayal, sympathizers and even participants can be brought around. Moreover, the government may offer some of these rewards immediately, without requiring people to wait for them until the fate of the revolution is known, though a corrupt government (such as we have assumed) operates under a peculiar limitation in respect to such current rewards. If it is corrupt, it may be quite difficult for the government to use the technique of offering rewards for information, because its low level police officials may be able to misappropriate the rewards. Indeed, quite senior policemen may be tempted if the amounts of money are large.

Looked at from the standpoint of the individual police officer, paying out a reward for information is an activity which generates a public good for the entire government of which he is a member; but if he can put his own hands on the money, it means that he would obtain a private good. This inverts the free-rider argument which we have been using so far that indicates that revolutionaries would be likely to provide information. If I, the chief of police in some prefecture, divert into my own pocket money which could be used to purchase information and pass on to the central government some false information — perhaps executing a few people in order to give it an air of verisimilitude, I probably do not increase the likelihood of revolutionary victory by very much. On the other hand, I may increase my own income very greatly indeed.

In a corrupt government, this is a very serious problem. This may be the basic reason that corrupt governments are apt to turn to the use of negative incentives, i.e., threats of imprisonment, execution, and torture, to obtain information rather than offering rewards. Certainly, it is not in any way the result of moral scruples.

It will be noted that the approximate result we get indicates that the individuals would ignore the public good aspects of the revolution in deciding whether to participate *and* on which side to participate. The important variables are the rewards and punishments offered by the two sides and the risk of injury during the fighting.

Entertainment is probably not an important variable in serious revolutionary or counterrevolutionary activity. People are willing to take some risks for the fun of it, but not very severe ones. If, however, we consider such pseudo-revolutions as the recent student problems in much of the democratic world, it is probable that entertainment is one of the more important motives. The students in general carefully avoided running any very severe risks of injury or heavy punishment, while the chance of rewards was also very slight because they directed the revolutionary activity toward such institutions as universities where little was to be gained. The fact that '$T_i$' is not readily measurable would raise problems in empirical testing. Fortunately it is a minor factor in serious revolutions. Thus it could be left out in testing the equation.

If we change from our approximate equation to exact equations, it makes really very little difference. Under these circumstances, the public good remains in the equation, but has very slight weight unless the individual feels that his participation or nonparticipation will have a major influence on the outcome. Since most participants in revolution should have no such illusions, it would appear that the public good aspects of a revolution are of relatively little importance in the decision to participate. They should, therefore, be of relatively little importance in determining the outcome of the revolution. The discounted value of the rewards and punishment is the crucial factor.

3. This is a paradoxical result. It immediately raises a number of questions in the mind of any reasonably skeptical scholar. For example, why is the bulk of the literature of revolution written in terms of the public good aspects rather than in terms of the private rewards to participants if public good aspects are, in fact, so unimportant? Second, may we not have obtained our results by oversimplifying the situation? Third, what is the empirical evidence as to the truth or falsity of what is, so far, a completely *a priori* argument? We shall take these questions up *seriatim*.

3.1. Beginning with the question of the image of revolution, we should note that this image is essentially an intellectual one. Consider a historian in his study contemplating the French Revolution. He is not going to be either penalized or benefited by participation in this revolution which happened some two hundred years ago. Under the circumstances, the only things that concern him are its public good aspects. He may have been benefited or injured by the change in society which resulted from the revolution. He surely was not benefited or injured by the system of rewards and punishments for participation in the fighting. The parts of the revolution which concern him, then, are almost entirely the public good aspects. As the potential participant disregards the value of the public good generated because its value falls to nearly zero in his personal cost-benefit calculus, the historian disregards the private payoffs to participants because their values fall to almost zero in *his* calculus. They are costs and benefits for other people, not for him.

Similarly, the reporter filing stories on a revolution or the editorial writer in the metropolis are affected, if they are affected at all, by the public good aspects of the revolution rather than by the private rewards/punishments which might lead to direct participation in the fighting. Putting the matter more directly, each participant or observer is interested in that part of the total situation which is of maximum importance for him. That part which is important for the observer is rarely important for the participant and vice versa.

There is one class of participants who also formally emphasize the public good aspect. A great deal of our information about revolutionary overthrows comes from the memoirs of people who have participated in them, either on

the winning or the losing side. These people rarely explain their own participation or nonparticipation in terms of selfish motives. Indeed, they very commonly ascribe selfish motives to rivals or to the other side, but always explain
their own actions in terms of devotion to the public good.[6] Thus, they present themselves in the brightest light and their opponents in the darkest. We
should not, of course, be particularly surprised by this quite human behavior
on the part of these human beings, but we should also discount their evidence.

If we turn to the arguments that are used during the course of a revolution
to attract support — either recruits to the fighting or, perhaps, foreign aid —
we will normally observe a mixture of appeals to public and private benefits;
In general the approach is much like that of the army recruiting sergeant. He
will undoubtedly tell his potential customers that joining the army is patriotic,
etc. He will also tell them a great deal about the material benefits of military
service. Indeed, this is a very common practice in all fields of life. I happened
one day to be walking through the Marriott Motor Hotel in Washington, D.C.,
at a time when they were engaged in instructing new waitresses in their duties.
As I walked by, I heard the woman who was giving the lecture explaining to
them what an honor it was to operate at Marriott, that the customers at
Marriott Hotels are superior customers, and that the employees there are
generally speaking exceptionally good. This appeal to what we might call the
public good aspect of employment is not uncommon in any walk of life.

Since the recruiting sergeants, the people asking for support for (or opposition to) revolutions, and the Marriott Hotels all make use of this appeal as
well as more individualistic appeals, it is clear they have some effect. I would
guess, however, that the effect is small. The army, in attempting to attract
recruits, puts far more money into the salary of its soldiers than it does into
propaganda about patriotism. Still, the joint appeal is sensible; people to
some extent are motivated by ethical and charitable impulses.

We have thus explained why the intellectuals and other nonparticipant
observers of revolutions normally discuss them almost exclusively in terms of
public goods. We have also explained why the participants probably are more
strongly motivated by direct personal rewards than by these public goods. I
should like to emphasize here, however, that I am not criticizing the intellectuals for their field of concentration. Clearly, if we are evaluating the desirability or undesirability of a revolution in general terms, the public good
aspect is the one which we should consider. It is only if we are attempting to
study the dynamics of the revolution that we should turn to examination of
the utility calculus of the participants. Generally speaking, intellectual observers have been making judgments on the desirability or undesirability of

revolution, rather than explaining the revolution. It must be conceded, of course, that in many cases they have attempted to use the public good criteria to explain the dynamics, too. This is unfortunate, but we cannot blame them too much. The public good aspect, for the reason we have given above, dominates the reports of the revolution by historians and reporters. Analysis have been misled by this dominance of public good aspects in the literature. As a result they have been led to believe that it also dominates the calculus of the participants. We should avoid this error.

Thus, if we choose to evaluate revolutions in terms of their general desirability or undesirability, we would look at Equation (1). If we are attempting to understand the activities of the revolutionists and their opponents, we should look at Equations (4) and (7). People planning revolution or a counter-revolutionary activity should use Equations (4) and (7) in their actual planning and Equation (2) in their propaganda.

3.2. So much for our first problem. Let us turn to the second problem — the possibility that we have oversimplified the situation. Clearly our equations *are* very simple and it is *a priori* not obvious that we have not left out some important variable. First, we have assumed a very simple revolutionary situation in which a vicious and corrupt government is being attacked by a pure and good revolution. Obviously the real world is not this simple. If we temporarily define revolutions as a violent overthrow of the government,[7] then it is clear that bad governments have been overthrown by good revolutions and good governments have been overthrown by bad revolutions; but in the overwhelming majority of cases, it is difficult to decide between the two parties. Historically, the common form of revolution has been a not-too-efficient despotism which is overthrown by another non-too-efficient despotism with little or no effect on the public good. Indeed, except for the change in the names of the ruling circles, it would be hard to distinguish one from the other.

In those cases where there is little public good aspect to the revolution, even the historians and observers discuss them in terms of the personal participant's gain. For example, most accounts of the War of the Roses pay little or no attention to the propaganda which was issued by both sides about good government, Christianity, ethics, etc. The only exception to this concerns the very successful propaganda by Henry Tudor about the viciousness of the man he killed at Bosworth Field.

Such revolutions are, of course, the overwhelming majority. If we turn to that more limited number of revolutions where there is a significant change in régime, I think it would be hard to argue that those cases in which the revolution was an improvement outnumbered those in which it was a detriment. In the judgment of most modern editorial critics, the military overthrows of the previous régimes in Greece, Brazil, and Argentina were all distinct reductions in the public welfare of these countries. Whether this judgment is correct or not is irrelevant for our particular purposes. Surely there are, in fact, many cases in which such overthrows are detriments. Further, it seems likely that the mere cost inflicted by the fighting and confusion is quite significant in most cases, and hence one would only favor a revolution for public goods reasons if one felt that the net benefit of the change of régime was great enough to pay this cost.

Thus our equations as they are now drawn should be modified to indicate that the public good values from the revolution may be negative. If the revolutionary party proposes to put up a less efficient system — let us say it is in favor of collective farming, and we know the historically bad results of that method of running agriculture — then, the public good term in our equations would be negative rather than positive. Again, however, this bit of realism does not detract from the conclusions which we have drawn. The individuals would participate in the revolution or in its repression in terms of the private payoffs with little attention to the public goods. Reporters, on the other hand, would talk mainly about the public good aspects.

Another aspect in which our equations might be thought to lack realism concerns their generalist approach. The public good in our equations as we have so far interpreted them is a public good for the entire society. Note that this is not a necessary characteristic of the equations. Let us suppose that some particular group within the society has some chance of gaining from the revolution and there is some other group that will probably lose. Here the public good would apply only to these two groups. This, however, would make no difference in our equations. Indeed, in this respect, our equation is very similar to Mancur Olson's analysis of pressure groups in political society.[8] Following Olson, we are in essence espousing the byproduct theory of revolutions.

Another element of possible unrealism in our equations is basic to most discussion of public goods. From the time that Samuelson began the current interest in this field, public goods have been normally analyzed in terms of their private benefits for the individual. Thus, if we regard the police force as a Samuelsonian public good and look at Samuelson's equations, I am benefited by the police force because I do not wish to be robbed, murdered, etc. I do not necessarily take into account the benefit to other people. Clearly, most human beings have at least some interest in the well-being of others and hence this is unrealistic. It is, however, an element of unrealism in almost the entirity of the formal public goods literature and is not confined to our analysis of revolutions alone.

This element of unrealism is not, however, a necessary aspect of the public goods literature. Further, individual scholars have avoided this particular simplification. My benefit from the police force is not entirely represented by the fact that I am protected against various crimes. I may also gain something from my knowledge that other people are also benefited. Clearly, most people are — to at least some extent — interested in the well-being of others.[9] Thus my evaluation of my gain from the revolution would include not only my direct personal gain, but also any pleasure or pain which I receive as a result of interdependence between my preference function and that of others. In this respect, the revolution would be much like any other charitable activity.

The issue here, however, is basically one of size. The scholars who have discussed public goods without paying any attention to this type of interdependence have been simplifying reality, but not by very much. As far as we can see, for most people marginal adjustment between benefit to themselves and the benefit to other people is achieved when something under 5% of the resources under their control is allocated to help 'others.' Thus we could anticipate that individuals might be willing to do something to aid the revolution for reasons of the benefit which this will give to other people, but probably not very much. We have here, however, a difficult empirical problem, the measurement of the degree to which individuals are willing to sacrifice for the benefit of others. The work that has been done so far is not very impressive. Still, it would have to be wrong by at least that much to make this particular aspect of our equation dangerously oversimplified. Indeed, the equations would not be incorrect even if it turned out that individual evaluation of the well-being of others was very high. It would simply mean that the public good aspect of revolutions would have a larger value than it would if the individual put little weight on the well-being of other persons.

3.3. This brings us to our third problem, the empirical evidence. The first thing that should be said is that there have been no careful empirical tests aimed at disentangling the motives of revolutionaries. The literature is overwhelmingly dominated by the 'public goods' hypothesis. Indeed, so far as I know, this paper is the first suggestion that it might be falsified. Under the circumstances, it is not surprising that no one has run a formal test.

Furthermore, no one has collected the type of detailed data which would be necessary to test the two hypotheses. It does not seem to me that formal statistical tests would be at all impossible, although they might be difficult. The difficulty would, of course, be particularly strong in the case of unsuccessful revolutions, since few records would have been kept. Still, approximating the ex ante value of the private rewards to be expected from participation in a revolution should not be impossible. It seems to me that such research would be most important and I would be delighted to see someone undertake it.

It is not, however, my intention to engage in such research here. Instead I propose to look rather superficially at the actual history of revolutions and see whether these data seem to contradict or support my byproduct theory of revolutions. First, it must be admitted that most revolutions do have some effect on government policy. The personnel at the top is changed and normally that would mean at least some change in government policy. It is hard to argue, however, that in most cases this was the major objective of the revolution. In most cases, after all, the new government is very much like the one before. Most overthrows are South American or African and simply change the higher level personnel. It is true that the new senior officials will tell everyone — and very likely believe it themselves — that they are giving better government than their predecessors. It is hard, however, to take these protestations very seriously.

One of the reasons it is hard to take these protestations seriously is that in most revolutions, the people who overthrew the existing government were high officials in that government before the revolution. If they were deeply depressed by the nature of the previous government's policies, it seems unlikely that they could have given enough cooperation in those policies to have risen to high rank. People who hold high, but not supreme, rank in a despotism are less likely to be unhappy with the policy of that despotism than are people who are outside the government. Thus, if we believed in the public good motivation of revolutions, we would anticipate that these high officials would be less likely than outsiders to attempt to overthrow the government.

From the private benefit theory of revolutions, however, the contrary deduction would be drawn. The largest profits from revolution are apt to come to those people who are (a) most likely to end up at the head of the government, and (b) most likely to be successful in overthrow of the existing government. They have the highest present discounted gain from the revolution and lowest present discounted cost. Thus, from the private goods theory of revolution, we would anticipate senior officials who have a particularly good chance of success in overthrowing the government and a fair certainty of being at high rank in the new government if they are successful to be the most common type of revolutionaries. Superficial examination of history would seem to indicate that the private good theory is upheld by this empirical test. Needless to say, a more careful and exhaustive study of the point is needed.

Another obvious area for empirical investigation concerns the expectations of the revolutionaries. My impression is that they generally expect to have a good position in the new state which is to be established by the revolution. Further, my impression is that the leaders of revolutions continuously encourage their followers in such views. In other words, they hold out private gains to them. It is certainly true that those people that I have known who have talked in terms of revolutionary activity have always fairly obviously thought that they themselves would have a good position in the 'new Jerusalem.' Normally, of course, it is necessary to do a little careful questioning of them to bring out this point. They will normally begin by telling you that they favor the revolution solely because it is right, virtuous, and preordained by history.

As another piece of evidence, Lenin is famous for having developed the idea of professional revolutionaries. He felt that amateurs were not to be trusted in running a revolution and wished to have people who devoted full-time to revolutionary activity and who were supported by the revolutionary organization. Clearly, he held a byproduct theory of revolution, although I doubt that he would ever have admitted it.

Last, we may take those noisest of 'revolutionaries' – the current radical left students. It is noticeable that these students, although they talk a great deal about public goods, in fact do very little in the way of demonstrating their devotion to such goods. Indeed, the single most conspicuous characteristic of their 'revolutionary' activities is the great care that they take to minimize private cost. Always and everywhere, one of the major demands is that no private cost be imposed on unsuccessful revolutionaries by way of punishment. Further, they normally carefully arrange their activities in locations – such as universities – where they feel confident that no great punishment will be imposed upon them. This is in spite of the fact that it is obvious that totally overthrowing *all* of the universities in the modern world would not significantly affect any government. The attack on a university may bring very little benefit – either private or public – but it is also accompanied by very small costs. Indeed, this may be one of the rare cases where the entertainment value of revolution is the dominant motivation.

I should not like to argue that the empirical information contained in the last few paragraphs is decisive. Clearly, however, it does prove that the evidence is not overwhelmingly against the byproduct theory of revolutions. Further, granted the fact that all previous theoretical discussion of revolutions have been based on the public goods theory, it is quite encouraging that material collected by scholars holding this point of view can be used to support the byproduct theory.

In sum, the theoretical arguments for the view that revolutions are carried out by people who hope for private gain and produce such public goods as they do produce as a byproduct seem to me very strong. As of now, no formal empirical test has been made of it, but a preliminary view of the empirical evidence would seem to support the byproduct theory. This, of course, is the paradox. Revolution is the subject of an elaborate and voluminous literature and, if I am right, all of this literature is wrong.

*Virginia Polytechnical Institute and*
*State University*

## NOTES

[1] See the table of algebraic symbols and their definitions at the beginning of the paper.
[2] P. Samuelson, 'The Pure Theory of Public Expenditure', *Review of Economics and Statistics* 54 (Nov., 1954), 387–9; 'A Diagrammatic Exposition of a Theory of Public Expenditure', *Loc. cit.* 55 (Nov., 1955), 387–389; cf. *The Collected Scientific Papers of Paul Samuelson*, R. Merton, ed., Vol. III, Cambridge, Mass., 1972; A. C. Pigou, *The Economics of Welfare*, Macmillan, London, 1920.
[3] In the real world, of course, there are various shades between the clear-cut alternatives, but our simplication will cause no great damage.
[4] For those wishing to make comparisons with Professor Scriven's treatment the basic equation is:

$$G(\text{Tullock}) = E - (I + C_R) \text{ (Scriven)} \cdot$$

[5] Note the rather peculiar algebraic role of $P_i$, the punishment the individual is likely to receive if he participates in the revolution and it fails. Because of the rules of algebra, this turns up as a minus quantity for the entire punishment with certainty, which is offset by a positive figure which is that punishment discounted by the probability of victory. It would be intuitively much simpler if our equation showed this expression in some more lucid way. It is still true, however, that increasing the weight of the punishment, something which is clearly within control of the government, would greatly reduce $G_r$.
[6] It should be noted that a somewhat similar phenomenon affects the nonparticipant observers like scholars and reporters. If they have become partisans of one side, they are apt to accuse the partisans of the other side of having individualistic motives.
[7] Some people seem to define 'revolution' as desirable violent overthrows of a government. With this definition, what we are to say below will not follow. Presumably they

would be willing to accept some other word to mean violent overthrow of government, regardless of its moral evaluation, and that could be substituted for 'revolution' in the rest of our discussion.

<sup>8</sup> Mancur Olson, *The Logic of Collective Action*, Harvard Press, Cambridge, Mass., 1965.

<sup>9</sup> Perhaps negatively. Kenneth Boulding has done a great deal to call attention to the role of malevolence in human life.

DAVID BRAYBROOKE

## SELF-INTEREST IN TIMES OF REVOLUTION
## AND REPRESSION

### *Comment on Professor Tullock's Analysis\**

In Professor Tullock's hands, axioms about rationality once again prove their fertility in generating arresting empirical hypotheses, which emerge from the very womb trailing plausible theoretical connections. I speak of 'axioms' in the plural, because there is a whole family of axioms to draw from. It will suffice, however, for my purposes in discussing the present example of Tullock's work, to have just one in mind: what I shall call "the gross axiom of rational action". Suppose that the alternatives to be chosen are reduced to two categories of action, exhaustive and mutually exclusive: doing $A$ or not-doing $A$; the gross axiom of rational action says that a person acts rationally only if he eschews the alternative for which the algebraic sum of the costs and benefits to himself is smaller. The axiom is gross not for want of delicacy, since among the benefits and costs the most refined philanthropic pleasures and the most delicate conscientious scruples may be counted. It is gross simply for want of the detail that other members of the same family of axioms bring into play: for example, one of the marginal principles for equilibrium in a consumer's budget.

Steady insistence upon the gross axiom of rational action implies steady insistence upon giving chief weight, in explaining even the most colorful of human events, to the returns that individual agents can expect to obtain from their own actions. Even if an agent were so benevolent as to have (say) ten times as much interest as the average agent in the welfare of his fellow citizens, raising the benefit $(G_i)$ that he may expect to derive from the public good of a successful revolution accordingly, in ordinary circumstances with ordinary powers he can have little — vanishingly little — to do with bringing the benefit about, however strenuously he acts. Furthermore, since the benefit is a public good, with which everyone can be supplied at no cost above the cost of supplying anyone, and from whose use no one can be excluded, the agent will benefit from it anyway (benevolently as well as selfishly) without having to pass any test about making a contribution himself. Consequently there is in ordinary circumstances, for men of ordinary powers — even when they are extraordinarily benevolent and in that way public-spirited — little or no weight to be given to the attraction of the public good as an effective motivation. It counts equally for doing $A$ and for not-doing $A$ and consequently

61

*H. J. Johnson, J. J. Leach, and R. G. Muehlmann (eds.), Revolutions, Systems, and Theories, 61–74. All Rights Reserved.*
*Copyright © 1979 by D. Reidel Publishing Company, Dordrecht, Holland.*

does not offer a distinctive motive for either alternative. Whether agents become active for a revolution (or against it), instead of remaining on the side-lines awaiting results, is to be explained either by showing that the agents' circumstances or powers were not in fact ordinary ones or by showing that the agents were moved by incentives relating to private goods — money, offices, safe-conduct to the border.

I am more than ready to give a sympathetic reception to the general hypothesis that a public goods motivation plays only a negligible part in the motivation of most agents in most revolutions. I think some of the particular suggestions that Tullock is led to by the hypothesis very likely come as close to being *a priori* hits upon empirical targets as a sound conception of scientific method could allow. It is not only an arresting suggestion, it is a suggestion unlikely to turn up on other approaches, that the people most likely to have a substantial net interest in taking part in a revolution are highly placed officials in the present government, though a revolution staged by such people is least likely to bring about a radical transformation of society and government. Again, the particular explanation suggested for the use of torture in the repressive activities of corrupt governments is surprising and (at least on an *a priori* view) penetrating: it is not just that every kind of bad thing is to be expected of governments once corrupt. Torture is a substitute for money rewards, which the governments cannot effectively use because corrupt officials would appropriate the rewards for themselves.[1]

I believe that hits like these could easily be multiplied in the course of extending the approach to take into account further aspects of revolutions, especially aspects of what might be called the dynamics of aggregation. Very likely Tullock himself has already done so somewhere in the writings from which his present contribution has been extracted. Let us consider his basic (approximate) equation for the net payoff to an individual agent for taking part in a revoluton:

$$V(i, r) \cong R_i \cdot p - P_i \cdot (1 - p) - J_i \cdot p' + T_i.$$

Would it not be sensible to add to the right-hand side of this equation a variable, $N_{(i, in)}$, standing for the penalty that the agent is liable to suffer at the hands of the revolutionists if he stands aside? I do not say, acts to defend the government; hence $N_{(i, in)}$ is not identical with $S_{(i, d)}$, which figures in another of Tullock's equations as the penalty that will be imposed on defenders of the government if the revolution succeeds. (No doubt, of course, this other penalty will often be meted out without much discrimination between having actively supported the government and having remained inactive on the side of the revolution).

The penalty $N_{(i,\ in)}$ will have to be multiplied by a probability, too; and since the penalty may not be exacted until accounts are settled by the revolutionists once victorious, the probability of the penalty, strictly speaking, will depend to some extent, like the probability of $S_{(i,\ d)}$ on the probability $p$ of victory. But there may be a high probability attached to the penalty already, quite independently of $p$ and of $S_{(i,\ d)}$, at least for agents who find themselves literally surrounded by revolutionists. Let the probability of suffering this penalty for inaction be represented as $p''$; then, taking the plus value of escaping the penalty as equal to the minus value of undergoing it with the probability $p''$, we add to the right-hand side of the equation the quantity $N_{(i,\ in)} \cdot p''$. The presence of this quantity will help explain how revolutionary forces, once they have a foothold in various sections or strata of the society, gather strength through aggregation: They gather it, in effect, by conscripting it, a common phenomenon found, for example, in the pressures exerted by patriotic mobs during the American Revolution as well as in the recruiting efforts of the Viet Cong in areas outside Saigon.

If the relationship between $p''$ and the probability $p$ of victory for the revolution is taken into account, the equation will show, as I think it should, a rise in the incentives for engaging in revolutionary activity as the revolution approaches victory more and more surely. Both probabilities, $p''$ and $p$, may in fact rise rapidly together. $p$ would rise if, taken together with the other variables, $p''$ in the period just concluded had been high enough for the prospect of $N_{(i,\ in)}$ to press a substantial number of people into the revolutionary cause; but then, both because there are more people to exert pressure on behalf of the revolution and because $p$ has risen, $p''$ will be still higher in the current period and bring still more people into the revolutionary aggregation. Indeed, once the penalty for inaction is taken into account, one may begin to wonder how a revolution could possibly be stopped, just as one might have wondered, given the unmodified equation, how it could possibly get underway. In fact, the negative quantities still present in the equation $(P_i \cdot (1 - p))$ — representing the penalty that the government might impose on anyone who engaged in revolutionary activity and $(J_i \cdot p')$ the dangers of injury in the course of the activity itself — may be heightened to the point of repressing such activity almost everywhere; and there will of course be sections and strata where agents find themselves surrounded not by revolutionists but by supporters of the government. If those are more important sections and strata to begin with, or they expand more rapidly, the revolution is not likely to get very far.

Tullock appears to take all the probabilities that he puts into the equation at their objective values; thus ordinary men in ordinary circumstances have (objectively) very little chance of affecting the course of the revolution in a significant way. It is true that what counts in motivating an individual agent would strictly speaking be his subjective estimates of the probabilities, were there to be any discrepancy between these estimates and their objective values (however determined); but Tullock may be assuming that there is a powerful tendency for subjective estimates to converge over time with the objective values. I think this is a reasonable assumption. However, there may be cases where the tendency (taken as a tendency in individual lives) hardly has time to operate, and the discrepancy is crucial to explaining the action.

Are not young people, who have had little experience of the difficulties of coordinated political action, likely to overestimate their individual chances of making an important, perhaps a decisive contribution, to the result? If they do not anticipate being leaders, they may nevertheless dream of being heroes, who will find themselves at a turning point of the revolution and carry the day. May not inexperienced people of any age, angered by a setback to their aspirations, or by some other kind of deprivation, lose sight, in the first moments of their enthusiasm for setting things right, of the true dimensions of their situation?[2] Not only may the value of the revolution as a public good, $G_i$, have to be brought back into the equation because these agents fail to reckon $\Delta p_i$ (the change in the probability of victory resulting from their respective individual contributions) at any reasonably small value; $p_i$ and $j_i$, the penalty liable to be imposed by the government and the injury liable to come in the course of the fighting, may not have the weight that they (objectively) deserve as deterrents because the agents, in their enthusiasm, ignore the rather high probabilities (objectively) associated with them.[3] Such discrepancies between subjective estimates and objective values might not continue for long; but suppose they exist long enough for the agents to cast their lot, visibly and irrevocably, with the revolutionary forces. Thereafter the soberest application of the gross axiom of rational action might well indicate that it would be more dangerous for them to defect from the revolutionary cause than to carry on as active revolutionists. The government might not welcome them back and their fellow-revolutionists will not take kindly to their leaving.

Che Guevara, in his quixotic attempt to rally a force to defend Guatemala City against the approaching hosts of counter-revolution led by Castillo Armas and supplied (it seems) by the CIA, might serve as an example of momentary aberration in subjective estimates. He could hardly be said to have expected a private reward in the form of an official post, or anything like it. He was an outsider, little more than a casual visitor from another country.[4] The prospects of success, with or without his intervention, were (objectively) very dim; and the danger of punitive action by the other side, considerable — in fact, after the event, Guevara's life was spared only because the Argentine ambassador had taken the initiative of bringing him within the protection of the embassy. There was, on the other hand, little or no pressure from the revolutionists (and so no substance in $N_{(i, in)}$); the disarray and disappearance of the revolutionists were precisely the factors that made the gesture of rallying them so quixotic.

Guevara's revolutionary career invites further reflection. How is it to be explained, consistently with the gross axiom of rational action, that he left, and never returned to, the promising career that his social connections and his medical degree presumably offered him in Argentina? If at any time in his wanderings, at least before he sailed with Castro to raise the flag of revolution in Cuba, perhaps even afterwards, he had weighed costs and benefits and probabilities, would not the practice of medicine in the milieu in which he was born have offered, and have seemed to offer, greater net benefits, unless perhaps we impute a bizarrely high quantity to 'entertainment value'? It is difficult to believe that any long-run estimates which Guevara might have made would have been so far off the mark which objective observers might have fixed as to persuade him that revolutionary activity accorded with his own interests.

Yet there is a way of applying the gross axiom of rational action even here, and of extending Tullock's approach to cover such cases, without having to set entertainment value at a bizarrely high figure. Tullock's equation does not, as it stands, carry on the face of it any limitation as to the scope of the calculations which it is to embrace; for all that it says to the contrary, every cost or benefit that fits under one or another of the heads mentioned, however remote, is to be taken into account. But is this always the right way to read the equation, or apply the axiom? Are there not agents who for a time at least, perhaps for years, maybe during the whole of their lives, act without making long-run calculations? Yet they may continually act in accordance with the gross axiom of rational action, applied successively to a succession of short-run agendas. Guevara seems to have acted in something like this way. He did not exactly renounce the practice of medicine after taking his degree; he rather put off beginning to practice, in favor of seeing a bit more of the world. He became increasingly curious, as he went from country to country, to see manifestations of reform and revolution. Then, in Guatemala, he passed from curiosity to commitment, though not as yet (thanks to the Argentine ambassador) irrevocable commitment. But even this passage was by stages: before intervening in the futile struggle against Armas, and the CIA, he had cared enough about acting to seek a job with the progressive government; though not enough to become a party member. Falling in with the Castro group, after his safe-conduct to Mexico, was just one more action on a short-run agenda – doing $A$ rather than not doing $A$, where not doing $A$ either did not include the alternative of going back to practice medicine in Argentina or at least did not bring to mind the long-run benefits to be associated with that alternative.[5]

It appears, then, that if some principle limiting in temporal scope the agendas to which Tullock's equation is to be applied is joined to the equation and thus to the gross axiom of rational action, such apparently unreflecting phenomena as Guevara's drift into revolutionary activity can be covered. I shall not try to determine here what the best choice of this extra principle might be, or how it is to be connected with such things as aspiration levels and conditioning; the principle may have a foundation of its own in rational considerations (themselves perhaps 'satisficing') having to do with reducing the efforts of calculation. I am here simply concerned to point out the equation will be a big success if it does no more than explain the motivation of most agents in most revolutions. The equation seems to be in a fair way of being able to provide such an explanation and enjoy the attached success. The extra principle will enlarge this success. The advantages of the extra principle, allowing for long-run drift through a succession of short-run agendas, are not confined simply to bringing more agents within the fold. They include the rather remarkable advantage of being able to extend the equation to explaining the motivation of revolutionary leaders. A theory of revolution that embraces Che Guevara as well as most ordinary agents is (other things being equal) appreciably more satisfactory than one that does not.

In Guevara's case, Tullock's equation can be made to serve in a reiterated short-run application if the discounted weights of the penalty for revolutionary activity and of the injury possibly to be suffered in the course of it fade out relatively to the positive incentives. We need not suppose that the penalty which the revolutionary forces themselves are liable to impose requires much weight in his case. We can give some special weight to 'entertainment value', and that might be enough to determine each decision. Should we not, however, think of revising $R_i \cdot p$, the variable for the private reward to the individual agent multiplied by the probability of victory for the revolution? An office to be gained after the revolution is a remote consideration here; the short-run agendas that we are discussing would embrace more immediate rewards — positions of leadership in the movement now or at least in a cell connected with it; reinforcing company, conversation, and applause; a girl from Peru.

It is not just Guevara that will be caught up by the extra principle about limited agendas; it helps capture the motivation of someone greater than he. Mao Tse-Tung did not as a young man have anything like Guevara's privileges or prospects. But he, too, seems to have drifted into full-time revolutionary activity through a series of decisions that had to do with short-run agendas so far as they were rational and reflective at all. In a professionalized revolutionary movement like Chinese Communism, the short-run rewards, all of which would be multiplied by a probability much higher than the probability of eventual victory, would in time include something like a livelihood — or at least the assurance of material support six months in advance. For Mao it may have been a better livelihood than he would have had as a peasant, a soap-maker, or a policeman. Even in the chaotic conditions of Chinese life at the time, a man of his talent might have expected to make in the long run a materially more rewarding career doing something else, for example, making a wholehearted job of being a teacher of teachers; but it seems reasonable to suppose that each successive short-run agenda offered the young Mao a positive incentive for entering deeper and deeper into revolutionary activity.

I think we might even do well to find a place in the equation for restoring the public-goods variable, on a short-run basis. From Mao's point of view each manifesto, each newspaper, each demonstration may have been itself a public good. They would have been public goods because they were thought to raise the probability $L_v$ of the ultimate public good of revolutionary social transformation; but if men choose to value changes in such a probability, why should the events thought to bring about such changes not be reckoned as public goods too?[6] Each of the goods in question would have been within the reach of a short-run agenda, and likely to depend greatly upon Mao's personal efforts.[7]

I have so far been able to avoid placing any bizarre or any even merely undue strain upon the variable for 'entertainment value', in showing how by suitable adjustments and changes of perspective Tullock's equation and with it the gross axiom of rational action can be extended to cover a wide variety of motivations. What, however, are we to say about the Ulyanov brothers? Like Guevara, they enjoyed a privileged background; like him, they had good prospects of leading outstanding professional careers. Unlike him, they made

their decisions to engage in revolutionary activity in circumstances that make
it well-nigh impossible to assume they did not reflect on long-run considerations.

Consider Vladimir first. Along with the rest of his family, he suffered some
embarrassment because of Alexander's arrest and execution; and the embarrassment may have multiplied the trouble that he created for himself by
taking part in a student demonstration at the University of Kazan.[8] His prospects were not ruined, however. On the contrary: in spite of being unable to
gain readmittance to university classes, he was allowed to proceed to the legal
examinations of the University of St. Petersburg as an external student. After
devoting a year to concentrated study at home, he wrote the examinations
and obtained a first class.[9] Then, when the question arose as to whether he
would have a full or limited license to practice, the police indicated that they
had no objection to Vladimir's being given a full license.[10] It is scarcely to be
believed that he would have put forward these efforts and gained these substantial successes without reflecting on the advantages of a conventional legal
career — in a society under strain but far from being so chaotic as to make
such a career look infeasible. It is hard to believe, on the other hand, that any
sober assessment of the life of a professional revolutionist, in and out of jail,
living poorly whether in or out, without a regular income or a regular family
life, unlikely to live long enough to enjoy personally any of the benefits of
the transformed society, could have held out advantages comparable to those
of a conventional career. Inescapably, to characterize Vladimir's agenda with
anything like substantial accuracy, it seems that we have to introduce into the
equation another variable, $A_i$, for the rewards of a conventional career, very
substantial in Vladimir's case, and multiplied in his case by a very high probability, $p_a$, the product counting as a dominant minus quantity. Nevertheless,
Vladimir's deliberate, long-run decision was to become a professional revolutionist.

Vladimir may be hard to explain; Alexander, executed in 1887 for conspiring to assassinate the Tsar, is harder. Consider three successive decisions taken
by Alexander: first, to enter the conspiracy; second, after capture by the
police, to shoulder as much as he could of the responsibility; third, after sentencing, to refrain from asking the Tsar for clemency. The first decision, to
enter the conspiracy, might be explained by bringing the public goods variable back into Tullock's equation and arguing that there was in fact a prospect
that Alexander's participation would make a substantial difference to bringing about that public good, the death of the Tsar. But Alexander himself did
not think that his participation was going to be very effectual in the end; he

seems to have thought that the enterprise was doomed from the beginning.[11] Nor did he have any reason to believe that if it succeeded, the death of the Tsar would so transform society that there would be no reprisals against the conspirators. Whether or not the Tsar was successfully killed, Alexander might rationally have expected to be giving up the scientific career on which his brilliant achievements at the university had launched him; seriously embarrassing his family, as well as breaking his mother's heart; and throwing away his chances of an agreeable personal life.

As regard the second and third decisions, there is not even a pretext for bringing in the public goods variable: for that variable by definition motivates only people who can expect to be around to enjoy the good once it is in being; and the actions that Alexander took following his second and third decisions were actions in which he gave up life itself. In terms of Tullock's equation, they raised the probability $p'$ of injury $J_i$ suffered in the course of revolutionary activity as close to certainty as made no difference. What is left in the way of possible counterbalance that we can draw on to explain these decisions? $R_i \cdot p$, the private reward to be obtained after the revolution, is either to be ignored or to be given negligible weight. If it counted for anything, would it not count in the way of impelling Alexander to stay alive in the hope of enjoying its benefits? All that is left is $T_i$, the term for 'entertainment value'. If we are to extend Tullock's approach to cover Alexander Ulyanov, we shall have either to count under 'entertainment value' a number of things that have little or nothing to do with 'entertainment' in any ordinary sense, or introduce a new variable.

Let us introduce a new variable. What might this variable $C$ stand for? I suggest that it might stand chiefly for various aspects of *conscience*, including chiefly a care for personal honor (to speak in a very elevated way), as founded upon notions about what I shall call the Other-Regarding No Sucker Principle. Tullock's equation allows, as he says, for other-regarding motivation in the value of the public goods variable; in effect, he allows for benevolence. But in the face of Alexander Ulyanov's decisions, it appears that there are further dimensions of other-regardingness to be allowed for.

Part of Alexander's motivation for the third decision, refusing to ask for clemency, was (like one of Socrates' reasons for refusing Crito's offer to help in escaping prison) that he felt it beneath his dignity (as a man of honor might well have felt it) to behave inconsistently with the defiant courage which he had displayed at his trial.[12] In his second decision, to assume as much of the blame as possible, part of his motivation seems to have been conscientious feelings about the mutual support owed his friends; and these feelings evidently assisted in bringing about his first decision, to enter the conspiracy.[13] Could he withhold his support, even in a desperate venture, if his friends were embarked upon it? But it was not merely that his friends needed his support; what they were engaged in was an attempt to promote something that Alexander himself believed in — the revolutionary transformation of Russian society.

It is in this connection that the Other-Regarding No Sucker Principle played a part — a part in Alexander's motivation that continued through all three decisions.[14] I suggest that like most people with a careful upbringing and expectations of social efficacy (in Alexander's and Vladimir's case, expectations grounded on among other things their father's career) Alexander had acquired rather deeply-rooted conscientious scruples about doing his part, carrying his share of the load, not letting other people do all the work, not playing for suckers other people when they put forward trustful initiatives. Thus the free-rider problem, which looms so large in the treatment accorded by Tullock and like-minded authors to the supply of public goods, is met to some extent by moral training which offsets the temptations that give rise to the problem; and this training extends beyond cases of public goods that the agent will enjoy himself to goods that will benefit other people only (his family; his friends; his countrymen).[15] The fact is, and Tullock's equation needs only one new discounted variable to cover the fact, men do volunteer for hazardous duties; and do on occasion lay down their lives, deliberately. While such phenomena occur, we must, I think, suppose that honor and conscience count for something; for Alexander Ulyanov they were evidently decisive.

Vladimir is easier to explain when we return to him from Alexander, though I am far from thinking that even so the explanation is as full as we would like. Vladimir evidently did not announce his decision at the time, and he was close-mouthed about the impression that Alexander's fate made upon him.[16] Yet it has seemed reasonable to his biographers to claim that his brother's fate was of crucial importance in Vladimir's decision, not, evidently, by way of revenge[17] but rather by way of furnishing Vladimir with an example of commitment and self-sacrifice which Vladimir could not conscientiously ignore.[18] I suggest that Vladimir, coming like his brother to desire a revolutionary transformation of Russian society, would have been ashamed not to commit himself as whole-heartedly as his brother had. To act otherwise, given their shared convictions, would have been something like playing Alexander for a sucker.

In its extended form, the form that covers the Ulyanov brothers, Mao, and

Guevara, as well as a lot of revolutionists young and old, who never counted
for so much or achieved such world-historical fame, Tullock's equation reads

$$V_{(i,\ r)} \cong R_i \cdot p - P_i \cdot (1 - p) - J_i \cdot p' + N_{(i,\ in)} \cdot p''$$
$$- A_i \cdot p_a + C_i + T_i.$$

In applications to short-run agendas, a public goods variable is to be reintro-
duced and the probability $p$ of ultimate success in the revolution replaced by
a probability associated with some short-run objective; and sometimes subjective probabilities rather than objective probabilities are to be used. The
adjustments that I have made to reach this position were easily predictable
ones; I think they might well be regarded as vindicating Tullock's approach
rather than refuting it. Some people might unkindly suggest, nevertheless,
that the adjustments have the effect of turning the equation inside out. For,
so the suggestion might run, they make room for all those romantic aspects of
revolutionary motivation that Tullock seemed so concerned to get rid of:
conscience, honor, emulation, zeal for the good of one's country, enthusiasm,
even dreams of heroism. It is true that the adjustments do make room for
these things; but the room that they make is chastened room, which (I am
ready to believe) will be no more room than is compatible with Tullock's
basic contention, interpreted as holding that for most agents in most revolutions private material incentives are crucial and indispensable. Vindicated on
this basic contention alone, Tullock will have achieved a dramatic reversal of
emphasis in the interpretation of revolutionary activity. If the adjustments I
have discussed are accepted (as I think they should be) as according with the
no-nonsense spirit of Tullock's approach and its basic assumptions about
rationality, Tullock would seem to be vindicated on much more than the
basic contention; though at a certain price. Tullock says, "Revolution is the
subject of an elaborate and voluminous literature and, if I am right, all of this
literature is wrong". I say, to be entirely right, Tullock must concede that the
other literature, which calls for some room in the calculus for a variety of
motives that he has not given any credit to, is not entirely wrong.

*Dalhousie University*


## NOTES

* I wish to thank Professor Roger Dial of the Department of Political Science and
Professor John Head of the Department of Economics at Dalhousie University for commenting on a draft of this comment.

[1] Along with the points just cited, I think we should itemize as an equally striking success Tullock's metatheoretical or metahistorical hypothesis ascribing the stress that historians and journalists put upon public goods motivations to the fact that the revolutions they write about, in other countries and other times, interest them as public goods, and not at all as prospective sources of private rewards.

[2] If some account is taken of discrepancies between subjective and objective probabilities, Tullock's equation can offer a more congenial reception to the most carefully worked-out behavioral theories of revolution, which attribute increases in revolutionary activity to increases in *relative deprivation*, defined as the agents' "perception of discrepancy between their value expectations and their value capabilities". See T. N. Gurr, *Why Men Rebel*, Princeton University Press, Princeton, 1970, p. 24 and pp. 46–56. Evidently increases in relative deprivation might figure as increases in the public goods variable, since the revolution would be expected to reduce deprivations; but the public goods variable, under Tullock's present treatment, is subject to such a drastic objective discount that it would drop out of the equation, increase or no increase; it could be saved as effective accommodation for increased relative deprivation only if the probability with which it is multiplied is understood as having an exaggerated, subjective value. The private reward variable might be used instead. However, it is confined to special inducements to revolutionary activity beyond the benefits (like reduced deprivation) that the revolution will achieve for everyone. More land, expropriated from the landlords, or a better job, displacing an undeserving idler, will not count as a private reward unless it is made a condition of obtaining such benefits that one be certified to have engaged in timely revolutionary activity. Even then the benefits will have to be assigned to the public goods variable and (given an objective probability) have to drop out with it insofar as there is some prospect of escaping the condition. A subjective interpretation might extend the accommodation offered by the private reward variable by letting it count when agents believed (mistakenly) that the condition could not be escaped. Yet this extension would not suffice to explain the behavior of people who do not believe that they face such a condition; and the objective interpretation of the equation could not use the private reward variable when no such condition exists. In these cases – which may be most cases in some revolutions – will not incongruously intensive use have to be made, in accommodating increases in relative deprivation, of $T_i$ 'entertainment value'? It hardly seems designed for the purpose; and certainly Tullock does not anticipate its having much importance. (My comments on the private reward variable in this note have been modified in response to a point made by Professor Michael Wallack in a discussion at the Memorial University of Newfoundland.)

[3] I am passing over the distinction between on the one hand, consciously making subjective estimates different from objective probabilities and on the other hand, simply ignoring for the moment the objective probabilities or the need for reckoning with them. The effect of ignoring can be represented in the equation by substituting an unsuitably high or low value at the appropriate places.

[4] A few months before, he had applied for a medical post with a rural development project sponsored by the Arbenz government; but he had refused to comply with the condition of employment, that he join what was in effect the Communist Party of Guatemala. See Richard Harris, *Death of a Revolutionary: Che Guevara's Last Mission*, W. W. Norton, New York, 1970, p. 25; for Guevara's efforts in Guatemala City just before its fall, and his rescue by the Argentine ambassador, see p. 27.

[5] For an account of Guevara's upbringing, wanderings, and gradual involvement in revolutionary activity, see Harris, *op. cit.*, Chap. 1.

[6] It is no argument against reckoning them so that they were intangible. A change in probability may be intangible, but they were not; and tangibility is not a necessary condition of being a good, public or private, anyway. Satisfaction taken as an approximation of a necessary condition, does not require tangibility; nor does the ultimately sophisticated test of revealing one's willingness to pay something for the good in question. People are willing to pay a good deal on occasion to have a verbal agreement.

[7] For accounts of Mao's origins and early years as a revolutionist, see Jerome Ch'en, *Mao and the Chinese Revolution*, Oxford University Press, London, 1965; and (in less detail) Stuart Schram, *Mao Tse-Tung*, Penguin, London, 1966.

[8] Nikolai Valentinov, *The Early Years of Lenin*, tr. and ed. Rolf H. W. Theen, The University of Michigan Press, Ann Arbor, 1969, p. 139, footnote A.

[9] Valentinov, *op. cit.*, p. 147.

[10] Louis Fischer, *The Life of Lenin*, Weidenfeld and Nicholson, 1965, p. 19. Fischer and Valentinov give incompatible dates for the period of study and for the examinations taken in St. Petersburg.

[11] Isaac Deutscher, *Lenin's Childhood*, Oxford University Press, London, 1970, p. 54.

[12] Deutscher, *op. cit.*, pp. 60–61; Valentinov, *op. cit.*, p. 100.

[13] Deutscher, *op. cit.*, pp. 55, 58, cf. p. 53; Valentinov, *op. cit.*, p. 99.

[14] See, again, Deutscher, *op. cit.*, p. 53.

[15] The species of moral training to which I refer here might be called 'generalization training'. The critical frenzy aroused by Marcus G. Singer's book *Generalization in Ethics*, Alfred A. Knopf, New York, 1961, may have had the odd effect of diverting philosophers' attention from the importance of such training, which substantially vindicates Singer's thinking. Singer's presentation seems to have had many defects, discovered during the controversy: he ignored 'threshold effects' and the need for a comparative form of his principle of consequences ('If the consequences of doing $X$ are undesirable, one ought not to do $x$') if the principle is to be convincing; he was mistaken in equating 'ought not' with 'has no right to'; he claimed too much in claiming that 'the generalization argument' was at the bottom of all moral reasoning. Yet it is a mistake on the other side to dismiss the argument that answers the question, "What would happen if everyone did that?", as "a minor moral argument of rather limited application" (Alexander Sesonske, 'Moral Rules and the Generalization Argument', *American Philosophical Quarterly* **3** (1966), 282. The free rider problem, which arises for every public good, shows how much of a mistake. The Generalization Argument reflects with substantial accuracy that part of moral training which, employing the Other-Regarding No Sucker Principle in a variety of formulations, is designed to cope with the free rider problem. The prescriptions for universal adherence that emerge are often more than would be needed if finer assignments of roles to agents could be made; they have to be resorted to just because information and the opportunities for legislation are so imperfect that the cruder device of requiring action or forbearance universally has to be adopted if there is to be any device at all. Even so, moral training is not always successful on this point, and the device does not work with everybody. Yet it works well enough to give some credibility to an alternative hypothesis explaining, for example, the use of coercion in collecting income taxes: Suppose, instead of supposing that everyone would evade paying the taxes if he could, that most people are prepared to pay them (at least on the next round or

two) anyway; they might still demand that coercion be used against the minority who are tempted to free-ride.

[16] Deutscher, *op. cit.*, pp. 64–67.

[17] Though revenge itself is not an unheard-of motive, and it is one that Tullock's equation has to be extended to embrace. (Valentinov conjectures that Alexander's execution aroused great hatred in Lenin for the Tsar and the Tsar's officials. Valentinov, *op. cit.*, p. 112. But Valentinov does not suggest that revenge was a primary motivation for Lenin's career as a revolutionist.)

[18] Deutscher, *op. cit.*, pp. 66–67; Valentinov, *op. cit.*, p. 112; pp. 125–126. Valentinov also, pp. 155–158, gives a good deal of weight to Lenin's self-confidence, heightened by his academic successes and by the admiration of his family and friends at home; and claims, "He lived in the constant sensation that he was standing on the eve of certain great revolutionary events in which – if he could only break away from Samara – a great role was waiting for him" (p. 158). No doubt some use needs to be made in Lenin's case of the public goods variable, with a relatively high value for the probability $\Delta p_i$ of making an effective contribution to obtaining it; but could he have rationally reckoned in 1891 or 1892 on making a substantial enough contribution to offset the rewards of a conventional career? Perhaps in youthful enthusiasm he undervalued these rewards; but are we to suppose that he treated them recklessly? If Lenin, with his intellectual capacity, time for reflection, and fateful circumstances, did not make a fully rational decision, who ever does?

ANATOL RAPOPORT

# ETHICS AND POLITICS

1. The word 'politics' and its derivatives is used in at least three different senses. First, it may refer to the exercise of power, second, to the allocation of power, and third, to a profession.

In the first sense, the meaning of 'politics' is closely related to that of policy.' In fact, Clausewitz's famous aphorism is sometimes translated as 'War is the continuation of *policy* by other means' and sometimes as 'War is the continuation of *politics* by other means.' In English, the word 'politics' is not often used in this sense, but it is so in other languages. The derivative 'political' often does refer to policy in English, as in the phrase 'for political considerations.'

In the second sense, 'politics' refers to the totality of activity in a society, where the prime concern is the allocation of power. Clearly, where power has been allocated once and for all, there is no such activity. It becomes important only in societies where on occasion power passes from some individuals or groups to others. In so-called democracies, this process takes the form of elections, formations of political parties, lobbies, etc. Elsewhere, allocation of power may be decided by intrigue or assassination. Allocation of power is not confined to the political process related to the government of a country. It takes place also in 'nonpolitical' organizations and institutions. All these activities are generally understood to be subsumed under 'politics' in its sense of power allocation, as in the phrase 'campus politics.'

In the United States, 'politics' frequently refers to a profession, so that it is natural to say of someone that 'He is in politics' as 'He is in show business' or 'He is in hardware.' The word 'political' in the phrase 'political career' has this sense.

In defining ethics, I shall not worry about whether the notion I am defining corresponds to what is understood by 'ethics' in philosophy or in various philosophies. It is a deeply ingrained habit among philosophers to invent a word and then inquire into its 'real' meaning. In my opinion, this aspect of philosophy is the least productive. I shall, therefore, eschew it and simply say at the outset what I shall mean by 'ethics' in this discussion.

Ethics, as I understand it, is concerned with incentives or restraints on behavior that stem from expectations of approval or disapproval by relevant

75

*H. J. Johnson, J. J. Leach, and R. G. Muehlmann (eds.), Revolutions, Systems, and Theories, 75–97. All Rights Reserved.*
*Copyright © 1979 by D. Reidel Publishing Company, Dordrecht, Holland.*

reference groups or individuals, including oneself, *rather* than from expectations of sanctions imposed by authorities invested with coercive power. Thus, if a man refrains from stealing because stealing is punishable by law, this man's behavior is not a matter of ethical concern; if he refrains from stealing because he wants to preserve his self respect or the respect of others, this is a matter of ethical concern. However, the *law* against stealing may be relevant to ethics, namely, the ethics of the society in which the laws is enforced. I shall also refer to the ethos of a society, to be elucidated below.

The approval or disapproval related to ethics generally involves notions of morality and for this reason the scope of ethics is difficult to circumscribe, because the scope of morality is not precisely defined. Breaches of convention are not generally thought of as breaches of morality. Such breaches are rather the concern of *etiquette*, which is sometimes mistakenly supposed to be etymologically related to ethics, i.e., 'little ethics.' However, the line between conventions and notions of morality is vague: some conventions do have their roots in notions of morality. For instance, respect for the conventions is sometimes motivated by considerations of other people's feelings.

Professional ethics is intermediate between rules of behavior imposed by law and those imposed by notions of morality. Breach of professional ethics may involve sanctions backed by the power of authority; for instance, expulsion from a professional society. But as a rule, adherence to professional ethics involves primarily concern for approval or disapproval by a relevant reference groups.

The relation of ethics to politics, then, can be examined in the three contexts of the meaning of politics: the juncture between ethics and the exercise of power; that between ethics and the allocation of power; the extent and sources of professional ethics, as it relates to the profession of politics. We shall examine these topics in reverse order.

2. Of professional ethics there are two kinds. *Internal ethics* concerns the relations of members of a profession to each other. *External ethics* concerns the relation of members of the profession to the society as a whole. In many professions, these distinctions are quite clear. Thus, the internal ethics of the medical profession involves circumstances under which it is permissible or impermissible for one physician to treat the patient of another. External ethics involves relations of physician to patient and, more generally, the social obligations of the physician. The ethics of the legal profession are analogous.

It seems natural to inquire whether the profession of politics admits of an internal and an external ethics. To pursue this inquiry, we must examine the nature of politics as a profession. Here we face difficulties, for the nature of this profession varies much more widely than that of others, namely, with the nature of the political system wherein politics is practiced. In a way, the nature of any profession varies with the nature of the society in which it is institutionalized. Nevertheless, where a profession is founded on certain technical knowledge and performs services relatively independent of cultural setting, we can expect to find certain invariant features in its ethics. With regard to politics, it is not easy to say whether it has such invariant features except in societies with similar political systems.

And so, lacking an anchorage for a generalization, I shall first confine myself to professional politics in the United States and to the bearing that ethics, internal or external, has or might have on its practice.

In every culture or society there is a dominant 'theme' that reflects the most important preoccupation of its members. At times, the preoccupation is reflected in a profession, whose practitioners are especially prominent or enjoy special privileges. Militarized societies are the most conspicuous examples. In the nineteenth century, the prestige of the military profession was reflected in the adoption of the military uniform as habitual dress by European monarchs. In imperial Germany, even the chief god of the ancient Germans was pictured in military garb, at least on the operatic stage.

Now, the 'dominant theme' rubs off, as if were, on other social functions and professions besides the one that embodies it. For instance, in imperial Germany, university professors appeared at ceremonial functions in quasi-military uniforms, complete with sword; both in Germany and in tsarist Russia, civil service contained a hierarchy of ranks exactly parallel to the military, just as in the United States the hierarchy of naval ranks parallels that of the army ranks.

The dominant preoccupation of a society has an ethos. An ethos is a more general concept than an ethics. It embodies an orientation, a world outlook, of which an ethics is a more concrete expression. For example, the ethos of traditional militarism embodies a certain conception of primary virtues, such as bravery, i.e., a disdain for personal safety; loyalty, i.e., obedience to superiors, reverence for certain symbols; leadership, i.e., the ability to elicit obedience of subordinates, etc. The ethics of the profession specifies rules of conduct that supposedly reflect the ethos. For example, in nineteenth-century Europe it was unethical for a military officer to decline a challenge to a duel.

In the United States, at least since the onset of industrialization, business enterprise has been the dominant theme. Business enterprise has an ethos. It embodies self-reliance, ambition, organizational abilities, and criteria of success. The ethos is reflected in business ethics: internally, financial responsibility, acceptance of competition, certain 'fair practices'; externally, contractual obligations, certain civic duties, at times responsibility for the quality of goods produced and services rendered.

The ethos of this dominant theme also rubs off on other social functions and professions. In the United States, one speaks more often of the 'entertainment industry' than of musical and dramatic arts. The term 'education industry' is widely accepted as a normal, not satirical, description of institutionalized education. The business ethos pervades also these activities. A successful film actor often acquires a business interest in a motion picture ('a piece of the action,' as the saying goes). A research scientist, after achieving prominence, often becomes an entrepreneur of research enterprises, etc.

It is interesting to note that in the United States the ethos of business enterprise has to a certain extent pervaded also the military profession. In American experience, the decisive factor in military operations has been logistics, the art of utilizing superior production capacity. The dominance of logistics over traditional military strategy (not to speak of personal bravery) has been demonstrated in the Civil War, later, even more dramatically, in both World Wars. Competence in logistics is in many respects akin to business competence. Accordingly, the organization of military effort in the United States is now entrusted largely to men with business competence, who brought with them a business ethos. The branches of the armed services act as vast, competing corporations.

Politics in the United States is a profession, and like any other is marked by a well defined ladder of success. For example, the hierarchy of elective offices graduates from membership in city councils to state legislatures, to Congress and Senate, the last being often a stepping stone to the presidency. Appointive offices have a parallel hierarchy. Advancement in the political career, especially along the elective path, is attained via the ritualized competition of elections.

Now, competence in any profession tends to be judged, at least in part, by the degree of prominence attained. Where successful competition is a factor in the profession itself, the degree of prominence attained is certainly a relevant criterion of competence. In some professions — competitive sports, for example — success in competition is the *only* objective criterion of competence. In the United States, where aggressive competition is part of the dominant ethos, successful competition is a dominant criterion of comptence. It is so both in business and in politics.

In that society, we expect, therefore, that the ethics of politics would be similar to the ethics of business. However, many restrictions imposed by business ethics do not apply to politics. We do not find, for example, well specified rules of political competition, defining 'unfair practices' and the like. Restrictions in campaign spending are imposed by laws, rather than by internal ethics, and reflect, in fact, the *absence* of internal ethics, that is, ethical restrictions on political competition.

This paucity of internal professional ethics is demonstrated not so much by the actual lack of restraint in political competition as by the apparent acceptance of a 'no holds barred' style of political campaigning. When Richard Nixon ran for the United States Senate in California in 1948, he insinuated that his incumbent opponent, Helen Douglas, was a covert Communist. Years later, when these tactics were cited as an example of 'dirty politics' (i.e., of a breach of internal political ethics), Mr. Nixon expressed dismay at the notion that it may have been his intention to slander Mrs. Douglas *personally*. It seems he took for granted that selecting a 'campaign issue' was simply practising the art of politics, that the truth or falsehood of allegations should not have been a matter of serious concern; smear tactics were just part of the game. The implication seems to be that people touchy about their reputations should not be in politics, just as people who are afraid of suffering financial losses, say, should not be in competitive business, or people queasy about injuries should not engage in dangerous sports.

The censure by the United States Senate of Senator Joseph McCarthy can be cited as an application of the internal ethics of professional politics. However, the conspicuousness of this incident points up its exceptional character.

A strong internal ethics reflects solidarity among the members of the profession. Apparently, the nature of professional politics has undermined even the sort of solidarity that is sometimes observed in the business world. One should note that, even in competitive business, prescriptions of internal professional ethics are still recognized, perhaps because business men do business with each other and business competition is not typically a 'fight to the death.' Success in business competition is quantitative. Success in elective politics, on the other hand, is typically all-or-none, as in prize-fighting: each victory or defeat is definitive, and a few defeats may spell the total demise of a political career. Moreover, success in professional politics is by and large evaluated *only* in terms of political victories. This aspect of competitive politics virtually removes the basis for an internal professional ethics.

External professional ethics is related to the services rendered by the profession. In the case of politics, these services are presumably related to the 'art of government.' It is noteworthy, however, that the 'art of government' and 'professional politics' are distinct concepts, at least in the United States. In common usage, 'statesmanship' designates the former, while 'politics' is most often used in the sense of professional competitive politics, as described above. Similarly, 'politician' and 'public servant' have distinct denotations and almost opposite connotations.

It would seem that at least in the case of a politician with a constituency, external ethics would prescribe efforts on behalf of the constituency or of its majority. However, even here, personal career considerations often override this universally recognized prescription of the democratic ethos, at least with regard to particular issues. For instance, obligations to constituencies would imply that the Congress of the United States would take effective action to end American military involvement in Indo-China, since in the spring of 1971, according to opinion polls, 73% of the electorate were in favor of quick and total withdrawal from Indo-China. But, as Noam Chomsky has pointed out, 'political' considerations (in this case related to political careers, not to policy) are very likely to prevent such action. For it is expected that a withdrawal would forthwith create a 'gut issue' in the form of charges of a 'stab in the back,' 'snatching defeat from the jaws of victory,' 'the first war lost by the United States,' etc. In subsequent political campaigns, adroit use of these phrases would provide formidable leverage for politicians who had *not* jumped on the peace bandwagon. The mood of the electorate being subject to quick reversals, effective action for ending the war might spell political death to its sponsors soon afterward, as it did for many who were accused of 'losing China' in the campaign of 1952. Therefore, the most prudent course, dictated by 'political considerations,' seems to be to express oneself vociferously against continuing the senseless war (thus giving the impression of discharging the responsibility to the constituency) but to shy away from any action which might later be cited as 'treason.' On the whole, considerations of this sort are regarded as perfectly normal in professional politics.

In short, the most common public image of the politician in the United States is that of someone engaged in a business, in which the wherewithal is influence or power, in the same way that in ordinary business the wherewithal of survival is money. And, just as it is taken for granted that in business, whatever other aims are served, the principal motivating force is the accretion of profit, so, in politics, the principal motivation is the accretion of influence and power. At the very least, the politician is considered to be entitled to safeguard his 'political life.'

3. The conception of politics as a competitive game, analogous to business, obscures what ought, perhaps, to be the central issue in the relation between ethics and politics, namely, the ethical issues that arise in the *exercise* of power. To bring these issues into focus, we must consider politics in the sense of the formulation and execution of policy, or as the art of government. But the conception of politics as the process of *allocating* power relegates to the background the relation between ethics and the exercise of power. A book by Harold Lasswell is entitled *Politics, Who Gets What, When, How*, and David Easton remarks that this "orientation has at least implicitly dominated the theoretical interest of most political research." (*A System Analysis of Political Life*, p. 474.)

The study of the allocation of power brings us into the realm of political theory, which may be either descriptive or normative (i.e., prescriptive). Descriptive theories center on the examination of the facts of political life and generalizations derived from them. Normative, or prescriptive, theories are primarily deductive and often rely on the formulation of 'first principles' or 'natural rights' or something of that sort. One would expect, therefore, that ethics would have greater relevance in the context of normative theories than in the context of descriptive ones. And so it has, for the most part. Nevertheless, there are normative theories that exclude a juncture between ethics and politics. On the other hand, descriptive theories can suggest ethically relevant questions.

An example of an 'ethically vacuous' normative theory is the so-called 'realist' theory of international relations or, more generally, of politics. For example, the theory of international relations embodied in Clausewitz's magnum opus *On War*, considered as a purely descriptive one, i.e., depicting how states act in pursuit of their interests, suggests the question as to whether states are not destructive of fundamental human values. To the extent, however, that Clausewitz's theory is prescriptive (and it is presented as such), it is relevant to ethics only in a purely negative way, as it were; for it deliberately excludes ethical components (as we have defined them) from the actions of states.

It can be argued that an ethical component is included in Clausewitz's prescriptions in the sense that a ruler who preserves or expands the power or influence of his realm gains the approval of his subjects. In the authoritarian nation state envisaged by Clausewitz, such approval is not backed by power, hence *is* relevant to our definition of ethical motivation. From this point of view, Clausewitz's 'realist' theory is not ethically vacuous in its prescriptive form, for it may be said to reflect the internal ethos of a nation state. The theory is ethically vacuous in its treatment of relations *among states*; for the only basis of power allocation among states, as it appears from Clausewitz's theory (and from modern 'realist' theories derived from it), is power.

Machiavelli's prescriptive theory embodied in *The Prince* is even further removed from ethical concerns than Clausewitz's, for it lacks even the nationalist ethos. Nevertheless, if *The Prince* is viewed as simply a *description* of how princes achieve and retain power, and ethical conclusion can be drawn from it, for instance, in Lord Acton's widely quoted aphorism.

'Realist' political theories in their descriptive sense are relevant to ethics in still another way. Contrary to certain views on the nature of science, it is not the case that questions of 'what is' can never be completely separated from questions of 'what ought to be.' To a very considerable extent, our beliefs determine our attitudes. Therefore, the assessment of the value of realist political theories as scientific theories is of importance in assessing their ethical import.

The strength of the realist position is that it takes due cognizance of power, which is quite as fundamental in politics as the concept of energy is in physics. The shortcomings of the realist position stem from two limitations. First, the realists tend to fixate on traditional or conventional conceptions of power and, so, often miss the implications of the changing sources of political power. Second, the realist position tends to ignore an opposite force in poltics, directed *against* power. By this force, I do not mean a counter-vailing power of the same sort, as the power of one political party or of one state pitted against that of another; of these confrontations, the realist position takes full account, of course. I mean forces that are not yet organized into power-wielding units, forces that are diffuse and contribute to the disintegration of existing power structures. Such are revolutionary forces in their incipience. It may be true that eventually revolutionary forces are 'organized' into a power structure and thereby cease to be revolutionary; so that historically they have been ephemeral. But it is in this transitional phase that the relation between politics and ethics is most clearly seen, for it is then that an emergent ethos is pitted against an established power structure.

The concept of 'social contract' characterizes an outlook that is in a way the polar opposite of the realist position. I shall refer to this outlook as the idealist position. It rests on an axiomatic base which includes concepts like 'natural rights,' typically of the individual. It pictures political arrangements as means by which such rights are realized. The idea is specifically expressed in the American Declaration of Independence: "We hold these truths to be self evident: that all men are created equal; that they are endowed by their creator with certain inalienable rights . . . That, *To secure these rights*, governments are instituted among men." The same document establishes the 'right of revolution.'

The weakness of the idealist position stems from its reliance on the conscious pursuit of goals by 'rational men' as a primary political force. It builds a model of society on elementary contacts between freely acting individuals in the same way that classical economics builds its theory on the coming together of individual traders in a 'free market.' This model has no historical foundation. There never was a 'free individual' in a state of nature of the sort pictured by Hobbes or Rousseau any more than there ever was the individual hunter, farmer, or craftsman going to a 'free market' with his produce. Man was already social when he became man; that is, he was already driven by forces other than those posited by Hobbes, Rousseau, and Adam Smith.

It seems to me that Karl Marx succeeded in avoiding the pitfalls of both the realist and the idealist positions. On the one hand, Marx clearly recognized the mortality of power structures — that every social order contains the seeds of its own destruction. On the other hand, Marx rejected the atomistic conception of 'natural rights.' He was particularly emphatic in pointing out the 'unconscious' bases of ethical notions, the rationalizations (as we would call them today) of class interests. Thus, the concept of 'natural rights' appeared in Marxist interpretation as the ideological reflection of the interests of a new rising class, the bourgeoisie. The factory system of production needed 'free labor,' i.e., 'hands' that could be hired when needed and fired when not needed, hence, 'free' to move about. The 'freedom' of the laborer freed also the entrepreneur, namely, from the responsibility for the laborer's subsistence, which the slave holder or the lord had assumed for the slave or the serf. This responsibility, in turn, had been an 'ethical spin-off' of the necessity for safeguarding property. As the economic necessity changed, so did its ethical overtones.

The industrial revolution and the bourgeois social order generated their own ethos. The 'freedom' of the entrepreneur and of the worker to enter a contractual relation became ideologized as 'individual freedom' and endowed with the new ethos. The ideologues of democracy were not hypocrites. They were genuinely convinced of the superiority of the new ethos over that of the feudal world. Nor should one dismiss the so-called 'bourgeois freedoms' as a sham, as some critics of the capitalist social order are wont to do.

It is not necessary to accept in its entirety the Marxist thesis that all ethos springs from 'social relations determined by the mode of production.' The important lesson to be derived from the Marxist conception of ideology is that ideologies are not given by God and are not necessarily rooted in human nature, whatever it is, but arise as consequence of social conditions. As for the latter, their origin is probably much more complex than the Marxists make them out to be.

The 'dominant themes' of societies change (from whatever causes). With them, the ethos changes. The ethos of a portion of a society may also change, possibily giving rise to a precursor of future ethos. Then the power structure of the society loses *legitimacy* for that portion of the society, and is challenged.

Legitimacy is that aspect of power than insures voluntary compliance to the directives issuing from the power source. Legitimacy may be, but need not be, spelled out in documents such as constitutions. A constitution is only the recognition of legitimacy. Actual legitimacy is a psychological, not a legal, state of affairs. Most political systems throughout history have functioned without constitutions. They could not, however, function without legitimacy.

The tyrant exercises his power not personally but through a network of enforcing agencies. At the distal end, these agencies may be armed soldiers or thugs. But even these can enforce the tyrant's commands only in virtue of the fact that their threats or occasional violence induce people to obey. Obedience is recognition of legitimacy, if only of the legitimacy embodied in the acceptance of the principle 'might is right.'

Strictly speaking, coercion is *physically* impossible. A person can be prevented by physical force from acting in a specific way, by being confined, for instance. But *positive* obedience, as in performing specific actions, is always a 'voluntary' act in which a person *chooses* to obey rather than suffer consequences. Whether these consequences are annihilation or merely disapproval is a matter of degree.

It is not usual to identify the criteria of legitimacy with simply the power to elicit obedience, but it is difficult to draw the line separating legitimacy from coercive power in isolated instances. Certainly it serves no purpose to say that a man who hands over his wallet to a gunman thereby recognizes the 'legitimacy' of the gunman's power. However, it would be misleading to identify the legitimacy of power with that conferred on it by constitutions.

Legitimate power is that which is *habitually* obeyed in a given society. Legitimacy is shattered when habits of obedience are shattered, whether the change is formalized or not.

The wide variety of political systems reflects a wide variety of concepts of

legitimacy in different cultural and historical settings. In contrast to its irrele-
vance to the struggle for power, ethics does have a direct bearing on legitimacy, and it is through this concept that the relation of ethics to politics can
be established in the context of the allocation of power.

Political assassinations, while not uncommon in the United States, do
not pave the way to legitimate power. They do elsewhere. Where they do
or did, they are or were practiced not exceptionally but routinely. In Russia,
for example, Stalin was able to consolidate absolute power by extensive
use of political assassination. The most important feature about these assassinations was that they were *legitimate* and, therefore, were called executions
rather than assassinations. Some, as if to emphasize their legitimacy, were
even preceded by public trials. Subsequently, Stalin was charged with vio-
lating socialist legitimacy, and certainly the Stalinist Constitution of 1936
can be so interpreted that the terror of the late 1930's and late 1940's appears as a breach of legitimacy. The crux of the matter, however, is that at
the time of the terror the constitution was *not* so interpreted. This means
that Stalin's absolute power was legitimate. The impulse of immediate,
unquestioning obedience was internalized by functionaries of all the organs
of government, party, and armed forces. Stalin's legitimacy had the soundest
political basis.

To take an example closer to home, let us examine the charge leveled
against Lyndon Johnson, and later against Richard Nixon, to the effect that
they usurped power not vested in them by the Constitution in committing
the United States to war in Southeast Asia. The fact remains that their commands were obeyed; that, moreover, even at present, when the 'legality' of
Johnson's and Nixon's actions is widely challenged, the war continues. Not
only is the possibility of impeachment proceedings quite remote, but even the
much simpler expedient of cutting off funds has not been resorted to. Therefore, according to our definition, the power exercised by Nixon and Johnson
remains legitimate, regardless of constitutional arguments.

Loss of legitimacy entails the loss of authority, that is, of the power to
elicit voluntary compliance. Denial of legitimacy to an erstwhile authority
entails a change in the state of mind of erstwhile subjects or 'law-abiding
citizens' which is usually irreversible, like loss of faith or the dissipation of a
superstition. Once denial of legitimacy has become widespread, a revolution
becomes possible. A revolution, be it noted, is to be distinguished from other
political changes in that the latter entail only the passing of power from one
group to another, while a revolution involves a change in the *way* power is
allocated. The difference is the social analogue of the formal political distinc-

tion between change of government and constitutional change. The question of legitimacy is a fundamental one with regard to the relation between ethics and politics in the contest over the allocation of power.

Although Marx, at least in his youth, had much to say about the ethical basis of revolutions, he later demonstratively uncoupled his theory of revolution from general ethical principles.

A social system is doomed, Marx argued, not because it is evil and is finally perceived as such, but because it gives rise to a new class with interests incompatible with those of the ruling class. The revolution, then, becomes a power struggle.

In taking exception to this position I do not thereby assert that a widespread ethical condemnation of a social system is *sufficient* to seal its doom. I simply assert that it is *necessary*. Nor do I deny the reality of power struggles as the final manifestations of revolutions. Rather, I ask, where does the 'power' in a revolutionary power struggle come from? Recall that, in the social context, power means the power to coerce, but there is never sufficient power to coerce, in the literal sense of the word. Power is coercive if it is accepted as such. The loss of legitimacy of a regime *is* the loss of power, that is, of the ability to coerce. And loss of legitimacy is founded, in the last analysis, on a change in ethos.

A case in point is the frequent contention that the predictions of Marx's theory failed in the industrially developed countries. The anticipated sharpening of the class struggle and the overthrow of the bourgeoisie by the 'working class' did not take place. Had it been simply a matter of a power struggle in the realist sense, one would have expected the prediction to be realized. Certainly the 'working class' (as Marx understood it) has more political power today than a hundred years ago. Why, then, was the capitalist system not 'overthrown' or why, at least, has not the class struggle become 'sharper,' in view of the fact that, in the political arena at least, the power of the two classes (if one can still speak in these terms) has apparently become more nearly equal? The usual explanations are that the 'capitalist class' still controls the state, the educational system, the press, etc., etc., and through them prevents the emergence of revolutionary class consciousness in the working class. These are *ad hoc* explanations. They do not touch the central issue, namely, that the revolutionary *ethos* of the nineteenth century has dissipated. In industrialized countries, the working class has joined the 'main stream.' As the abundance of mass production permeated the majority of the population, so did the aspirations characteristic of the bourgeois ethos — personal comfort and security, apoliticalization, and de-ideologization. In short, for the majority in industrialized capitalist societies, the power structure characteristic of that society never lost its legitimacy.

Most significantly, we find now that the challenge to the power structure comes from sources other than those predicted by Marx. In the United States, the challenge comes predominantly from three sources: a sector of the youth, a sector of the intelligentsia, and the rejects of the industrial system. None of these sectors resembles the 'revolutionary working class' of Marxist theory. One could, of course, insist that for this reason the challenge does not constitute a revolutionary potential, but this, of course, remains to be seen.

Neither the rebellious youth nor the intelligentsia are at the bottom of the economic scale and so do not qualify as the 'oppressed' classes. The rejected (that is, the poor, predominantly black) are at the bottom of the economic scale, but they also fail to qualify as the oppressed in Marx's sense, because their poverty is not the result of appropriation by the capitalists of the surplus value of their labor. On the contrary, those who work regularly in industry and its vastly ramified institutions, the so-called 'wage slaves,' are far from poor, either by historical or by present standards. The poor are poor not because they are exploited in the classical sense but because they are rejected. They are, of course, *robbed*, by gouging landlords, by usurers, etc., but it is not this sort of exploitation that keeps them poor. They would continue to be poor even if they paid no rent and no interest on borrowed money. They are poor because they are not needed. Were they to disappear, the economic life of the country would go on unimpeded, in fact, would become less burdened.

The problem is primarily ethical, because the ethos of the capitalist system demands that money should be dispensed in sufficient amounts to guarantee comfort, security, and dignity only as *payment*, and, moreover, whether or not it is needed by the recipient. Where money is dispensed not as a payment but because it is *needed*, it must be limited so as at least to deny dignity to the recipient. The economy of capitalist society does not determine this limitation. Whatever else it is, the economy is not one of scarcity. In fact, its 'proper' functioning actually demands systematized waste of labor and materials, as in planned obsolescence and in the upkeep of military establishments. There is no question, therefore, that the money dispensed to the rejected — those that do not fit into the scheme of remunerated activities — could be easily doubled or quadrupled without making the economy in the least less abundant. But the business ethos prohibits such a 'solution' to the 'problem of poverty.'

And so the quality of oppression in an advanced capitalist society, such as the United States, is different from that envisaged by Marx. It stems not from economic necessity but from the dominant ethos. The poor are oppressed and degraded because the ethos demands that anyone who cannot fit into the scheme of remunerative activities *must* be subjected to certain indignities.

As for the rebellious young and the dissenting intellectuals, is it proper to speak of them as 'oppressed'? Certainly not in the traditional sense of political or economic oppression. Yet the anguish of these people, especially of the young, is as real as that of the poor. It is also the anguish of the rejected. Let us examine its sources.

A by-product of abundance in modern advanced societies has been a vast expansion of higher education. Nowhere has the expansion been more dramatic than in the United States. The main contributing factors to this expansion are well known: on the one hand, the increasing demand for intellectual skills or, at least, of college graduate status in the world of industry and business; on the other, the habitual resistance to flooding the labor market.

However removed these pressures are from the ethos of higher education professed by some dedicated educators (who would see its goals to be emancipation and enlightenment), it was inevitable that some of this ethos should concentrate in some 'pockets', at least, of the vast higher education complex. In other words, the expansion of the educational system made it inevitable that an intelligentsia would have arisen in the United States with an ethos of its own, and it was inevitable that this ethos should have clashed with the dominant one.

Elsewhere I have raised the question of whether intellectuals have a class interest. The question is, of course, answered in the negative by an orothodox Marxist, for whom class interest springs by definition from the role of the class in the productive process, either that of a producer or that of an expropriator. By stretching the definition of expropriation, the class interest of at least a segment of intellectual workers can be defined in Marxist terms. For instance, the 'product' of the scientist can be said to be 'expropriated' by being diverted to the needs of the power elite, such as to military uses. But I have chosen instead to redefine class interest so as to make it independent of the classical confrontation between producers and expropriators. I have argued that the power elites in the process of protecting their monopoly of power subvert and degrade the value to which the intellectuals with a certain historically continuous outlook are committed: emancipation and enlightenment. When the clash between these values and the prerogatives of the power elite become sharp and explicit, the intelligentsia becomes revolutionary. From its point of view, the power elite loses its legitimacy. This happens the more surely, the less the product of the intellectuals is of use to the power elite.

Consider the different historic roles of the intelligentsia in Russia and in Western Europe in the nineteenth century. Russian aristocracy had little use for the services of the intelligentsia. It ruled the peasantry (which constituted over 80% of the population) by the whip. In Europe, on the other hand, because of the needs of the bourgeois social order for science and of the constitutional governments for administrative skills, the intellectuals could be to a large extent co-opted into public life, as producers of cultural values, as educators, as scientists, and, in a certain extent, as bureaucrats. It is not surprising, therefore, that in Russia the intelligentsia became revolutionized to a far greater degree than in Europe. There was no 'official philosopher' in tsarist Russia, like Hegel, to glorify the autocracy as the ultimate manifestation of the Absolute Idea. Odes to reigning monarchs were still written in Russia in the eighteenth century by court poets, imitating their Western European colleagues, but no longer in the nineteenth. The ethos of the Russian intelligentsia became a countervailing ethos directed sharply and openly against the ethos of the autocracy, which demanded only silence, obedience, piety, and toil from the masses. The intelligentsia glorified freedom, deplored 'the power of darkness,' and delved into the intricacies of human relations, as in the remarkable flowering of Russian literature in that century. There was no common ground between the autocracy and the intelligentsia, and it is not surprising that revolutionary leadership sprang from among the ranks of the latter.

The United States is an example of an intermediate case. Initially, the intelligentsia played a revolutionary role, rejecting the legitimacy of the monarchy and formulating a political system on an explicitly declared ethos, already mentioned. With the ascendance of the business ethos, the services of the intellectual were at first utilized to a limited extent by the business elite, largely in an educational system providing training requisite to some professions. There was hardly any need for an explicit formulation of an official ideology couched in a sophisticated terminology (as, for example, there is in the Soviet Union). 'Americanism' was absorbed in the course of daily activities, in which, being pragmatically oriented, it was firmly rooted. The exploited classes, the Negroes and, for a long time, predominantly imported labor were not easily identified as 'The People.' The 'American People' were the free, the enterprising, the aggressive, not the burdened, the humble, and the patient. The latter shrank in number as skilled workers lost the stigma of foreignness and increased their share of mass-produced abundance.

In short, the need to reiterate and to rationalize (in philosophical terms) the dominant ideology was, until recently, not as sharp in the United States as it was, say, in nineteenth-century Europe or in the present day Soviet Union. On that score, therefore, the services of the intellectuals were not needed in the United States.

Next, the American power elite never had the cultural aspirations, or at least the pretensions, that characterized the European elites, who liked to beautify their cities, to support the arts, etc. On the contrary, the dominant attitude in the American business community toward purely esthetic values was often that of disdain, at best, a patronizing philanthropy. So, also on that score, the services of the intellectual were not needed.

One would expect, therefore, that if an intelligentsia arose in the United States it would, as in Russia, develop a countervailing ethos. Sharp social criticism by perceptive individuals was, of course, in evidence in the United States throughout its history. However, the full fruition of a countervailing ethos occurred in the United States only after two conditions were fulfilled: (1) the number of people engaged in intelletual work increased many-fold in consequence of the expansion of higher education; (2) the brutal and genocidal aspects of United States global policy became obvious.

The first condition created a niche for the intellectually inclined. Traditionally, intellectuals were either members of a leisure class or served the cultural aspirations of the privileged. In the United States, in spite of Thorstein Veblen's theory, there was never a traditional leisure class. The rich worked as hard at making money as the poor in keeping body and soul together. And, as we have seen, the cultural aspirations of the privileged were not expansive. With the hypergrowth of the universities, suddenly a place was made for the intelligentsia, who were thereby enabled both to make a living and to exercise the option of not serving the power elite.

It is true, of course, that the extent of this option varied with the institution and with the academic field of endeavor. It is also true that many did not exercise the option, even if it did exist. In fact, the universities were to a very great extent co-opted as research centers into the service of business and the military. Moreover, as the prestige of science increased and as the halo effect spread to the social sciences, academicians were rectuited also as policy advisers to the power elite. Nevertheless, to the extent that the option not to serve power remained, the academe became the natural habitat of the countervailing ethos and eventually the base from which the very legitimacy of the power establishment was challenged.

Here we must deal with the question of whether the ethos of the rebellious student youth, among whom anti-intellectual sentiments are so often heard, can be considered as part of the same countervailing ethos that sprouted among intellectuals. Possibly not. But, then, it is important to recognize that the current challenges to established power, although stemming from two different sources, have a common base.

One source is the 'ancien régime' nature of the superpower establishments. Like the Bourbons, their supreme leaders never learn anything nor forget anything. The arrogance and the mendacity of their supreme leaders is matched only by occasional outbursts of incredible stupidity. Moral depravity, as manifested in the genocide in Indo-China and in the preparation for a nuclear holocaust, are seen as consequences of absolute corruption by absolute power, the traditional source of anguish of the intellectual committed to reason and analysis and appalled by senseless cruelty and shameless hypocrisy.

The other source of the current challenge to establishment power stems from the onslaught against some fundamental human needs; for instance, the need for esthetic experience and for effective identification with other human beings rather than a self-submerging identification with organizations or institutions. Here the challenge is directed not so much at the power establishment itself as at the whole fabric of life in atomized, competitive, consumption-and-success oriented society. The stifling and debilitating effects of this mode of existence is felt especially keenly by the young of the affluent society, for whom the problem of earning daily bread or starving is not a continual nagging presence. In fact, this circumstance has been hurled as an accusation against the rebellious young. Their rebellion has been declared to be the result of permissiveness and pampering. The significance of the accusation is not to be denied, but whether it is a basis for censure depends, of course, on whether one accepts or rejects the dominant ethos, in which leisure is regarded with chronic suspicion. Indeed, the rebellious student youth, with its indifference to the conventional goals of education, is a sort of analogue to a leisure class. And the revolutionary ferment in it is as much a consequence of the rejection by the dominant society of the countervailing values of the young as of the rejection by the rebellious young of the dominant Calvinist ethos.

Since this mutual rejection is more directly linked to the direct personal experience of the young (e.g., family relations, sex attitudes, life style, etc.) than to ideational factors (as it is with mature intellectuals, whose life style has already been established), the rebellious young have no strong needs to intellectualize their attitudes, to engage in polemics, to construct theories, and so on — the traditional activities of ideology-conscious intellectuals. Since the most conspicuous power structure in the experience of the students is that of the university and since, for the most part, the university remains integrated into the established order, the rebellious student young often reject intellectual values along with those of the dominant ethos.

Nevertheless, the challenge to established power by a sector of the American intelligentsia and the rebellion of the young has a common basis. Both challenges are ethically grounded; both were to a large extent precipitated by the Vietnam War. The young, of course, were directly affected by the war. Many of them lived under the constant, ugly threat of the draft. But the intellectuals beyond the draft age were not so threatened. Moral indignation was the principal instigating factor in their so-called 'alienation' from so-called 'national interests.' Nor can there be doubt that profound disgust with the moral depravity of 'the establishment' was a principal contributing factor in the so-called 'alienation' of the young. It is impossible to say how far the erosion of legitimacy of the entrenched power establishements of our era will go, or what sort of social changes, if any, it portends.

4. Our last topic is the relation of ethics to politics in the context of the *exercise* of power. Of the three issues we have singled out, it is the oldest, for it was raised even in societies where there was no 'political profession' nor even a sphere of social life called 'politics,' at least, no awareness of it, hence, no problem of allocating power. Power was concentrated or perceived to be concentrated in an absolute ruler, and there was no question of its legitimacy. The only issue was to what end that power was exercised, and that is an ethical issue. In this context, the use of power to achieve ethically approved ends is equated with justice.

It was not long, however, before the issue of justice was linked to that of allocating power and, therefore, to the question of legitimacy. We find, already in the Old Testament, King Saul deprived of legitimacy for having abused his power. Eventually, the concept of the just ruler became supplanted by that of the just social order, that is, a just allocation of power. Plato's Republic is, of course, a classical example of this concept. In his *Politics*, Aristotle, comparing types of political systems, associates the monarchy with the justice (or virtue) of one, the oligarchy with the virtue of the few, and democracy with the virtue of the majority. On that basis he draws a conclusion unfavorable to democracy.

Ultimately, the issue of power allocation became overwhelmingly dominant in political philosophy, the implicit or sometimes explicit assumption being that a 'just' allocation of power guarantees the just exercise of power. Such was the implicit assumption of the authors of the American Constitution and the rationale of the doctrine of proletarian dictatorship.

That these assumptions were illusory is, I believe, evident to anyone who still keeps the central ethical issue in focus. There is no denying, however, that for many this issue no longer exists. The defenders of Soviet orthodoxy insist that because power in the Societ Union has been in the hands of the working class since the victory of the Great October Revolution, it follows that power is exercised in the interest of social justice; in other words, that the State or, at any rate, the leadership of the Communist Party, *constitutionally defined* as the 'most advanced sector of the working class', can do no wrong — the modern version of the Divine Right of Kings.

Similarly, in the United States, the belief persists that, because of formal constitutional provisions, political power is exercised in the public interest and, therefore, in the interest of social justice.

In both conceptions, legitimacy of power is equated with social justice instead of being recognized as only a necessary prerequisite of it. Thus, we read in the *Confessions of Lieutenant Calley* the following justification of the massacre at My lai:

I'll do everything the American people want me to do . . . Even if the people say, "Go wipe out South America", the Army will do it. Majority rules . . . If a majority tells me, "Lieutenant, go and kill one thousand enemies", I'll go and kill one thousand enemies . . . I'm an American citizen.

This is only an extreme, vulgarized version of the so-called positivist philosopher of politics. A highly respected version of positivism in the philosophy of law was expressed by Oliver Wendell Holmes: "The prophesies of what the courts will do and nothing more pretentious are what is meant by law." (*The Path of Law*, 1897.) The quotation is used as a motto to introduce Edward McWhinney's article in Volume 2 of *The Strategy of World Order* ('Soviet and Western International Law and the Cold War in the Era of Bipolarity'). The content of the article might be summarized thus:

"What the *litigants* will do and nothing more pretentious is what is meant by international law."

In short, both dogmatism, with its ideology ossified in rhetoric, and positivism, with its pretension of having emancipated science from ideology, lead to an ethically vacuous conception of politics. The same can be said for what I would call a rationalist theory of laws, where what is legal and what is not is deduced from the existing body of codified law by logical argument and a delicate distinction of categories.

An instructive example is Telford Taylor's book, entitled *Nuremberg and Vietnam: An American Tragedy*. Professor Taylor examines the applicability of the Nuremberg precedent in international laws to the conduct of war in Southeast Asia by the United States. He concludes that there is sufficient evidence that war crimes were committed by Americans in Vietnam. His conception of a war crime, however, has hardly any relevance to the most important ethical issues of our day. A war crime, in the narrow legal definition, is a violation of the rules of war precisely specified in treaties and conventions. These rules prohibit the wanton killing of civilians, mistreatment of prisoners of war, and the like. Thus, the massacre of civilians, the torture and killing of prisoners are unquestionably war crimes and, as such, violations of international law. However, Professor Taylor rejects the larger implications of the Nuremberg Trials, the implications, for instance, of the punishment inflicted on Nazi leaders convicted of crimes against peace and humanity. He absolves the United States of any analogous guilt, in spite of the documented evidence (which the United States government unsuccessfully attempted to suppress) that the United States political leaders made extensive preparations for waging aggressive war in Vietnam and Laos, contrary to the provisions of Article 2 of the United Nations Charter, which, according to the United States Constitution, is part of the supreme laws of the land.

Lawyers, it seems, are most at home with law when it specifies with sufficient precision what is allowed and what is prohibited. Thus, in judging war crimes, the specifically prohibited and clearly demonstrable atrocities are singled out for attention, while crimes against humanity are ignored because recognition of such crimes depends on a commitment to an ethos *in addition* to available evidence, no matter how convincing. But it is just these precise specifications that remove the ethical dimensions from a crime. Examining the so-called rules of war, we find that it is permissible to kill an enemy soldier when he is asleep and unarmed but not permissible to kill him if he surrenders. We find that it is permissible to bomb cities designated as military targets (at the discretion of the commander) regardless of how many women, children, or aged are in it, but it is impermissible to kill civilians 'wantonly,' whatever that means. It is permissible to use nuclear weapons and napalm and 'anti-personnel' bombs filled with steel splinters (since they have not been prohibited by treaty) but impermissible to use gas or bullets filled with glass, because these weapons happen to have been prohibited by a treaty over three quarters of a century ago.

Professor Taylor defends the 'laws of war' because, in his estimation, they save lives and are a reflection of a respect for humanitarian values even in war. But how is one to estimate the number of lives 'saved' by refraining from using bullets filled with glass and making do with antipersonnel bombs instead? Is it not reasonable to view the so-called 'rules of war' as a by-product of the *institutionalization* of war in the world of politics, which confers legitimacy upon it?

In short, the major ethical issues related to the exercise of power are only rarely examined in contemporary discussions of politics or political theory. Here are there an issue is pressed to the surface, mostly by people outside of politics, law faculties, or departments of political science, but on occasions also from inside.

I was impressed by some articles written in the last few years by Hans Morgenthau, a political scientist of the 'realist' persuasion, juding by his past writings. Professor Morgenthau speaks of a confrontation between truth and power. If I understand Professor Morgenthau's thought correctly, the exercise of power necessarily involves the suppression of truth at some point, and therein lies the tremendous corrupting effect of power. The suppression of truth becomes the more urgent, the more serious is the threat that the legitimacy of the power will be eventually challenged.

It may, therefore, turn out that the question "How is power to be used for ethically approved ends?" contains an inherent contradiction, at least if one is convinced that mendacity, by undermining trust among men, defeats whatever 'ethical' ends are envisaged. No one today asks "What is a just ruler?" — a question that seemed eminently relevant to the exercise of power in the era of unchallenged, absolute rule. Perhaps, in time, the question "What allocation of power guarantees a just social order?" will also lose its relevance. The very notion of power, as it is now understood, may be revealed to be incompatible with the notion of social justice.

Naturally, the problem of the relation of ethics to politics will not thereby evaporate. The age-old questions will still be with us — all related to the dialectic opposition between individual freedom and the collective weal, between preservation of values and their transformations as a consequence of social change, between the self-defeating use of coercive force and the necessity of restraining those who would use coercive force. We can only hope that restoring ethical issues to a central position in politics, where they belong, will give us a fresh perspective on these problems of social life.

*University of Toronto*

---


## AUTHOR'S REPLY TO COMMENTS
## OF CHARLES TAYLOR, McGILL UNIVERSITY

I appreciate both the supportive and the critical comments by Professor Taylor. I should like, however, to dispel some possible misconceptions about my views. The first concerns the attribution to me of an attempt to formulate questions of ethics on a pragmatic basis, supposedly because science is or ought to be 'value-free.' I do not believe that science is or can be value free, least of all, social science. What I believe is that science, in order to deserve the name, ought to be objective. The difference between 'value-free' and 'objective' is a fundamental one. The scientist must be objective *because* he cannot be 'value free,' which is to say, because, being human, he hopes and fears, hates and loves, and must see to it that these passions do not influence his conclusions about what is objectively true. His values do and ought to influence his commitments to *what* he shall investigate and to what purposes. For example, I happen to believe that race is not correlated with general intelligence, that the size and complexity of a country's military establishment is negatively rather than positively correlated with security from the ravages of war, and that the general theory of relativity will continue to be corroborated when put to increasingly more severe tests. I know that at the basis of these beliefs are my contempt for racism and for militarism and the esthetic gratification I derive from the mathematical and philosophical aspects of relativity theory. If I were a social scientist or a physicist, I would be strongly motivated to seek evidence in support of my views. In this sense, since is not value-free. However, aware of the pressures and committed to the values of science itself, I would have to be especially demanding with respect to the evidence I happened to find and especially careful of my methods of investigation. In fact, sound medical and psychiatric research is usually conducted 'double blind,' where neither the administrators of treatments to be tested nor the evaluators of the results are aware of which subjects received the treatment and which were the controls. The precaution illustrates the relation between commitments to values and objectivity.

In addition to motivating and directing scientific activity, not only of individuals but of entire societies, values enter the social sciences also in another way, via the so-called self-predictive assumptions. Professor Taylor spoke of the moral optimists, those who believe that it is possible to have an organized society without the imposition of violence. Whether or not it is possible may well depend in considerable measure on whether sufficient numbers of people believe it. Moreover, to answer questions of this sort, one resorts to activities not usually subsumed under science. One tries to bring such a society into existence, instead of thinking up reasons about why it is or is not possible or even gathering historical evidence which may be of questionable relevance. Activity, coupled with a critical evaluation of results, is what, I believe, Marx meant by praxis.

I agree with Professor Taylor that in my paper the dilemma of ethics and politics has not been brought into sufficient focus, and I am grateful to him for stating it so well. At the same time, I have grave reservations against rehabilitating Machiavelli and also against defining great statesmanship. The difficulty with defining great statesmanship is that most of the problems faced by great statesmen become irreversibly obsolete. Wherein was the greatness of Moses, one of Machiavelli's heros? In welding a mob of nomads into a military machine by instilling in them a belief that their tribal god could lick the tar out of all other tribal gods? In what contexts are such skills of value in politics, except to demagogues? Wherein was the greatness of Cyrus, another of Machiavelli's heros? In having invented an effective imperial administration machine? Who needs it?

Yes, there is indeed a dilemma of ethics and politics, and perhaps it is the very dilemma of the human condition. Possibly some coercive component is necessary to achieve cooperation among humans. At the same time, Lord Acton's immortal aphorism remains frightfully convincing.

CHARLES TAYLOR

# ETHICS AND POLITICS

## A Rejoinder to Professor Rapoport

1. I agree with a great deal in Prof. Rapoport's interesting paper, and yet I feel the need to give the issue a somewhat different focus.

In fact I think there are some unstated notions and demands which lie behind Prof. Rapoport's discussions of the relation of ethics to politics — which indeed almost invariably underlie such discussions — and which are not entirely admitted in his paper. I'd like to start by trying to bring these out.

Prof. Rapoport wants to define ethics for the sake of his discussion as "concerned with incentives or restraints on behaviour that stem from expectations of approval or disapproval by relevant reference groups or individuals, including oneself, *rather* than from expectations of sanctions imposed by authorities vested with coercive power". Now this definition has the property of being 'value-free', it uses concepts which do not rely on valuations for their application, and as such it rings well in the arena of 'social science' of our day. But of course, it is not the interesting definition of the ethical, it is not the one which is relevant to Prof. Rapoport's problem, and is not the one he eventually will rely on throughout his discussion.

That this is not an illuminating definition of the ethical appears at once in the following paragraph of Prof. Rapoport's text, where he quite correctly sees that this definition is too broad, and covers ranges of convention, like those of etiquette, which we want to distinguish from ethics. So that Prof. Rapoport is led to extend the definition by allowing that "the approval or disapproval related to ethics generally involves notions of morality . . .". And here the difficulty re-enters. Ethics can not ultimately in any interesting sense be defined by conventions, approval, or disapproval, and the like; for all of these are capable of operating on both peripheral and central matters. And on the less important, peripheral matters, conventions, approval, disapproval, etc. are precisely not considered ethical. In the definition of the ethical, there has to be some restriction to matters of true significance, of inescapable import to man, or something of the like. And once we admit this, then the hope of a value-free definition of the ethical disappears.

And good riddance, in this context at least! For in discussing ethics and politics, we are not interested in such general notions of the ethical, or they are at best of only partial relevance to our problem. We can of course hope to

99

H. J. Johnson, J. J. Leach, and R. G. Muehlmann (eds.), Revolutions, Systems, and Theories, 99—111. All Rights Reserved.
Copyright © 1979 by D. Reidel Publishing Company, Dordrecht, Holland.

arrive at a general, 'value-free' notion by leaving the question of significance to the people we study in each case. That is, we can say that those matters will be considered of ethical import which people in any given society designate as such. We therefore have a criterion which escapes the unselective triviality of the first definition, while at the same time not taking a position ourselves. And this is, of course, a standard move in social science. This is the way the closely-related concept of legitimacy is generally handled in political science: legitimations are what people 'buy' as legitimations. Prof. Rapoport follows this line in saying that "legitimacy is that aspect of power that insures voluntary compliance to the directives issuing from the power source".

Now although there are questions at this level which will be relevant to our problem, this kind of 'neutral' definition of legitimacy and the ethical is nowhere nearly adequate to our problem. Why are we all, including Prof. Rapoport, very interested and concerned by the relation of ethics to politics? It is not because we are interested in general in the presence and absence, rise and fall of legitimacy beliefs or ethical standards. Questions about the rise and fall of certain such beliefs and identifications prove very relevant to our quest, but this basic problem cannot be stated in terms of them. Rather it is the seeming inapplicability of certain very definite ethical standards in the political realm which worries and concerns us. It is not some general problem of the lack of congruence between legitimacy beliefs and political reality which arouses disquiet but the lack of congruence of political reality to some very definite ethical standards which are our own.

Thus, there is some evidence that in the Soviet Union the majority accept such principles as, e.g., that the Soviet Union has a duty to protect other people's democracies from counter-revolution, that writers who publish abroad are unpatriotic, and so on. There may be a high degree of congruence between Soviet practices and widespread legitimacy beliefs; but to us such practices pose the same anguishing problem as their counterparts in other countries where they are less accepted. They pose a problem because they clash with a specific powerfully-held ethic. And this is of course what comes to the fore at the end of Prof. Rapoport's paper where he speaks of the moral revulsion against our politics, of the intellectual "committed to reason and analysis ... appalled by senseless cruelty and shameless hypocrisy" (p. 91).

What is the conception of ethics which underlies the questioning about ethics and politics? It is not easy to characterize tightly, but can easily be roughly designated. It is in fact the central tradition of our civilization, variously nourished by the Natural Law tradition, and what is loosely called the Judaeo-Christian ethic, and enriched by certain crucial developments of the Enlightenment and the Romantic period. It calls for respect for human life and welfare, for man as a conscious being capable of knowledge, and in the developments since the C18, for respect for man's power of initiative and freedom. Now there are certain important differences between us today concerning the application of this ethical code in certain cases; the case of abortion provides an example. But the startling thing is how localized these disagreements are, and how impressive the unanimity in interpretation of this ethic across whole ranges of cases in inter-personal life.

All the more striking then is the gap between the inter-personal standard and that which reigns in politics. Some of the greatest political monsters, a Stalin, a Hitler, might flinch from committing for personal gain or any personal motive, one hundredth of what they order without reflection as heads of state. If we were ruled by Caligulas, then the problem of ethics and politics might be substantially simpler: how to replace them with moral men. Of course, we might find that any man on assuming power became a Caligula, and we would then find ourselves forced to an Actonian formulation of our predicament: that power corrupts.

But although there is a lot of truth in this dictum, we know that it is far from the whole truth, and that the greater problem remains when we have enunciated it. We may indeed try to comfort ourselves with the assurance that political evil is simply the moral corruption bred of power; but this is clearly not adequate. We all know incorruptible men who do thoroughly evil things — evil being judged by the central core of inter-personal ethic which they and we all accept — starting with one whose sobriquet was 'l'Incorruptible'. And these men all plead a kind of necessity, that their acts are the inescapable consequence of loyalty to values we find it hard to repudiate.

And this is much more worrying, since it seems to present the political realm as one where precisely the best men will not allow themselves to flinch from evil, the realm of 'dirty hands'; and yet it is a realm from which we cannot escape except in the coward's way, leaving others to do our dirty work for us.

The question, in other words, arises: how much the ethical, in the quite specific sense of the central core of our commonly-accepted inter-personal morality, can penetrate the political realm: is politics fundamentally and irremovably refractory to this morality?

I think this was the question Machiavelli was tackling, as against the more fashionable view that he presents us with a non-moral theory of statecraft. Machiavelli's ethical outlook is reflected in some of the uses of the protean word 'virtù'. But beyond this, he used the terms 'good' and 'evil', and a whole host of related concepts in exactly the sense of the central core of morality in the version regnant in his day. I do not believe that there is any irony or 'inverted commas' in Machiavelli's use of *"efferate crudeltà e inumanità"*, *"infinite scelleratezze"*, in connection with Agathocles, for instance.[1]

The brunt of Machiavelli's point depended, I believe, on this serious use of ordinary ethical language. For it gives us one of the most powerful formulations of the negative answer to our question above, the view that politics is refractory to morality. Politics in fact has its own intrinsic values, those of *virtù*, and these are not simply the values of personal success for Machiavelli, as can be seen from the pattern of men he admires in history. Rather politics is the realm in which men can attain to the dignity of agents, or else sink to the status of victims. The greatest statesmen are those who have founded polities in which men were for a long time agents: Moses, Cyrus, Romulus, Theseus; they were not men who simply aggrandized their own power.

But the exigencies of great statesmanship require that one be free of total allegiance to the central core of morality — not that one simply be bad. It is useful "to appear compassionate, faithful, humane, upright, religious, and to be so. But [the Prince's] mind should be disposed in such a way that should it become necessary not to be so, he will be able and know how to change to the contrary"; "he must not separate himself from the good, if he is able, but he must know how to take up evil, should it become necessary".[2]

Machiavelli gives us a picture of a clash between two ethics neither of which can be simply repudiated, which are not always opposed, but which enter from time to time into unavoidable collision. Politics can never be moral in the sense of the central core. To believe this is to console oneself with illusion while courting inevitable defeat — not only personal defeat, but also of all that one values in the political realm. This is the immensely disquieting doctrine of Machiavelli, and this is why he has been much more worrying than any author of a do-it-yourself manual for aspiring putschists.

2. Machiavelli's has been a minority voice; it is strange how much of our tradition of political theory avoids facing this problem of politics and evil. The political theories of the Enlightenment, for instance, which have sought a convergence of interest in order to find a legitimate basis for society; and in so doing have shaded out of their picture the politics of power and the play of appearance which are in fact inseparable from political life.

But even today influential theories would have us reject the dilemma of politics and morality.

2.1 For instance, the heirs of the utilitarians would want to reformulate all moral questions as calculations of good and bad consequences. In this formulation, the dilemma can be made to disappear. The right thing to do is that which has on balance better consequences. It is irrelevant what quantities go into the positive and negative side of the scales provided the balance is positive. In given cases the bad consequences of lying, bombardment of civilians, judicial murder will be outweighted by the good which results. The balance being positive we should go ahead, without agonizing over a supposed 'dilemma' any more than the man does who invests $100 to get back $120.

But this homogeneization of all moral questions to the common coin of consequences cannot be sustained. We sense that there are certain acts whose rightness or wrongness cannot be exhaustively characterized in terms of the consequences which flow from them in the chain of events in which they figure. Their moral quality, if I can use this expression, is more a function of what quality of will they embody. The wrongness of dropping napalm on a village of noncombattants has not been measured when one has counted the number of dead in order subsequently to balance them against the number of lives saved; something of moral moment already lies in the fact that we are ready and able to calculate in this way over the lives of children, say; we have to be hardened, to be pushed a little closer to the monstrous, to be able to make this calculation and act on it. There is a certain moral degradation intrinsic to this range of action, that is, which is not simply consequence downstream in the chain of events.[3]

It is the fact that political life frequently seems to demand this kind of hardening, an acceptance and entrenchment of this degradation, which poses the dilemma of ethics and politics. But this in itself suggests another apparent way around the dilemma. An action will have not only morally relevant consequences downstream in the chain of events, but will also entrench or alter the quality of will of the agent. It will have not only consequences, but issue, as I propose to call this other form of outcome. And when we are dealing with political action, with action which ramifies through structures and engages many agents, the issue will affect not only the initial agent, say, the President or general who orders the bombing, but may alter the quality of will throughout the society. History can offer examples of whole societies undergoing moral degradation and becoming willing to accept the formerly unconscionable. Thus when the Republican government accused Gen. Franco of ordering the bombing of the residential quarters of Madrid in 1936, this kind of thing was considered so horrible that the Franco forces had to treat the accusation as an unjust calumny. Today this kind of thing is all in a day's work and can appear in operational reports.

To be aware of issues as well as consequences is to see political action in a new light. The most striking case of a political leader in our century who had this double focus is perhaps Gandhi. Civil Disobedience campaigns which for all one knew at the time might have had the intended consequences, independence, were called off because they were turning violent, and their issue would have been moral degradation, a falling away from *ahimsa*. For Gandhi the issue was ultimately more important than the consequences.

2.2 Gandhi's was a success story in the sense that the consequences came anyway, and this example can give rise to another unfounded hope of avoiding the dilemma: we can easily make ourselves believe that any worthwhile consequences can be got without moral degradation, that any which must be obtained at this price are not worth it. It is all the easier to do this if we work it out in some general argument without too close attention to historical examples: what value is independence if the kind of society we live in would filled with violence, hate, strife? But actual history does not fit as neatly into these categories. I have not yet heard a satisfactory answer to those who argue that Gandhi's methods would not have worked with the Japanese, that their success depended on the English, for a variety of reasons, lacking the ruthlessness to ride roughshod over non-violent resistance. Similarly, these methods will do nothing for those who are unhappy in the present Soviet Empire.

But this is not to say that Gandhi deserves any less our admiration. His action really does represent one of the important turning points of contemporary history. For anyone else, playing the game as it was universally understood before Gandhi, would not have called off the civil disobedience campaigns. By risking the consequences, Gandhi managed to bring off an expectedly great moral outcome. Paradoxical as it may sound, true followers of Machiavelli should hold Gandhi among the highest in esteem of 20th-century political leaders, because he understood where no one else did that a certain price did not have to be paid, and in this he was closer to the "*verità effettuale della cosa*" than those who are more usually called 'Machiavellian'. Political greatness is surely measured by this, that one not only leaves consequences more favourable, but a higher issue in one's wake. Once more, the figures cited as models by Machiavelli could be thought to have achieved just this: Moses, Cyrus, Romulus, Theseus.

But the obverse of this point is that disaster and even greater degradation can ensue from trying to maintain a level of moral purity which the political life of the time can not sustain. And this not just by the classical mechanism whereby the best retire and leave the field to the worst. There is also the mechanism we are witnessing today, where unrealistic standards demanded of a political process make it lose the allegiance of great numbers of people, with the result that it is less and less able to function and tends to be replaced with another form of political process which may be much worse. Something like this is operative today, though it may not go the full limit: thus, great numbers of people, particularly young people, profess to have lost faith in any political process which proceeds through elected legislatures. This is condemned as being inherently élitist, as stifling more immediate expressions of ordinary people's will and aspirations. Yet I doubt very much if there can be a process which is even as close to democratic as our own very imperfect one which does not incorporate as part of it — but by no means the whole — elected legislatures. To look for an improved model beyond the process of elections is to demand of politics a degree of spontaneity and free-wheeling immediacy which it can never give, at least in large polities.

But the widespread demand that it give more can easily lead to such a widespread falling away of allegiance to legislatures whose legitimacy is based on election, that they could no longer sustain themselves against those who represent themselves as more direct expressions of the popular will — a Bonaparte, or a vanguard party, or a military clique. We have seen enough of these in recent history to know well what kind of 'improvement' they represent. The imperious demand for more reason, fellowship and freedom, can bring force and cruelty in its wake. The consequence can be a putsch, and the issue a profound degradation of political morality.

2.3. The drive to an illusory perfection is the source of a third attempt to deny the dilemma of ethics and politics. From the standpoint of the higher ideal, the present reality is so penetrated by evil, is so abandoned by the good that no act one can commit in it, however *prima facie* bad, can be condemnable. It cannot add to evil in a world which is already absolutely so. It can only, as it were, redistribute evil, and if this redistribution may have as consequence the collapse of the system, then it is totally justifiable. The dilemma is overcome not by denying evil, as with the utilitarian solution above, but rather by holding that the present reality is so saturated with evil that it is impossible to initiate any further evil. Whatever one does one is not responsible for any further evil, since one is caught in a chain of total evil; and since

the evil of the present system is total, refraining from action has just as condemnable an outcome as committing the most heinous 'crime'. This latter is
therefore totally justified if it brings us even a hair's breadth closer to the
destruction of the 'system'.

This, as we readily recognize, is the morality of many contemporary terrorists. Thus the apologists of Laporte's murderers always replied to any
condemnation by invoking the 'violence of the system'. For instance construction workers die on inadequately protected sites because employers frequently
omit the necessary precautions. The rhetorical reply of terrorists: "and what
about the construction workers?" is a good *ad hominem* point. In fact not
much fuss *is* made by newspapers and the public about perfectly avoidable
accidents. In fact judges *are* often lax in condemning employers for breaches
of minimum precautions, or slow to award damages. In part this argument
is intended to rout the opponent in a flutter of guilt. But it is more than just
a debating point: it is actually felt that the 'violence of the system' makes it
not wrong to kidnap and murder. And this conviction will even survive a
relatively convincing demonstration that the kidnap-murder of Laporte is
unlikely to have any effect on safety standards for construction workers, and
may even serve to entrench the 'system'. What underlies the relevance of this
reply is really the conviction that the "system" is so totally violent and evil
that acts of violence within it do not constitute any additional evil; one is
not at the origin of any evil in so acting, but simply transmitting it, as it were;
and since in a totally violent and evil society inaction is just letting it be transmitted through the usual channels, there is no moral difference between
crime and inaction. But where no evil is originated, how can there be wrong?

This is the terrorist solution to the dilemma. But it is as illusory as that
of the utilitarian and the moral optimist. The terrorist can only blind himself
to his own responsibility, his own origination of evil, by maintaining a semi-
hysterical state of burning indignation at the system, one which melts down
to a solid jet black all the impure alloy of moral ambiguity and contradiction
which almost any human society, bar a few limited situations, contains. And
this total vision is in turn fed by unrealizable dreams of perfection, from
which standpoint all wrongs seem of equal import, the most trivial and the
most heinous, mendacious advertising on a par with intimidation and with
judicial murder, all blocked together as *'le terrorisme du système'*.

All these evasions of the dilemma are dangerous because they fudge a
crucial distinction. Political action requires that one balance consequences
and issues and act frequently in conflict with morality. To try to escape this,
to embrace what Weber called an ethic of ultimate ends, is to read oneself

out of effective politics. But this is not to say that everything is calculable, that *any* act should be weighed in its consequences and issue and hence in some possible circumstances could be recommended. The ethic of responsibility cannot suffice by itself. As Weber himself says, the man who follows the ethic of responsibility "somewhere reaches the point where he says: 'Here I stand; I can no other' ". And he continues:

That is something genuinely human and moving. And every one of us who is not spiritually dead must realize the possibility of finding himself at some time in that position. In so far as this is true, an ethic of ultimate ends and an ethic of responsibility are not absolute contrasts but rather supplements . . . .[4]

The notion that there is an absolute stopping point, that there is a line over which one cannot allow oneself to step, can be presented as the view that there is some level of moral degradation for which nothing can repay; that acts which cut us off from all contact with human good cannot be justified, for no consequences can be that good interwoven with such terrible issue. At some extreme level, we all, or almost all, rejoin the moral optimists.

But the problem of where to place this qualitative threshold cannot even arise if one accepts one of the above ways of burying the moral dilemma of politics. For the utilitarians, there are no qualitative differences, while for the optimists, one need never engage with evil at all; and for the terrorists, evil is so pervasive that there are no further distinctions to be made. But for myself, I think the hypothesis plausible that a refusal to recognize a threshold of this kind aids and abets the process of moral degradation in history, even or perhaps especially if this refusal is born of high, even perfectionist, standards. Thus the Bolsheviks, just because they were dedicated to the bringing to birth of a realm of integral freedom, found no ground of moral distinction between the politics and practice of Tsarism at its worst, and Liberal democracy at its best. This is not without relation to the fact that they have ended up outdoing Tsarism in its horrors, rather than liberal democracy in its limited freedom.

3. But the problem of ethics and politics is not exhausted once we have explored the choices we can be faced with between moral allegiance and political effectiveness. It is implicit in what was said above about moral degradation and its opposite that political contexts can differ greatly in the choices they impose, in the degree and nature of morally repugnant action they require. Central Italy under the Borgias, the Soviet Union of the 20's and 30's, and contemporary present-day Canada present quite incommensurable contexts. We may judge the first two to have been near the nadir in brutality

and violence, and yet they differ radically from each other in the type of action appropriate. The third context is still well above the nadir, although the events of October 1970 show how easily and rapidly we might sink in that direction.

Political action can alter or maintain the context, which was the point of introducing the notion of an 'issue', as distinct from consequences, above. And our greatest admiration should perhaps be reserved for those, like Gandhi, who transform the context for the better, that is, into one where the moral choices are less cruel and repugnant. But as to what contributes to altering contexts, very little coherent can be said in general terms. To understand this fully would be to understand the mainsprings of human history. The search for a cross-contextual 'general theory' is at best premature and probably in principle a monumental waste of time, as can be gleaned from contemporary attempts of this kind in political science.

It is a viable objective, however, to come to understand a particular context, its possibilities, the transformations it is undergoing or has undergone. And it is certainly of the greatest importance to aim to understand our own. Part of the urgency of the concern with the question of ethics and politics today is that we sense that in our society things are slipping. And in this we are not wrong. Not very long ago many people believed that advanced Western democracies were coming to a kind of historical home port in which ideological passion fed by glaring contrasts in life-fortune would abate, and politics would settle down to the civilized adjustment of non-fanatical interests. Moreover the sanguine could believe that this was the eventual fate of all societies when they reached the appropriate point on the economic growth curve which all must inevitably attain sooner or later. These hopes are dashed today when we see that 'ideological' politics, as this is understood by the utilitarian orthodoxy in our universities, is on the rampage again, and that violent solutions, or solutions which would destroy the fabric of peaceful adjustment of differences, are no longer unthinkable in our societies, that growing numbers are thinking of them.

It is important to understand why this is happening, and far from easy to do so. Prof. Rapoport's paper has the merit of biting into this question, and I should like to close my comments by some remarks on the hypotheses he puts forward.

Of course, Prof. Rapoport doesn't put the question in the way I have. He is examining the challenge to the power structure which is coming in the United States from the poor, youth, and the intelligentsia, and he tries to cast some light on the proferring of these challenges at this moment in history.

The aspect that I am singling out is that these challenges tend to see them-selves today not as directed just against the unjust or condemnable polities, like the Vietnam war, or the neglect of the cities, and not even just at the 'system' understood as the structure of economic power where major deci-sions are in the hands of large corporations in collaboration with a compliant government and military establishment; rather they often see their target as the 'system' in a sense that englobes what Americans used to call the "demo-cratic process" − that is, the set of structures and procedures of representa-tive democracy − and takes in the judicial system for good measure. These structures are seen as being so corrupted and vitiated by their interweaving with economic power as to be at best sham, and perhaps even necessary cogs in the mechanism of manipulation of people by power and privilege.

But of course the declining allegiance to these procedures is part of the growth in vogue of recourse to violence or solutions imposed by direct action. Should this trend continue, we will undergo a transformation in political context in which 'order' (for all societies require order of some kind) will be maintained more and more by repressive measures, such as those we glimpsed briefly with the imposition of the War Measures Act of October 1970, and re-form and revendicative movements of all kinds will be induced to have greater recourse to violence, which in turn will call forth more repression until the situation stabilizes in a new context, one in which deprivation of liberty, blackmail, violent coups, assassination, etc. will be more fully integrated into the normal operation of politics. Those engaged in political action in this context will have much crueler choices than our present politicians or most of our present 'revolutionaries' face.

Of course, having asked a somewhat different question than Prof. Rapo-port, my answer is bound to be different. I cannot do justice in this space to the richness and complexity of his treatment of the growing rebellion in the three milieux he singles out, poor, youth and intelligentisia. But the impor-tant difference is this: an important weight in explaining the alienation of intelligentsia and youth is put on their 'moral revulsion' at the 'ancien régime' nature of the superpower establishments. "The arrogance and the mendacity of the supreme leaders is matched only by occasional outbursts of incredible stupidity", Prof. Rapoport continues (p. 91).

This explanation does not convince me. First, because the reactionary and oppressive nature of American power abroad is not from yesterday, but the revolt is. In 1954, Eisenhower organized the overturn of a progressive régime in Guatemala, and was even able to boast about it in the next Presidential election, and no-one turned a hair. Second, because the turning against the 'system' in the late sixties does not explain why the 'system' is frequently defined in such a way as to include the procedures of representative democracy, why the 'power structure' is so little and so globally and frequently simplistically understood, why the moral revulsion, and the sense of denial of certain needs, like those for 'aesthetic experience' and 'affective identification with other human beings', has carried many young people to a more total rejection of their society.

As to the first point, why the rebellion now and not say in 1954 or at any time earlier, a common answer is the growth of affluence, which frees a rising generation of young from the "problem of earning daily bread or starving" (p. 91). Prof. Rapoport takes up this answer. But I'm not sure this is adequate as it stands, since it leaves unanswered the question why the threshold of affluence is the one attained in, say 1965, and not 1955 or 1975. I would like to have a satisfactory answer to this question myself, but I confess I do not.

As to the second point, it is often answered that the revolt against the system is global, because the system itself is global, because "there's no way you can change it", "it's all rigged", and so on. This is, I suppose, where the real argument starts, and I haven't space to do justice to it in this reply. But using brevity as an alibi for dogmatism, I should like to say that such arguments to impotence repose either on unrealistically purist expectations of politics − for instance, there *is* obviously no way that all the evils of U.S. imperial involvement will be stopped overnight − or on sloppy thinking about the nature of democratic procedures, their implications with the present structures of power, and possible alternatives to them.

If I am right about this, then the globality of the response cannot just be explained by the globality of the situation. My guess is that the answer lies at another level. A context reasonably free of violence and brutality requires widespread allegiance to a self-image of society which shows it to be connected to what are generally held to be important goals or valuable ways of life. In speaking of a self-image of society I mean not just a set of ideas in the minds of its members; to be effective some of these ideas must be woven into its public life in that they are constitutive of some of its institutions and practices. This is integral to the problem of legitimacy, much discussed in political science, and which Prof. Rapoport rises (pp. 84ff).

One of the powerful self-images which has held together Western liberal democracies, and perhaps the U.S.A. more than other, is that of society as an association of producers, linked by relations which were both rational and subject to continuous negotiation − this being in part an image of what was and in part the goal to which all effort and reform tended. This linked up with an important set of final goals for modern men: the sense of dominance over fate and nature, the turning towards the future as new creation, the freedom of the individual in a rational world, and so on.

Recently we are seeing a collapse of the allegiance to this image of society and a growing uncertainty about the underlying goods. It is possible that this will turn out to be only a temporary eclipse and that the march of modernization will resume after a decade or two, but at the moment the crisis of loss of faith is quite severe among the young. It is against the background of this collapse that we should see what I called above the globality of the response to injustice and the attendant growth in attraction to violence and direct action.

If this is so, then we are in a time of inevitable contextual transformation, and one therefore in which creative politics is at a premium. By creative politics I mean one which issues in a higher moral context. But if I am right, then the path to such a context certainly doesn't lie in feeding the moral absolutism or global responses of young rebels; nor in lecturing these same young rebels on their lack of appreciation of democracy. Rather a new self-image of technological society has to grow to provide the basis for a renewed civility, and this kind of development is much harder to produce to order.

I think a new self-image of this kind is in fact growing. I have tried rather inadequately to gesture towards it elsewhere,[5] using the rather inappropriate term 'contemplative' to point the contrast with our present model of technological society. But it needs to be constantly disengaged from a lot of cant, dreaming, charlatanry and *Schwarmerei* if it is to emerge effectively onto the stage of history. It will also need a vehicle and propitious political situation. I actually think it could find both in this country, which is why Canadian politics fills me alternatively with hope and despair, but to pursue this would take us far from the theoretical level of this symposium.

*McGill University*


NOTES

[1]  *The Prince*, c. viii.
[2]  *Ibid.*, c. xviii.
[3]  Cf. the penetrating discussion of latter-day utilitarianism in Stuart Hampshire's Leslie Stephen lecture, *Morality and Pessimism*, Cambridge, 1972.
[4]  *From Max Weber: Essays in Sociology* transl by H. H. Gerth and C. W. Mills, Oxford University Press, N.Y., 1946, p. 127.
[5]  'The Agony of Economic Man' in *Essays on the Left, in honour of T. C. Douglas*, ed. by Laurier Lapierre *et. al.*, Toronto, 1971.

LIONEL RUBINOFF

# THE LOGIC AND METAPHYSICS OF EVALUATION IN POLITICAL THEORY

*A Response to Professor Rapoport*

1. Professor Rapoport takes issue with all approaches to the study of political behaviour which presuppose a distinction between political science and ethics. He wants to argue that in addition to describing the phenomenon of political behaviour in terms of means-ends relations political scientists must be concerned with evaluating it as a species of moral conduct. Thus while the main substance of his paper consists of describing the ethical dimensions of politicaal behaviour in so far as it offers itself as a candidate for explanation, he appears at the same time to be implying that the very concept of political science as science is logically tied to the *evaluation* of that behaviour. Before commenting on the implications of his analysis I will first attempt to reconstruct it.

Professor Rapoport identifies three senses in which politics is concerned with ethics. Each corresponds to one of the three main senses of politics as such. Politics refers first of all to the 'art of government' or 'the exercise of power'. In this sense, according to Rapoport, 'politics' is closely related to 'policy'. Secondly, politics refers to the 'allocation of power', the process whereby power is transferred from individual to individual and from group to group. Included in this process are the factors affecting the attitudes and obligations of those who are governed towards those who govern. Finally, 'politics' refers to the various processes constituting the 'profession' of politics. We can therefore identify (1) the ethics of the exercise of power, (2) the ethics of the allocation of power and (3) the ethics of the profession.

By 'ethics' Rapoport means the rules of a particular 'ethos' whose very essence is defined by "incentives or restraints on behaviour that stem from expectations of approval or disapproval by relevant reference groups or individuals including oneself" rather than by rules backed up by sanctions. It thus follows that in so far as the professional exercise of power is concerned politics involves behaviour which is not only goal-directed but directed towards goals of a primarily ethical nature. The rationality of the exercise of power is thus a species of moral reasoning and to the extent to which that rationale is the subject of 'scientific' inquiry it is studied qua moral behaviour. This is the first main sense in which the subject matter of political science may be regarded as falling within the domain of ethics.

113

*H. J. Johnson, J. J. Leach, and R. G. Muehlmann (eds.), Revolutions, Systems, and Theories, 113–123. All Rights Reserved.*
*Copyright © 1979 by D. Reidel Publishing Company, Dordrecht, Holland.*

The same considerations apply to the processes of the allocation of power. Not only does the dominant ethos determine the rules according to which power is awarded, but the same ethos determines the attitudes that may be expected in so far as claims to power are supported or rejected. In other words 'legitimacy' depends not simply on consent but on consent offered in the interests of realizing certain moral commitments, while loss of legitimacy, which is the sole justification for revolution, depends upon withdrawal of support in the interests of preserving the very same morality that constitutes the basis of consent.

The ethics of the allocation of power, then, may be analysed in the following contexts: (1) the ethics of the award or transference of power, (2) the ethics of consent constituting an affirmation of legitimacy and (3) the ethics of protest, resistance and revolution, constituting a rejection of legitimacy. This is not the precise program laid down by Rapoport but it is the kind of thing suggested by his analysis.

Finally Rapoport makes the point that the 'ethos' dominating a particular society tends to be reflected by one particular form of life, such as, for example, the business enterprise, or the military enterprise. In the United States the dominant theme of its ethos is derived from the business enterprise. Accordingly there is a parallel (especially when it comes to the competitive atmosphere in which power is allocated) between the ethics of politics and the business ethic. But, Rapoport insists, this should not "obscure what ought to be the central issue in the relation between ethics and politics, namely, the ethical issues that arise in the exercise of power". In other words, if I understand Rapoport correctly, notwithstanding the influence of the business ethic on the ethos of a given society, the source of the ethical principles from which political conduct is to be appreciated go beyond the mere conventions that define the conduct of business. We must distinguish, in other words, between the game of politics and the ethics of politics.

Given these observations about the juncture between ethics and politics, what can be said about the role of political theory? On the one hand political theory may choose to concern itself with a description and analysis of social and political behaviour rather than with prescriptive evaluation. Presupposed by this dogma is the belief that not only is there a clear cut distinction between 'means' and 'ends' but it is possible to consider the relation between means and ends without evaluating that relation from the standpoint of ethics. As Max Weber once put it ". . . It can never be the task of an empirical science to provide binding norms and ideals from which directives for immediate practical activity can be derived . . . . To judge the validity of values is a matter of faith . . . . An empirical science cannot tell anyone what he *should* do — but rather what he can do — and under certain circumstances — what he wishes to do".[1] In keeping with this dogma some political scientists thus argue that to the extent to which political science is 'scientific', that is to say, capable of 'objectivity', then "it may be expected to show us what will result from that, but it cannot be expected to tell us whether the results will be good. It is for the use of both the wicked and the virtuous, of the just and the unjust".[2]

If we turn to Professor Rapoport's paper we find that he is not satisfied with merely describing the implications of belief on political conduct. The bulk of his paper is concerned with identifying the causes of revolutionary action. In this regard he seeks not only to contrast competing alternate theories of causation but to evaluate what he understands to be the intentionality underlying the behaviour of revolutionaries in such a way as to elicit either sympathy or disdain for the justice of their cause. Rapoport's thesis is that all revolutionary action derives from a conflict between the ethos or ideology of established power and the emerging ethos or ideology representing the general will upon which the legitimacy of power is based.

But if political behaviour is to be evaluated in terms of the ethos, upon what basis is the ethos itself to be evaluated? Rapoport rules out all theories that ground ideology in the transcendental realm of the *a priori*. Political science, he argues, must proceed on the assumption that the ethos springs from 'social conditions' which are historical. Ideologies are neither God-given nor rooted in an *a priori* human nature but arise as a consequence of historically changing social conditions. But then the problem is, as Rapoport himself acknowledges, to define clearly what is meant by social conditions in such a way that their ideological products can be evaluated. For if by social conditions is meant nothing more than whatever happens to be the case (that is to say, whatever happens to result through the successful satisfaction of desire) then we fall into the relativism of being unable to distinguish between what exists merely and what ought to exist, between what is *desired* and what is desirable, between mere *weltanschauung* and *weltanschauungslehre*. But it is only on the basis of such a distinction that we can establish the conditions of legitimacy (in so far as political power is concerned) as well as evaluate the ethics of revolution.

If on the other hand we distinguish between the merely existent and the ideally existent according to a pre-existing conception of what is good and therefore desirable, with the result that history becomes the mere vehicle within which reality is revealed, then we would appear to have fallen back into the dogmatic a priorism from which we originally sought to escape. In order to support the thesis that the conditions of legitimacy depend upon meeting moral as well as political-legal considerations it is necessary to provide an analysis of the ethical which provides for the possibility of distinguishing between the sociology of competing claims on the one hand and the logic and metaphysics of ethically valid claims on the other. In short, if ethics is to mean more than the sociology of knowledge then it can only be on the basis of a conceptual analysis of the ethos which assigns a *synthetic a priori* status to the resulting ideologies, while at the same time recognizing the historical context in which they evolve.

Implicit in Rapoport's paper then is the recognition that the concept of legitimacy in political theory parallels the concept of 'good' or 'desirability' in ethics. Just as moral approval and disapproval presuppose a concept of 'good', so political assent and dissent presuppose a concept of 'legitimacy'. Just as *morally good conduct* must be distinguished from conduct which is *compelled by fear of punishment* so *recognition of legitimacy* must be distinguished from *obedience through force*. The essence of morality and political legitimacy does not lie in the power to elicit obedience. On the contrary, morally right acts are acts done with the intention of so acting, and legitimate authority is that which is habitually obeyed through conscious choice. Legitimate power is thus exercised only when it elicits voluntary compliance, and denial of legitimacy entails a voluntary change in the state of mind of the citizens upon whose consent that authority rests. To so reject authority is the condition of revolution, and it is in this sense that a loss of legitimacy is said to be grounded in a change in the ethos.

The problem to which this analysis draws attention may be stated as follows. Granted that failure to elicit voluntary compliance is a necessary condition of loss of legitimacy, it is clearly not a sufficient condition, any more, that is, than failure to obey the moral law necessarily invalidates that law. At best such a description — withdrawal of voluntary compliance — may constitute a definition of revolution. But this is far short of being either an explanation of or a justification for revolution.

Now although Rapoport's paper has the virtue of raising the questions and issues stated above, the bulk of his analysis consists in offering an explanation of the sources of revolution in contemporary industrial society. And although a justification of this behaviour would seem to be implicit in Rapoport's causal analysis the question of the logic of justification as such is nowhere raised. It is, I take it, with a view to drawing attention to this difficulty that Professor Taylor begins his comment with the charge that while Rapoport's explicit definition of ethics may ring well in the arena of the social sciences, it is not a particularly interesting one for the ethical philosopher, nor is it in fact the definition which he (Rapoport) implicitly relies upon throughout his discussion.

2. Rapoport initiates his discussion of the ethics of revolution by rejecting the Marxist theory that all revolutions are power struggles between the ruling class and the oppressed class. Marxism fails today both as an explanation of alienation and as a prospect for change because unlike the situation in the nineteenth century the working class has today been co-opted into the main stream, and the power structure thus retains its legitimacy in so far as that legitimacy rests upon the consent of the working class. The challenge to the power structure now comes from sources other than those predicted by Marx, namely, from youth, a section of the intelligensia, and the rejects of the in-dustrial system. None of these sectors, according to Rapoport, resembles the revolutionary working class of Marxist theory.

The most significant of these alienated groups according to Rapoport are the rejects. Their poverty is a result not of genuine economic necessity but follows rather from the ethos of the capitalist system which demands that money should be dispensed in sufficient amounts to guarantee comfort, security and dignity only as payment, whether or not it is needed by the beneficiary. In short, poverty is moral rejection masquerading as necessity, and since the problem is primarily ethical, it follows, for Rapoport, that the resulting revolutionary activities of these groups should be understood as motivated by a desire to re-establish a sense of justice.

But to point out that political behaviour is motivated by ethical motives is not equivalent to evaluating the justice of that behaviour as Rapoport seems eager to do. Surely Rapoport would have to agree that if justice is on the side of revolutionaries rather than the establishment then it can only be because the behaviour of revolutionaries coincides with a standard of justice which in some sense 'transcends' the ethos. Rapoport claims that moral value systems are ideologies and arise, therefore, as a consequence of social conditions, and his point is that in the case of some revolutionaries their values arise in the context of their passionate rejection of the legitimacy of a corrupt social system. This perhaps explains the genesis of their ideology but it does not yet justify it — unless by justify we mean nothing more than the extent to which the origin of a value or belief can be explained. But Rapoport contends that the ideologies of the rejected are morally praise-worthy, which suggests that the justification of their ideologies derives from factors which are logically independent of the social conditions under which they arise.

In other words, Rapoport would seem to want to deny that the ethical dimensions of political behaviour are nothing more than rationalizations of the social conditions which determine the context in which that behaviour is enacted. Yet as he has so far stated his case his views would appear to be perfectly consistent with the reductionist argument that while the revolutionary classes may appear to reject the power elite for 'moral reasons', the motivation underlying their choice of morality is nothing more than a rationalization of their rejection; nothing more, that is, than the morality of rejection.[3] If against this possible interpretation Rapoport wants to argue that (1) the disaffection of revolutionary movements is motivated by moral indignation, (2) this indignation is further aggravated by their rejection, and (3) the basis of this indignation is morally sound, then he is implying that the moral soundness of their position is logically (though not historically) independent of the sociology and psychology of the situation.

There is thus implicit in Rapoport's discussion a second definition of ethics which, when elicited, might be characterized as "the science of the rules of conduct derived from principles whose validity is logically independent of the historical conditions to which they apply." The ground of these principles is transcendental and *a priori* while their *meaning* is historically contingent and is therefore dependent upon the social conditions to which the principles apply; which means, in effect, that any explication of their meaning must include some reference to these conditions. Thus, for example, the validity of the categorical imperative — treat others as ends and never as means — is transcendental in the sense that it may be derived from a logical analysis of the concept of man *qua* man, while the meaning of this principle depends upon understanding the historical conditions of its applicability. For while the categorical imperative defines the concept or ideal type of the moral act it does not specify either the conditions under which it may be expected to obtain or what counts as an appropriate embodiment of it in any specific social situation. In other words, the question remains, what does it mean to treat persons as ends in America or Canada in the 70's, in the here and now of life as it is lived today? This cannot be deduced from either an abstract definition of the principle or from an historical understanding of its applicability on past occasions. The understanding of the meaning is to a large extent dependent upon an intuitive apprehension of the principle implicit in a detailed sociological-historical description of the social conditions in question. Rapoport's analysis thus points in the direction of a phenomenology of social existence with a view to determining the *a priori* structures on the basis of which the changing social conditions can be evaluated as well as described.

To illustrate the point I am making let us consider for a moment what is involved in any attempt to apply a principle like the categorical imperative to any specific situation. Traditionally, the categorical imperative has been interpreted so as to exclude any decision which conflicts with the principle of 'reverence for life as such'. During the past few years, however, it has been interpreted in such a way as to lend support to a 'quality of life' principle. The implications of these differing interpretations for the world of practical action and decision making are profound, and the question therefore arises, "Which is the correct interpretation?" This question cannot be answered on the basis of either a purely logical and conceptual analysis of the categorical imperative or a merely historical description of its past applications. The question can only be answered on the basis of an analysis which is both conceptual *a priori* and phenomenological-historical; which pays attention to what follows logically from the universal concept of man qua person (or, as Kant put it, man conceived as a rational being) while at the same time evaluating the result in the context of the particular social and historical circumstances which obtain at the moment and which determine the nature of the climate of rationality within which the evaluation takes place. In such an analysis the *a priori* constitutes a necessary but not a sufficient condition of the possibility of a phenomenological-historical analysis, while the phenomenological-historical analysis constitutes a necessary but not sufficient condition of comprehending the meaning of the *a priori*. Only in this way — to cite the most extreme example I can imagine — could we expect to justify a decision to withold life supporting devices for a life in jeopardy on the basis of an appeal to 'quality of life' while at the same time conforming to the logical requirements of the categorical imperative which in previous ages has been correctly interpreted as requiring the contrary decision. I am not by this example suggesting that the 'quality of life' principle is in fact a morally justified principle for our particular generation, and is more likely than the 'reverence for life' principle to express the true meaning of the categorical imperative. My remarks are intended merely to clarify the conditions under which an evaluation of universal moral principles can be undertaken at all, and to show that such evaluations are both *a priori* and phenomenological-historical.

The final topic in Professor Rapoport's review of problems pertaining to the relation of ethics and politics is the 'exercise of power'. Rapoport takes issue with traditional positivist dogmas such as that a just allocation of power guarantees the just excercise of power. The mistake, he argues, has been to equate legitimacy of power with social justice instead of recognizing it as simply a necessary pre-requisite. This leads to such confusions as believing that whatever is done by a legitimate authority is right and just: a complaint which, in my opinion, is well substantiated by the following editorial from the *Wall Street Journal*:

We do not deny that the junta is, on the record, repressive. It has squashed freedom and other liberties associated with a free society. It relentlessly punished political dissent. On these scores it is presumably repugnant to most Americans, including U.S. policy-makers.

*Yet to make such repugnance the criterion of policy would be to indulge in diplomacy by emotionalism* — never a wise exercise. *Diplomatic recognition, or its recision, should not depend on emotional reactions but on considerations of the national interest.* (my italics)

If Washington can use whatever influence it has to induce more democratic conditions in Greece, that is worth doing. But the administration has evidently decided, so far, that for strategic and international political reasons, the present basic policy is in this nation's interest. For that evaluation, it seems to us, it does not deserve chastisement.[4]

But while Rapoport draws attention to this sort of confusion he does not explain how it arises. What are the factors which mediate between the perception of 'legitimate authority' and the perception of the conduct of that authority as 'just'? I would suggest that the answer lies in recognizing another more basic confusion which results from the identification of the essence of rationality *per se* with one particular mode of rationality which I shall designate, following Karl Mannheim, 'functional rationality'.[5] Functional rationality, like Plato's 'technē', and Heidegger's 'calculative thinking',[6] is the rationality of means-ends, the rationality involved in the organization of means towards the accomplishment of ends, regardless of whether those ends are morally desirable or politically just. This may be constrasted with what Mannheim calls "substantial rationality" which like Plato's 'aretē' and Heidegger's 'meditative thinking' thinks in terms of what is right, proper and just, and is capable, therefore, of distinguishing what is desirable from what is merely desired. To the extent to which consciousness is governed by substantial rationality it is subject to the *cogito ergo sum* but to the extent to which it is dominated, by 'functional rationality' it is rather a *facio ergo sum*.

The pathology of functional rationality derives from the fact that the agent becomes obsessed with means and techniques and is virtually anaesthetized by this into adopting an attitude of passive indifference towards (or acceptance of) the goals. What gives the enterprise the pretence of rationality is the fact that it is *organized*. Thus Eichmann, for example, in his pursuit of the 'final solution' regarded his actions as rational because he had organized a repertoire of technologically functional means toward the solution of a specific goal, and any action which is experienced as having a functional role to pay in achieving a goal is, by virtue of this fact alone, regarded as rational. The agent sets out to solve a problem and achieve a goal, for the sake of solving a problem and achieving a goal. The nature and content of the goal are secondary to the satisfaction of achieving it.

Not only is the nature and content of the goal secondary to the satisfaction of achieving it, but the agent's perception of the rationality of the goal itself is determined primarily by the success and efficiency with which it is achieved. If it is *possible* to achieve a given goal, then the goal itself must be rational.

It is thus that one acquires a completely false sense of rationality. Just as Hume pointed out in his famous analysis of causation, that we confuse the psychological experience of 'fulfilled expectancy' with the perception of 'necessary connection' or 'force', so the bureaucrats and technocrats confuse the psychological experience of the means bringing about the end with the reason or rationality for the sake of which the end exists.

It is thus, also, that human action becomes the agent of what Hannah Arendt has called "the banality of evil", the capacity for engaging in evil without experiencing it as evil, for performing evil acts as part of one's job description. Such behaviour, as Hannah Arendt and others have so ably pointed out, is not so much the expression of innate aggressiveness or sadism, as it is the result of the agent's inability to challenge whatever discrepencies and irrationalities he might perceive between his moral beliefs and what he actually does. This is especially true of the way in which certain acts of violence become assimilated to the agent's perception of what is rationally appropriate.[7]

The corruption of the exercise of power may thus be explained as following from a corruption of the very idea of rationality. Admittedly this is not a complete explanation but it points, perhaps, in the direction of the kind of analysis (in this case a sociology and phenomenology of reason) which might conceivably account for the confusion between the allocation of power and the excercise of power to which Rapoport has drawn attention.

There are other problems connected with the excercise of power to which Rapoport has not drawn attention in this paper but which should be acknowledged nevertheless. There is, for example, the problem of the way in which the excercise of power is experienced by the agent. It could be argued that the experience of power is ambivalent and that the desire to excercise power for its own sake is as compelling as the desire to use it as a means for accom-

plishing certain goals. To analyse the experience of power in this way would
be to draw attention to the dialectic inherent in the process whereby conduct
is converted from "using power *because* the ends justify its use" to "ration-
alizing the need to accomplish such ends *in order to* employ power". It might
also be argued that such tendencies, inherent in the *a priori* structure of
power as experienced, are reinforced by certain social situations which encourage the temptation to rationalize experience in this way. And in this
connection it would be found that bureaucratically structured social situations are more likely to encourage such behaviour than non-bureaucratic
ones. Once again the analysis points in the direction of a phenomenology and
sociology of power, an enterprise which is different in character from the
approaches illustrated in this volume, but which is clearly called for by the
approach taken by Rapoport's paper.

3. Rapoport's paper demonstrates the kind of concern for the relation between ethics and politics which in my opinion should be the duty of every
philosopher and political theorist to explore. Alas, as Rapoport rightly com-
plains, such issues are rarely explored in a field which is dominated by a
concern for describing and quantifying behaviour and for evaluating it only
in so far as its chances of success are concerned. In short contemporary
political science is preoccupied with developing strategies and policies based
on quantitative research rather than with social theories concerned with the
ethics of the implementation of such strategies and policies. Contemporary
political scientists would thus seem to be following the advice of Max Weber
and Pareto and so concern themselves with a description and analysis of
· social and political behaviour rather than with prescriptive evaluation. From
this approach the pathology of political behaviour becomes a problem of
technique. Whereas for Rapoport the pathology of political behaviour derives
from a corruption of moral consciousness. And for this reason Rapoport's
critique rests on an analysis of what is morally acceptable. His thesis then
is to the effect that legitimate political power rests first of all upon a just
allocation of power, secondly upon an integrity of commitment to the ethics
of the profession and thirdly, upon a wise and judicious excercise of power
in accordance with the historically grounded but nevertheless logically autonomous standards of morality. Failure to comply with any or all of these
requirements constitutes an *a priori* withdrawal of legitimacy and constitutes
therefore a justification for revolutionary action. In order words, failure to
elicit approval becomes a basis of denial of legitimacy *only* when that state
of affairs coincides with a violation of the standards of morality.

I have argued that if this is indeed Rapoport's thesis then he is arguing that not only does political behaviour have moral implications but that politics is in fact *grounded* in ethics and the concept of legitimacy is therefore grounded in a concept of the morally good. In other words, justice is a moral and not simply a political-legal term.

The implication of this thesis for political theory is that not only does political theory point to ethics, it points as well to metaphysics. For the consideration of the concept of the morally good as logically distinct from the historical conditions in which it develops is the task of metaphysics. At the same time, I have argued the need for a phenomenology and sociology of political behaviour which explains the sources both of corruption and of value, and which accounts therefore for the contexts in which the logical distinction between desire and desirability can be applied.

*Trent University*

## NOTES

[1] *The Methodology of the Social Sciences*, transl. and ed. by E. A. Shils and H. A. Finch, The Free Press of Glencoe, New York, 1949, pp. 52, 54, 55.

[2] G. E. G. Catlin, *Science and Method of Politics*, Archon Books, Hamden, Conn. 1964, pp. 347–48.

[3] A classic example of the reductionist approach to the morality of political behaviour is a paper by J. R. Fishman and F. Solomon called 'Youth and Social Action: Perspectives on the Student Sit-in Movement', *American Journal of Orthopsychiatry* 33, (1963), 872–881. For a critical discussion of this approach see Paul Goodman, 'The Ineffectuality of Some Intelligent People', *Commentary*, June 1962 and L. Rubinoff, *The Pornography of Power*, Quadrangle Books, Chicago, 1968, Ch. II, sect. 2.

[4] 12 January, 1970, p. 12.

[5] *Man and Society in an Age of Reconstruction*, Routledge and Kegan Paul Ltd., London, 1966, p. 52.

[6] *Discourse on Thinking*, transl. by J. M. Anderson and E. Hans Freund, Harper & Row, New York, 1966, and 'Letter on Humanism', transl. by Edgar Lohner, on W. Barrett and H. D. Aiken (eds.), *Philosophy in the Twentieth Century*, Random House, New York, 1962.

[7] On this question see Stanley Milgram, *Obedience to Authority*, Harper & Row, New York, 1974.

FREDERIC SCHICK

# ATTENDING TO INTERDEPENDENCIES

Democracy is government by the people. This is usually taken to mean that all decisions are to be based on the preferences of those involved. The preferences here are their *actual* preferences, the ones they currently have.

This sees democracy very narrowly. I want to argue for a broader view, one that would allow us to attend to certain sorts of conditional preferences along with those that are actual. The first section of this paper develops the concepts we need. The second section shows how these provide for a new approach to democracy.

1. Our basic concept is that of *conditional preference*. The idea here is obvious. A person prefer $p$ to $q$ *conditionally upon r* if and only if he would prefer $p$ to $q$ wherever he believed $r$.[1] If a preference is conditional both upon $r$ and upon not-$r$, I shall say it is *vacuously* conditional upon $r$.

Note that a conditional preference need not be a preference at all. It *might* be an actual preference: if a person prefers $p$ to $q$ conditionally upon $r$, and also believes $r$, it follows from our definition that his preference is both conditional and actual. But this is a special case. A typical conditional preference is conditional only.

Certain sorts of conditional preferences will be called *dependent* preferences. Only these will concern us here. A conditional preference is a dependent preference when it is conditional upon someone's having some specific preference, or conditional upon his not having that preference, or upon some conjunction or alternation of such preference-propositions, or upon some compound of such compounds. I would prefer having dinner with the Jones' to having dinner with the Smiths' if I thought that my wife preferred the Jones' company to the Smiths'. I would enjoy playing the piano after eleven If I thought that my neighbor liked to go to bed at ten. My preference for the Jones' over the Smiths' *depends upon* my wife's preference for the Jones' over the Smiths'. My preference for playing the piano late *depends upon* my neighbor's preference for going to bed early.[2] So also if I prefer $p$ to $q$ on condition that everyone else or most other people do.

Any group of people some of whom have preferences dependent nonvacuously on some of the preferences of the others will be said to be *interdepen-*

125

*H. J. Johnson, J. J. Leach, and R. G. Muehlmann (eds.), Revolutions, Systems, and Theories, 125–134. All Rights Reserved.*
*Copyright © 1979 by D. Reidel Publishing Company, Dordrecht, Holland.*

*dent.* The examples above reveal that my wife and I form an interdependent group, and also my neighbor and I. The interesting cases involve larger groups. In a large interdependent group, many of the people might have no preferences nonvacuously dependent on those of any other person. Then again, every member of the group may have some preference so dependent on other members' preferences. There are various types of intermediate cases. We shall want a way of representing the distinctive character of the interdependence of a group, or at least, the distinctive character of its interdependence with regard to some set of alternatives.

Several additional concepts will be useful. An *actual ranking* is a set of actual preferences. A *conditional* ranking is the set of all those of a person's conditional preferences that are conditional upon some specific proposition, the ranking being *conditional* (or *founded*) *upon* the specified proposition. Suppose that Jones prefers $p$ to $q$ conditionally upon Smith's preferring $r$ to $s$, and that he prefers $s$ to $r$ upon the same condition. Then both of these conditional preferences belong to Jones' ranking conditional upon Smith's preferring $r$ to $s$. Suppose also that Jones prefer $t$ to $s$ conditionally upon Smith's preferring $v$ to $w$. Then this conditional preference belongs to Jones' ranking conditional upon Smith's preferring $v$ to $w$. A derivative concept is that of a conditional ranking *of a given set of alternatives*. The conditional preferences in this case focus on these alternatives only.

I shall refer to certain sets of conditional rankings as preference *perspectives*. Suppose again that Jones prefers $p$ to $q$ conditionally upon some simple singular preference-proposition, say the proposition that Smith prefers $r$ to $s$, and that this dependence is not merely vacuous. Then the three propositions that Smith prefers $r$ to $s$, that he prefers $s$ to $r$ and that he is indifferent as to $s$ and $r$ compose one of Jones' *dependence sets*. The conjunction of one proposition from each of some set of dependence sets is one of Jones' *dependence expansions*. Consider now only those of Jones' dependencies that depend nonvacuously on those preferences of the other people that focus on whatever alternatives are at issue. Jones' *perspective* on the alternatives at issue is the set of the conditional rankings of them he founds upon the dependence expansions obtained from these dependencies and upon the various alternations of the dependence expansions so obtained. If none of a person's preferences with regard to the alternatives is nonvacuously dependent on those of the others, his perspective will be said to consist simply of his actual ranking of these alternatives. (It will be useful to think of this ranking as conditional upon some logically true proposition.)

If Jones' only nonvacuously dependent preferences are those focusing on

$p$ and $q$, on $r$ and $s$ and on $t$ and $u$ cited above, he has two dependences sets. Label these $\{x_1, x_2, x_3\}$ and $\{y_1, y_2, y_3\}$. There are nine dependence expansions: $x_1$-and-$y_1$, $x_1$-and-$y_2$, $x_1$-and-$y_3$, $x_2$-and-$y_1$, . . . and $x_3$-and-$y_3$. If all the propositions cited are among the current alternatives, Jones' perspective consists of 511 conditional rankings. These are the rankings he founds upon the nine expansions above — label these expansions $e_1$, . . . $e_9$ — plus the rankings he founds upon $e_1$-or-$e_2$, $e_1$-or-$e_3$, . . . $e_2$-or-$e_3$, . . . $e_1$-or-$e_2$-or-$e_3$, . . . and $e_1$-or-$e_2$-or-$e_3$-or-$e_4$-or-$e_5$-or-$e_6$-or-$e_7$-or-$e_8$-or-$e_9$. Note that a person's perspective reflects not only what he would prefer if he held the various possible *specific* beliefs about the preferences of the others, but what his preferences would be if he believed only that the others' preferences were *either* this *or* that, etc. Note also that one ranking here (as always) represents a total uncertainty regarding the others, a suspension of all (factual) belief. This is the ranking founded upon the (logically true) alternation of all the dependence expansions.

We defined perspectives in terms of preferences nonvacuously dependent on simple singular preference-propositions. If some of a person's preferences depend nonvacuously on negations of such propositions, or on conjunctions or alternations of them, or on compounds of such compounds, we can take the propositional constituents of the propositions depended upon to generate dependence sets. Or rather, we can do this with their *essential* propositional constituents — with those that cannot be left out of any logically equivalent restatement. If a preference depends nonvacuously on $r$-or-not-$s$-or-$t$-or-not-$r$, both $s$ and $t$ can be taken to generate dependence sets, but $r$ cannot.

The set of everyone's perspectives reflects the nature of the group's interdependence with regard to the alternatives. The average number of rankings in all the perspectives reflects the extent of this interdependence, or the *incidence* of dependence in the group. The pattern of cross-reference among the perspectives models the *cohesion* of the group, the dependencies either binding the group together or dividing it into subgroups or making for some intermediate state. The cross-references also reflect the *distribution of influence* — whether there is some person or small group of people on whose preferences those of all the others depend, or whether no one has this much of a say; whether every person's preferences are dependent on those of some small number of people (different, perhaps, for each), or whether each person looks to many. We shall return to some of these matters in the next section.

Turn now to the sets of rankings composed of one ranking from each perspective. Some of these sets have special characteristics. Consider first the *equilibrium sets*. Generally speaking, an equilibrium is a situation from which no one will move unless he thinks that some of the others will be elsewhere too. A set of rankings $S$ is an *equilibrium set* if and only if, were all the rankings in $S$ concurrently actual, each would be founded on a true proposition. No one in the group will believe any proposition incompatible with the one on which his ranking in $S$ is founded unless he thinks that the actual rankings of some of the others will not be their rankings in $S$. Thus no one will incompatible to a ranking founded on any such proposition unless he thinks that some of the others will actualize rankings other than *theirs* in $S$.

This has the flavor of game theory, but the ideas are not the same. In the game-theoretic case, an equilibrium identifies a set of possible actions, one for each person involved. The equilibrium is defined in terms of everyone's actual ranking of the junctures of the actions in each such set (or in terms of the various utilities assigned to each of these junctures). On our analysis here, an equilibrium identifies a set of conditional rankings, one for each person involved. We define an equilibrium in terms of the truth values of the propositions on which the rankings in these sets are founded. A set of rankings is in equilibrium if and only if, were all the rankings actual, each of these propositions would be true.

There must always be at least one equilibrium set. Whatever the circumstances, the set of the rankings founded on logical truths is bound to be in equilibrium. There may be several equilibrium sets, some of them more appealing than others.

Consider two of a person's conditional rankings. Suppose that this person prefers the proposition on which the first ranking is founded to the proposition on which the second is. Then he would rather things were such that, if his beliefs reflected the facts, his actual preferences would be those making up the first ranking. We might express this in terms of his *preferring to prefer p to q*. But let us think of the rankings *in toto* and say that he *favors* the first ranking over the second.

This provides for a concept of a *least constrained* equilibrium set. Consider again the sets of rankings composed of one ranking from each perspective. A set $S$ will be said to be a *least constrained* equilibrium set if and only if $S$ is an equilibrium set and, for every second equilibrium set $S'$, the number of people who favor their ranking in some set other than $S'$ over their ranking in $S'$ is not exceeded by the number of those who favor their ranking in some set other than $S$ over their ranking in $S$.

There is always at least one least constrained equilibrium set. There may be several such sets, and further distinctions could be made. But we shall stop here. We have the distinctions we need.[3]

2. Let us turn to some of the ways in which all this might be used. I suggested at the outset that the idea of democracy does not require that social decisions be based on people's actual preferences. We can now make a case for a more inclusive basis.

It is easy to see that, where there is interdependence, decisions based solely on actual preferences may well be unstable. Were everyone to be informed of where everyone else stood, some people might so change their own positions that the decision would no longer be appropriate. It seems to me that the disclosure of the facts on which a decision is based ought never itself to lead to such changes that the decision must also be changed. The soundness of a decision ought not to hinge on the secrecy of the ballot. But the only way of assuring this is to base decisions on preferences in equilibrium, whether or not these preferences are actual. I shall call the procedural rule involved the *principle of equilibria*.

Consider the following hypothetical case. A city is planning the erection of a stadium. The sports fans are a small minority, but all the others support the project in the conviction that the fans are for it. But this conviction is in fact false. Most of the fans do *not* want the new stadium, and were this to get to be known, most of the others would not want it either. The actual preferences are overwhelmingly in favor of construction, the conditional preferences in equilibrium overwhelmingly against. The principle of equilibria would say that the project ought to be dropped.

Closer to home, many of the reforms debated today would have more backing if those who oppose them were to discover that those who support them are not all either hippies or professors. Though the consensus seems to be against these reforms, they might be urged on the grounds that the consensus is not in equilibrium, and that the conditional preferences in equilibrium mostly favor them.

This last is of course conjectural. The claim that the reforms would have more backing if people knew more of one another may be no more than wishful thinking. There have been no surveys of the dependent preferences on any of these issues, and so we cannot be certain of how things stand. Plausibilities are not to be scorned. Still, many more surveys of dependencies are needed before our principle of equilibria can be put to any decisive use.

In the meantime, the principle expands our horizon. It prompts us to attend to more than the standard theory of democracy does. And it allows us to argue (if only inconclusively) for measures and policies that are clearly ruled out on the standard view. For purposes of advocacy, our principle is indeed rather weak. But we can easily strengthen it.

Consider a package of proposals, with something in it for everyone. Everyone supports the package, but only because he knows that the others do. No one is happy about supporting it, each person wishing that the others had better sense. The package has unanimous support, but if, somehow, it were rejected, the news would make for relief all around.

Here both the set of the actual preferences in favor of the package and the set of the conditional ones opposed to it are in equilibrium. The principle of equilibria would have nothing to say. Yet the preferences in favor are the less compelling, for these are only held reluctantly. It seems to me that, given equilibrium, *non*reluctant preferences should count for more than reluctant ones. One way of assuring that they do is to base all decisions on preferences in a *least constrained* equilibrium. I shall call the rule that requires this the *principle of least constrained equilibria*.

Our second principle absorbs the first and inherits its difficulties of application. It also runs into snags of its own, for there have never been any surveys of how people rank their rankings. So clear-cut test cases are out of the question. We must make do with what seems plausible.

Take an example from history, the prohibition amendment. At the time this was passed, prohibition had widespread support. But the support was rarely wholehearted. Conjecturing: everyone knew that many supported the proposed amendment, and many of those who supported it did so *because* they knew this, wanting to stand among the righteous, since righteousness was winning anyway. Conjecturing further: many of these people regretted the passing of alcohol. They wished that the others opposed prohibition, in which case they too would have opposed it. If these (and other similar) surmises are correct, the principle of least constrained equilibria would say that prohibition was wrong.

Or consider the current attitudes toward pornography, prostitution and the like. There is a good deal of support for the policy of clamping down. But it may well be that many of those who support this policy do so only because they know that the others support it, and that they not only would prefer *laissez faire* if they thought that the others did but would be delighted to hear that the others had come around. If all this (plus some more) is in fact the case, our principle would call for freedom in these matters.

The line I am taking is not entirely new. It recalls, in part, the approach of the classical idealist philosophers. Rousseau, Kant and the rest believed that, aside from his actual ranking, each person has some conditional ranking that would be actual if he were rational or sensitive or clear-sighted, and that the set of these *ideal* rankings deserved a special consideration. The analysis I offer follows the idealists in this. (Though not all the way: there may be more than a single set of least constrained equilibrium rankings.)

But my position nonetheless differs from the idealists'. The idealists held that each person's ideal ranking was identical to that of everyone else. Nothing of the sort can be expected here. Our principle does not presuppose any unanimity. The problem of reconciling differences remains.

There is one curious item in this connection. It turns out, on our analysis, that populist democracy ought to be uniquely attractive to idealists. For if everyone preferred one course to another whenever he believed that the majority preferred the first to the second — or whenever he believed that two thirds, or four fifth or everyone did — then there would always be several equilibria in which all the rankings coincided. (There would be as many such equilibria as there were possible distinct rankings of the propositions at issue.) Our analysis does not endorse unanimity even where everyone is a populist, for none of the sets of unanimous rankings need be least constrained. Everyone might prefer the majority (or the two thirds or four fifth or whatever) to have remained indifferent, and the rankings founded on the indifference of the others may be in equilibrium too. But if we extended our analysis along idealist lines, and held that only the preferences in a least constrained equilibrium set *of unanimous rankings* deserved to be considered, then only where everyone was a populist could our principle always be applied.

The idealists held also that the ideal rankings have some sort of a moral edge, and that social decisions based on them are therefore morally right. Here too we part company. There need be nothing meritorious about a ranking in a least constrained equilibrium set. The rankings in such sets are distinguished from others solely in terms of each person's preferences, though not solely in terms of his preferences over the alternatives at issue, and not independently of the other people's preferences. Whether a person's ranking in a least constrained equilibrium is morally superior to his actual ranking depends on the character of all his preferences. Equilibria may occur at low levels of morality. And a least constrained equilibrium need not be any more admirable than the rest. The adoption of our principles would not always make for decisions that are morally compelling.

I do not want to overstate this. Since our principles themselves are moral directives, subscribing to them cannot be morally neutral. The point is rather that procedural principles such as ours do not exhaust the subject of morality, and that decisions squaring with these principles may still be faulted on other grounds. Let almost everyone prefer one course to another, all in a least constrained equilibrium. The course preferred may still be cruel, unjust or destructive. Where this is so, we would have to consider our moral priorities. The adoption of the principles proposed would not have settled things.

Turn now to some problems of a purely theoretical sort. In default of the requisite data, we cannot ever single out any least constrained equilibria. But it may be thought we can get around this, for we make use of the information at hand. We listen to one another. We read the results of polls. We study the otucomes of elections. All this allows us to adapt our preferences to sounder beliefs about the others and so provides for some groping in what we hope is the right direction.

In cases like those presented above, this process steers us straight. In others, however, it does not. Consider the following situation. A group contains two cliques. The $A$'s prefer $p$ to $q$, believing (correctly) that the $B$'s prefer $q$ to $p$. They would prefer $q$ to $p$ if they believed that the $B$'s preferred $p$ to $q$. The $B$'s prefer $q$ to $p$, believing (*in*correctly) that the $A$'s prefer $q$ to $p$. And the $B$'s would prefer $p$ to $q$ if they thought that the $A$'s did. The actual preferences are not in equilibrium, and however long the people involved collect information about one another, revise their preferences, correct their beliefs and revise their preferences again, they cannot reach an equilibrium. (There is of course an equilibrium where no one has any beliefs about any of the others, but this position cannot be reached in the course of picking up information.)

Here is a problem of the *preconditions* of democracy. In what contexts of interdependence can an equilibrium always be worked out? In what contexts is this not always possible? The case just considered provides an answer to the first of these two questions. The preferences of the $A$'s are spiteful, and it can be shown that a sufficient condition of the attainability of equilibria from every initial position is that there be no spite, whether actual or conditional. But this is not a necessary condition. Suppose that the $A$'s are as above, that the $B$'s prefer $p$ to $q$, believing that the $A$'s prefer $q$ to $p$, and that the $B$'s would prefer $q$ to $p$ if they thought that the $A$'s preferred $p$ to $q$. Everyone is spiteful here. Yet if the $B$'s found out about the $A$'s, they would revise their preferences, and all would be in equilibrium. Nor would any other initial beliefs make for a permanent disequilibrium where these dependencies hold. So the absence of spite is not essential to the invariant attainability of equilibria. Since nothing else suggests itself, the second of our questions remains. Or more directly: I have no idea how to answer this question.

A few words on the problem of what might be called the *effectiveness* of democracy. One argument for democracy is that everyone knows best where his own shoe pinches, and that letting each person's voice count will therefore serve people's interests better than any alternative would. Democracy is held to be effective because it yields the essentials. In giving people what they *want*, it gets them what they *need*. At least it provides for more of their needs than any other form of government would.

Interdependence makes for doubts on this point. Consider a situation in which the preferences of all but one person depend on that one person's preferences. (Suppose, for instance, that whatever people think his preferences to be are also theirs.) In a case of this sort, all but one are inattentive to their own needs. Each person knows where his shoe pinches, but all but one are looking somewhere else, and so the presumption in favor of effectiveness fails. Where there are several, but still a proportionally small number of people influential in this way, the effectiveness of democracy must likewise be in question.

The unevenness of the distribution of influence may seem to be the source of the trouble. If Jones' preference for $p$ over $q$ depends nonvacuously on one of Smith's preferences, Smith has more influence than Jones has on the issue of $p$ versus $q$ — unless Smith's preference on the issue depends on one of Jones' preferences, in which case they are even. We could take the number of preferences that depend nonvacuously on his, plus the number of those that depend on the preferences dependent on his, etc., as an index of the influence a person has on an issue. (Or we might restrict this to those dependencies that focus on the same pairs of propositions and that order then in the same way.) This would permit us to set up some index of the unevenness of the distribution of influence in the group — the standard deviation would do — and to go on to reflect on the maximum unevenness likely to be compatible with effectiveness.

But this would not go to the heart of the matter. If all of everyone's preferences depended on someone else's and were in turn depended upon by some still other person's preferences, influence would be evenly distributed, and yet the chance that people's needs were being reflected would be small. The problem is one of *autonomy*, where this is understood in terms of the proportion of those of a person's preferences that are *not* dependent on the preferences of others. The trouble above is that no one has any autonomy. Likewise in the preceding case: a society of leaders and followers is one of little autonomy. This is true by definition, so it does not say anything new. But it suggests that effectiveness cannot go along with too much interdependence.

How much interdependence is likely to be compatible with effectiveness? We cannot begin to consider this until we have some index of effectiveness,

and nothing of the sort is around. So here is another question that remains
unanswered. But answers may yet be found. One virtue of the concepts presented above is that they provide for the questions. They allow us to raise
some old issues in some new ways. The concepts themselves do not solve any
problems. They do help us to think things out afresh.

*Rutgers University*

## NOTES

[1] Here and throughout, all variables stand for propositions, or hypothetical states of
affairs.
[2] In extenuation: my neighbor has a dog who barks all day.
[3] An earlier version of the analysis in this section appears in my 'Democracy and Interdependent Preferences', *Theory and Decision* 3 (1972), 55–75. For a different body of
concepts that serves the same purposes, see my 'Beyond Utilitarianism', *Journal of
Philosophy* 68 (1971), 657–66.

MARX W. WARTOFSKY

# POLITICS, POLITICAL PHILOSOPHY AND
# THE POLITICS OF PHILOSOPHY

Philosophy has its own politics. That is to say, the 'society' (or the 'profes-sion') of philosophy and of philosophers has its roles and rules, its means and ends, its conflicts and mediations, its forms of governance, its modes of dominance and subordination, its varying 'constitutions' which determine legality, legitimacy and due process. This analogous 'politics of philosophy' has its counterpart in the politics of the larger society in which philosophy functions, and the relation between the 'inner' and 'outer' politics — between that of philosophy and that of society (or of a given society) — may well be instructive concerning both polities. It is not simply that (the profession of) Philosophy is Politics writ small, or that Politics is Philosophy writ large, though the Platonic metaphor is suggestive. Rather, it is that the study of the state of philosophy reveals something about the state of Society at large, and *vice versa*.

Now this is harmless enough, because vague. It also has little to do with the narrow sense of academic politics, i.e., 'professional' or 'departmental' politics; as little as, say, political theory has to do with Boston politics. The latter, we may say, is the *reductio ad absurdum* of the former. (Or, more reductively, one may argue that the 'politics of the wards' is the place where the universals of political theory are deflated, and brought to ground in good nominalist fashion.) But if we are not speaking here of the intramural politics of the profession, in the narrower sense — e.g., who is getting what job, and being published by what editor, or being fired for what reasons of stringency, politics or competence — then what is the politics of philosophy? If politics in general is the context in which theory and practice ought most closely to be united, and if intramural and internecine 'politics' is not the practice, what is?

I want to propose the view that the politics of philosophy has its actualiza-tion in the doing of philosophy, i.e., in philosophical practice. Philosophical practice is the actual (and normal) work of philosophers — what they speak about, argue for or against, publish and teach, in the context of their pro-fessional activities *as* philosophers. This 'politics' then has its issue in any of the subdisciplines or fields of philosophic activity — metaphysics no less than ethics, philosophy of science no less than aesthetics, logic no less than

135

H. J. Johnson, J. J. Leach, and R. G. Muehlmann (eds.), *Revolutions, Systems, and Theories, 135–153. All Rights Reserved.*
Copyright © 1979 by D. Reidel Publishing Company, Dordrecht, Holland.

political philosophy. Thus, theory and practice are, here, the theory and practice of philosophy. The particular philosophical practice I will discuss happens to be political philosophy, and the thesis I will argue is that political philosophy, in its fads and fashions, as well as in its deeper modes, maps the politics of philosophy accurately.

If it seems that political philosophy *as a practice* is several steps removed from politics proper — i.e., from the larger human concerns and actions most appropriately characterized as political — then this is because it is a philosophical practice, or indeed a theoretical practice, and this need not be held against it. What may be held against it is its deformation of the content with which it is theoretically, or pedagogically engaged. The first serious critique of such a deformation was leveled by Feuerbach against his own mentor, Hegel. In his *Critique of Hegelian Philosophy* (1839) Feuerbach took Hegel to task for mistaking form for content; in particular, for mistaking the formal reconstruction of consciousness (in the *Phenomenology of Mind*) for the actual content or activity of consciousness itself. In effect, Feuerbach criticized Hegel for substituting the reflected-upon abstraction, in thought, for the actual content or the thing of which it was the abstraction. Hegel had reified the activity of the *philosopher*, substituting it for the 'real' activity of human consciousness.

Marx's critique of Hegel followed a similar pattern, but he followed it with a critique of Feuerbach, whom he also accused of 'abstracting' the activity of human beings. The very 'consciousness' which Feuerbach had tried to naturalize, in his conception of it as more than what is represented in philosophical reconstruction — i.e., as feeling, willing, needy, dependent consciousness, and not simply as the self-activity of reason — was seen by Marx as itself hopelessly abstract, in that it did not ground this consciousness itself upon the actual needs and actions of human beings in concrete historical and social contexts. Feuerbach, said Marx, had criticized the 'Holy Family' — i.e., the religious conception of human needs, hopes and desires hypostatized in the Gods, who represent these needs, hopes, etc. to human consciousness not as its own activity, but in the form of other 'beings.' But, Marx continued, now it was time to do a critique of the 'Earthly Family'; i.e., to reveal the ways in which human social relations were hypostatized, or 'fetishized' in the institutional forms of the state and politics, and in the economic formations of the marketplace and the workshop. The 'deformation' which Marx alleged — most specifically in theories of Political Economy — was the self-same 'mistake' of taking the outward forms, or the appearances yielded by the institutionalization of social and economic life, for the very relations into which human beings had entered within these forms. Classical Political Economy, Marx argued, had hypostatized the present transient and historically developed modes of human social, economic and political organization and had thus taken them as 'essential' or 'universal' or 'eternal' features of human organization, deriving from 'human nature' itself.

Why this digression? Does it bring us any closer to the critique of Political Philosophy, or give us any new insights into the Politics of Philosophy? After all, what is accomplished in a critique of *practice*, when one reflects upon the reflections of Marx upon the reflections of Feuerbach upon the reflections of Hegel? Isn't this more of the same game? Namely, the game in which the actual *content* of politics remains hermetically sealed off from an internal 'critical' history of theory, or of reflection? Indeed, even if we were to accept the 'inner' politics of philosophy as a politics of ideas and criticisms, how is it then to be related to the larger human politics?

The answer, I think, lies in the character of this philosophical politics itself. Ideas and criticisms don't follow each other in some internally tight-knit dialectic, *except* within schools or modes of philosophizing. If Hegel, Feuerbach and Marx, in some respects, constitute a consequent series of critical ideas, one feeding off the next, then it is because, in some respects, they are continuous in their conceptual framework to the extent that the critique shares the language and the methodology of what it criticizes. This delimits what one may call a 'school' of philosophy, or a 'movement' or even a 'style'. To be sure, within a 'school' or a 'style', there may occur the most fundamental disagreements, not alone in what follows from premises, but on premises themselves. Yet, when a critique is sharp, and effective, it concerns what is commonly understood by both critic and victim. The character of philosophical politics is that it is a politics both within 'schools' and 'styles', and among them. What counts as an issue within political philosophy may therefore be either a debate within a 'school' — e.g., on what counts as justice within the framework of contract theories of government — or between 'schools' — e.g., on what are the sources of political obligation, say, between deontologists and pragmatists. This presupposes that, even when the premises are different, and even the style and language of philosophy are different, there is at least a commonly understood *problematique* — that is to say, the question being asked is regarded as both meaningful and legitimate by both sides. But thus far, we are still 'inside' philosophy, and the practice we are describing is familiar and relatively unproblematic. The question to be answered, however is a different one: namely, how is all this 'internal' practice of criticism, analysis and debate to be related to the larger human politics, in which alternative *conceptions* of political right, power, obligation find their actualization in different policies and practices in human affairs? Here, the crucial distinction is not that between one analysis and another, or even one school or style and another, but in what is regarded as a meaningful and legitimate question — i.e., what is accepted as *problematique*, and what is rejected.

It is time to be at least minimally concrete about all this. For these purposes, it will be useful to sketch, or even to caricature the current scene and its history, in terms of political philosophy. First, the setting: it is the university, for that is now where political philosophy gets done, for better or worse. Political philosophy was occasionally practiced by statesmen and politicians. Jefferson was a political philosopher, as were James Madison and John C. Calhoun. (I have trouble coming up with others, if one is to retain for the term 'philosophy' something of its connotations of conceptual sophistication, systematic construction and analytic rigor.) Now, however, political philosophy is almost exclusively practised within an academic setting, at least in the United States. It has, in effect, become Professional. In this setting, it has exhibited the fads and fashions of Academe, and of philosophical academe in particular. More than a generation ago, political philosophy meant the *study* of political philosophers, notably such classic ones as Plato, Aristotle, Hobbes, Spinoza, Locke, Burke, Hegel, and perhaps even Marx. What marked them off as political philosophers was that the accepted range of 'political-theoretical' questions was discussed by them. These included such unexceptionable questions as the nature and origins of the state, the rights and obligations of the citizen, the alternative forms of rule and their justification, the right to revolution, etc. After World War II, and during the Cold War, political philosophy added to its classical repertoire a systematic concern with 'Fascism, Communism, and Democracy' (sic) in which the category-mistake vied with the vulgarization of political theory for dominance. 'Ideology', barely differentiated from 'political philosophy', lived cheek by jowl with sheer political journalism, and worse — (rhetoric and explicit low-level propaganda) — as a new generation of students toyed, in pubescent foreplay, with a polite relevance. Quite suddenly, as these things go, the Sexy Sixties were upon us, and the Academy discovered the world: real Politics intruded upon the classroom, as student and faculty civil-rights workers returned from the South, as the Viet-Nam War exploded into the classrooms and onto the campuses, as the Third World revolutions and counterrevolutions came closer and closer to home, as Presidents and Presidential candidates were assassinated, and as campus political movements turned to demonstration and confrontation. Political philosophy in the classroom responded with a new

cast: Che, Mao, Marcuse, and the litany of 'first-name' leaders of Black Liberation: Stokely, Eldridge, Huey, Angela and paradigmatically, Malcolm X. Old
timers like Marx, Lenin and Stalin, formerly included discretely in antholo-
gies, well guarded and surrounded by more traditional theorists, were now
screamingly available in full panoply. The more esoteric figures of the left –
Lukács, Luxemburg, Korsch, Gramsci, Althusser – became more familiar.
Political philosophy, certainly in the outposts of academic activism, but even
in the politer precincts of Academe, had gone Marxist, or something like it.
The older demarcations between 'Political Theory' (the precinct of 'Political
Science' departments, kept there as a precocious and not always manageable
orphan) and 'Political Philosophy' were no longer easy to maintain; moreover,
sociology no longer could be kept from the borders of philosophy, especially
when continental political philosophy – e.g., in Germany and France –
merged with critical sociology, and as 'sociology' became the cover under
which political philosophy was done in Eastern Europe. (As an aside, sociology and anthropology had already intruded across the philosophical borders
earlier, but under an immigration law which admitted only Aryan types: i.e.,
candidates for citizenship in the then still formalistic precincts of 'Philosophy
(or Methodology) of the Social Sciences.'

This is admittedly a caricature, hard to resist. I use it for one purpose only,
since caricatures are one-dimensional – (really two, but the jargon seems suitable here), – and leave out all detail in order to preserve quickly identifiable
features. That purpose is to show that the shifts in *problematique* within
Political Philosophy are *not* the results of a merely internal critical or ideational dialectic; nor even the products of the dominance of one or another
graduate school in producing the 'going style' in philosophy. If this were so,
then the Politics of Philosophy, as it concerns Political Philosophy at least,
would be that hermetically sealed-off 'inner politics' we spoke of earlier.
Rather, it seems clearly to be the case that the problem-shifts are related to
politics in the large. But before one jumps to the vulgar conclusion that the
domain of Political Philosophy is but a microcosm of national or world
politics, let us recall the setting: namely, the university. The university, as
an institution, mediates Politics with a capital P, and mediates it crucially. It
is not Politics *tout court* which determines the problem-shifts in Political
Philosophy, but rather Politics as *it* is transformed by the institution, the
polity, the constituency of the university. And here, as the Yiddish proverb
goes, is where the dog lies buried.

Two conclusions are going to follow from this, and I think I should state
them *before* I argue to them: *First*, that the current fad and fashion in Politi-

cal philosophy of dealing with such central questions as Violence, Race, War and Revolution is, in fact, Political Philosophy's response to real Politics. But it is not yet a real response. *Second*, that this response not only *mediates* real Politics through the filter of the university; it mystifies Politics once again, in good academic tradition, by pretending to solve in the head (or on paper, or *within* philosophy) problems whose solution lies *beyond* philosophy, beyond philosophical *practice*, and certainly beyond the university. In short, Political Philosophy has tended to reify Politics, even while it has accepted Politics (rather than merely political theory) as its proper domain.

(1) As to the first conclusion: Why should not Political Philosophy's response to Politics be a 'real' response? Is this a matter of feigning, or of insincerity on the part of political philosophers? It may be that, to some extent, the preoccupation with contemporary political questions, (or with traditional political questions in their contemporary setting) is fake, or at least faddish. The inner politics of philosophy can explain that much. Bandwagons, as we all know, have a special fascination in our profession. To be *au courant* is to exist. But I think that the large majority of professors and students who are engaged in this contemporaneity are not only sincere, but serious in their intentions. They quite rightly take these issues to be legitimate and crucial issues for philosophical analysis and critique, and want to enlarge classical Political Philosophy beyond the confines of some essentialist or merely historical approach. Then why is this not a 'real response' to Politics? One may argue that it is not 'real' in the sense that it is not profound, or solid, or long-lasting, as an attitude; that however sincere it is, its seriousness is a seriousness of the moment, a flirtation which will pass when the mood or the political atmosphere changes. Marx taught us that the petty bourgeoisie are essentially fickle, first swaying to this side, and then to that, because of their relations to the class struggle. Well, who is more petty-bourgeois than a College professor or an intellectual? His bread is buttered first on this side, then on that, or on both, or on neither, and he isn't ready to cast it upon the waters because of sheer prudence, (to mix a few metaphors). From this, it ought to follow that professors and students alike may be serious and well-intentioned enough in their concerns in Political Philosophy, but that their social and class position makes them prone to vacillation. For example, one might argue that the response to Politics is not 'real' precisely in the sense that violence, racism, war and revolution have been our lot long before the Sixties, and that it was only their effect *upon the University* that made these viable issues for academic Political Philosophy. (The student-draft, *or* student-exemption; white guilt in the face of racial violence, or in the heyday of the Civil-Rights move-

ment; or simply boredom with played out and non-vital repetitions of a classic curriculum, etc.) A 'real' response would therefore be based on an abiding understanding or commitment, and not simply respond to Politics for the occasion – the occasion being the intrusion upon the university in specific and historically unique ways, likely to change.

Yet I think that none of these explanations – faddism or opportunism of the moment, petty-bourgeois vacillation, or the intrusion of Politics into Academe – is what condemns the current concern with real Politics as not yet a real concern. Let me say why not, and then say what I think *is* the 'unreality' of political philosophy. First, however temporary or circumstantial or *ad hoc* the current concern may be, it is perfectly clear that professors – even professors of political philosophy – can learn from experience. Whatever the circumstances of the 'politicalization' of political philosophy, however they are mediated by the university setting, they were and are real circumstances. Their reality may be highly specific, and not at all the stuff of so-called 'real Politics' – i.e., political action in sustained organizational forms directly bearing on the nitty-gritty issues of the war, racism, violence, revolution, or whatnot. Yet, even apart from what one may characterize as 'movement' politics, which certainly had its place on the campus, Professorial experience is not so far removed from national life as to be totally immune to political issues, or totally incapable of seeing their relevance to one's own discipline. One may want to hold to a rigorous unity of theory and practice: 'No political theory without political practice'; and thereby denigrate any political philosophy which is not itself tied to the practice of 'real' (as opposed to 'academic') politics. Yet, this seems to me to be at once too severe and too mechanistic a requirement, and also an evasion of the critical question as to why political philosophy fails to realize the political. It is entirely conceivable that a political philosopher be immersed in 'real' political practice, and yet emerge merely wet, but not baptized. There may be no learning without experience, but there may very well be experience with no learning. Therefore, I would hold that the current concern for 'real' politics in terms of issue-orientation in political philosophy is a real reflection of the larger politics, and within the constraints of Professorial existence, an honest one. If it is not yet the 'real' response which I held up vaguely as a criterion, it is not because the concerns are not real, nor is it because it fails to eventuate in 'real' political action. The latter is a separate question, to be dealt with, but not in this context where I think it is irrelevant. Rather, I want to argue that it is not a 'real' response because it is *philosophically* inadequate: inadequate both as a positive and critical activity of political theorizing, *and* as *philosophical practice.* One need only read the current work being published in political philosophy in the United States to recognize how raw and untheoretical it still is, at least with respect to anything vaguely identifiable with current concerns with politics. Historical, systematic and analytic studies fare better, in terms of sheer competence or adequacy, but they represent the traditional philosophic response: the reflection upon reflection, within the dialectic of the schools. Thus, Hobbes, Mill, Spinoza, Contract theory, and even the more exotic reaches of academic Marxism (or 'Marxology'), among other themes, have generated a laudable literature, by any academic standards. Just War, Racism, Women's Liberation, Black Liberation, the Strategy and Tactics of student and anti-war movements have begun to pass over the border from humanist rhetoric and (even quite decent) political journalism to philosophy, but in no way have as yet produced deep or systematic works. The distillation of a decade of political activism is small indeed, in this regard, if one takes the term 'philosophy' seriously. The failure to give a 'real' response to Politics is therefore the failure to give an adequate *philosophical* response.

But this failure may be inevitable, at the moment. There is no tradition of active, critical, normative political philosophy upon which an adequate response could build. The political detachment of analytic philosophy, for more than three decades certainly did not prepare it for the task, though there are signs of life from that quarter. Yet, they are feeble, since the very language and stance of analysis has deconditioned a whole generation of the most able young philosophers, by a fatal confusion of methodology and content in the analytic movement. If there was anywhere a reification of methodology it was here; and the loss is all the more poignant since analysis is the sharpest tool of philosophical criticism, and there is nothing intrinsic in the method to keep it from being an instrument of political criticism. Socrates and Plato wielded it thus, but then, so did Marx in his devastating *analytic* critiques of the theories of his opponents. Unfortunately, analysis became misidentified with political detachment, and took its *problematique* to be the small and timeless world of 'concepts' or of 'language' conceived either in literary or logical terms. 'Use' and 'Action' promised to spill over from their analytic contexts into the social and life-forms of language. But the abstraction remained too severe, and still does. The Professoriat had successfully turned a means into an end, in the search for a self-justification for philosophy.

Phenomenology had promised more. From 'rigorous science' in its severer Husserlian moods, it had become socialized, existentialized, even historicized;

but it remained apolitical, or became politicalized only in the luxuriant literary-professorial contexts of France, where its politicalization was more a function of its Hegelianization, in Sartre and Merleau-Ponty, than of any more original approach to political philosophy. That is to say, it discovered its road to politics in practice, during the resistance; but theoretically, through Hegel and Marx. Phenomenological Marxism was attractive precisely in its emphasis on the self-dependence and the formative activity of the subject, which had been neglected by more orthodox Marxism. Lukács had shown the possibility of uniting activist political philosophy and practice with phenomenological subtlety, and was able to revive the humanist and dialectical content in Marx's own work, in direct application to practical political questions of revolution and class-consciousness, the analysis of the role of the Party, and of the organizational forms of class-struggle. Marcuse, too, had theorized a revolutionary role for the students, the intelligentsia, the alienated professional classes and the Blacks, in a pessimistic Marxism which saw the power of 'Totalitarian Democracy' in emasculating the revolutionary impulses of the working classes in advanced capitalist countries. Out of 'phenomenological Marxism' and 'Critical Theory' (of the Frankfurt School of Adorno, Horkheimer, Marcuse, and more recently, Habermas), there has arisen a kind of political philosophy, but one as yet so exotic, so eclectic and so academic in its theorizing flights, that it can not yet be characterized as adequate to the task of giving 'real' responses to Politics.

Popperian political philosophy, where it is not simply a philosophical reflection of the virtues of the British Constitutional Monarchy, is mainly negative: it eschews its scarecrow versions of Plato, Hegel, and Marx, and comes out for the individual. Hooray! Hardly a response to the complex, historically unprecedented and traumatic politics of our time, though methodologically on the side of rationality and critical intelligence.

So-called 'Radical Philosophy' has tried to take the bull by the horns, combining activism with the radical critique of philosophy, and of political philosophy in particular. It is conglomerate, newly formed, and involves some of the most promising young philosophers, many from analytic backgrounds, and many serious new students of Marxism and of alternative political-theoretic traditions. 'Radical' is the name for an attitude, here, and not yet for a philosophical method nor for a philosophical program. It rather functions as a nominalist 'term', designating the individuals who have joined together for discussion, study and philosophical work, and not as a realist 'essence' denoting a clearly articulated set of principles, premises and goals. But the promise seems great here.

In summary, then, my own reason for stating that political philosophy has not yet given a real response to politics is that the responses it has given are philosophically raw, as yet, hindered by the lack of a political tradition in political philosophy. One may ask: What about the Marxists themselves? Well, what about them? In the United States at least, that tradition was broken especially in the Fifties, and though here, as in England, Marxist theory had had some philosophical competence in literary criticism, history of philosophy, aesthetics, and in social history, it did not yet provide the firm basis of colleagual work and high scholarship required as a foundation for a philosophical movement. Communist politics, as well as anti-communist politics left the tradition of Marxist scholarship enfeebled, especially in the field of political philosophy, where one should think it would be strongest. Yet here too, the heightened interest in Marx's writings, and in Marxism generally over the past years, is promising; and the contributions of contemporary Marxists and Marx scholars — (e.g., Schaff, Coletti, Marković, Avineri, McClellan, Kolakowski, Petrović, Stojanović, Dupré, Schmidt, Heller, Nowak, Althusser, Mandel, among others) — to questions of political and social theory may yet engender serious works in American political philosophy.

(2) So much for my sketch-argument to my first conclusion. The second is a deeper conclusion, I think, and requires a knottier argument. The second conclusion, it will be remembered, charges contemporary political philosophy with *mystifying* politics. Now what is *that* all about?

'Mystification' is a term current in Marx's critique of classical Political Economy, i.e., of what he considered as the bourgeois theory of capitalism. It is directly borrowed from Feuerbach, and while it may make perfectly clear sense in its ordinary connotations, it is in fact a technical term. In the earlier sketch of the critique of Hegel by Feuerbach, and of Feuerbach by Marx, I suggested what this 'mystification' comes to. Here there is a need to be more systematic. To *be* mystified, is to be taken in by false appearances, or, in good old fashioned epistemological terms, to mistake the appearance for the reality, the way a thing *looks* for the way it *is*. Thus, to think that the sun is the size of my thumb, because I can visually cover it with my thumb is to be mystified. No mysteries there, and nothing untraditional. Now, *to mystify* is to present the appearances as if they were the things themselves. But this won't do, for example, if one argues that things are as they appear, where 'appear' is not bound to the naive phenomenalism, e.g., of the sense-datum theory, but where 'appearances' are themselves the products of our active construction in perception, and where the way a thing appears is in fact the way it appears to me mediated by my theoretical or scientific understanding and by my history of practical understanding. (Theory-laden Observation, and all that sort of thing.) This non-naive 'appearance' is the closest I come to knowing the way things are, given the limitations of human knowledge and its fallibility. In this non-naive context, a discrepancy between appearance and 'reality' can come about only in the context where what appears to you is different from what appears to me, and we both take it to be the same thing we are observing. Should the Athenians think the Sun is a God, while Anaxagoras thinks it is a hot rock, then what appears to the Athenians is not what appears to Anaxagoras, and there is no neutral 'datum' which both have, the interpretations of which they may then argue over. To claim that something is a *false* appearance then is to claim that the appearance-as-understood — (and there are *only* appearances-as-understood, and no appearances-*en-soi*) — is wrongly understood. It is taken to be something which it is not. It thereby may be said to 'mystify' the observer-understander, who takes it for something it is not. But here we are beyond phenomenalism, and are caught in the domain of truth-claims. In one mode of appearance, we come to understand *correctly* — i.e., truthfully — what the appearance is an appearance of (or better, what-it-is that appears thus); in another, we fail.

Suppose now that what it is I have to understand is my own action, or the action of others; and in this context, the relations between myself and others in these actions. The form in which my action takes place is not my private construal, but is understood by me in terms of rules, or social expectations, or more concretely, in terms of institutional or societal structures or procedures. In order for me to be able to *understand* the socially-structured action, or relation, it must be objectified for me — simply speaking, it must be something which I come to know as an object of consciousness. If — to take a favorite example from contemporary discussion — I go to the polls to vote with the conviction that the way I vote will serve my interest, then the construal of the voting-action and of the whole structure of elections is embodied for me in the institutional *form* of an election. This is what I understand an election to be. The 'object' — the *election* — is taken as an embodiment of my own actions, intentions, understanding, insofar as its very meaning, and its social existence as an 'object' (or structure, or procedure) are constituted by the relations I enter into in voting. Now suppose this is, in fact, how I understand 'election'; and in good faith, on this understanding, I conscientiously deliberate on how I should vote, make every effort to go to the polls, etc. If it can then be shown to me, for example, that my votes are not even counted, that the 'results' are manipulated by deceit, that the exercise is a pure 'show' (*Schein!*), and that what is going on in the black box into which I cast my ballot has no relation whatever to the fact that I cast my ballot, or how I voted, then my good faith has been violated, and if I persist in voting in the unswerving belief that things are as they had been taught me to appear, I am a fool. I am 'mystified' by the ballot box, by the concept 'election', and am in effect taken in by false appearances. Were I to understand the concept 'election' properly, in such a case, I would take it to mean something like "periodic exercise in deception of the 'electorate', in order to keep it in the belief that the government is chosen by it to represent its interests, and thereby to legitimate the continuing non-representative power politically, and to avoid dissension and disruption." (Marx's example is quite different, of course: there, the 'real' relations between human beings, in the social relations of production, give the appearance of being an equitable exchange of value for value, in the medium of exchange, i.e., money or wages; but this 'false appearance' masks or 'mystifies' the real exchange, and therefore hides the worker's exploitation by the capitalist under the form of 'equivalence of value', or in Gompers' famous slogan, "A fair day's work for a fair day's pay.")

Now what heinous deception is our innocent and well-meaning political philosophy passing off as true coin? Who is being 'exploited' and what 'false appearances' are being perpetrated?

Suppose now that the issue before philosophy is the political issue of just and unjust war. The issue has been raised because *real* politics has intruded into the classroom or the study, the Viet-Nam war, or the Cambodian bombing, or the Israeli-Arab Six-Day war is at issue. The real political question is one of justification, or of justice, and the political consequences of a resolution of the question in one or another way are that both in thought and action, the war will be supported or defied. Just-War Theory is studied, the issues are analyzed, the arguments examined, historical examples are scrutinized, the concepts and the internal coherence of the theory are subjected to logical reconstruction, the normative premises are gone through in their various theological, ethical, and political variants, articles are written, classroom debates rage, counterarticles are written, a major work appears, it is reviewed critically, panel discussions are held inviting lawyers, statesmen, representatives of both sides of the actual conflict. There is a veritable 'just-and-unjust war' boom in academe, and even one or two non-philosophical journals and one Sunday Supplement carry the news beyond the Groves. First one philosophical school holds the upper hand, having demolished the thesis that 'wars' can be either just or unjust — a reductionist methodological individualist school, for example. Then the essentialists and social-organicists take the lead, having made the case that 'war' is a social entity whose very character it is to be normative, 'justice' being the most basic of all social norms, etc., etc. The issue is resolved first this way, then that. Proponents are led to hold views they did not hold before. Relevance reigns. Minds are changed. Philosophy bakes bread, at long last.

So far no deception, and no mystification. No one has been led to take something to be what it is not. Philosophical practice set itself the task of engaging in philosophical study, critique and debate of an issue taken from contemporary politics, with its roots in ethics, political theory, theology. The notion of a 'philosophical resolution' of the issue is clear: one way or another, for one person or another, a particular intellectual stance on the question has been determined, on the grounds of philosophical analysis and argument; certain convictions have been arrived at, and perhaps they will be acted upon beyond the philosophical contexts. They will certainly inform the attitudes which eventuate in action of one form or another.

What is wrong? Thus far, nothing. Insofar as philosophy has taken upon itself a real question of politics, and has dealt with it within the confines of philosophical practice, it has provided an essential component of theory, of self-conscious reflection on practical political questions, necessary for a theorized practice. True, the *practical* question of just and unjust war has not been resolved by this theorizing and analysis. The practical question comes to be resolved by actual political practice, hopefully made rational and clear-headed by the philosophical discussion.

Whence comes the mystification, then? I think it has two sources: one, within the mode of philosophical practice itself, and another, in the substitution of a philosophical for a political resolution of the issue. Within the mode of philosophical practice itself — i.e., within the theoretical analysis of the issue — the very notion of justice, and of just and unjust war may come to be treated as if it were merely a philosophical question, i.e., a matter of conceptual analysis. Wars are concrete historical and social events, and whatever there may be in common between the Punic Wars, the Wars of the Roses and the Viet-Nam war, the questions of justice cannot be dealt with abstractly but only in the contexts of the actual historical and social circumstances of those wars. Thus, for example, Catholic Just War Theory abstracts from contexts in its question-begging first criterion: the war must be in a just cause. The virtue here is that war is made a matter of conscience and of justice. But that is at best a heuristic, and not yet a theory of justice. For an abstract analysis of the concept of justice is not yet a theory of justice either, no more than abstract vector analysis is physical theory. The analysis must, somehow, relate

to or be interpreted in the concrete context. In historical-social contexts, and
in political contexts, the danger is that questions of justice, of rights, of obligation will come to be treated in *no more than* an abstract, conceptual way,
and thereby hide or mask the limitations of the particular abstractions used.
Thus, for example, on the legal interpretation of Just-War Theory, a war is
unjust when it violates international agreements or treaties, when it constitutes an act of aggression by one nation against another, where aggression is
defined as a violation of the sovereignty (territorial, political) of one nation
by another by force, and not in self-defense against a prior aggression. The
conception here is abstract enough to cover the widest variety of cases. It is
complicated further by considerations of alliances and mutual defense treaties.
It was in such a context of legalism that the fiction of a war of defense against
a prior aggression was assiduously maintained by the United States, in the
name of treaty obligations in Viet-Nam. Could one reasonably be said to be
doing an adequate job of political philosophy, in such a case, if the concrete
circumstances and history of the conflict were not themselves used to test
these legal-conceptual abstractions? The policy arguments by the United
States Government during the Viet-Nam war, regarding treaty obligations,
and the fiction of the legitimacy of the South-Vietnamese government, as a
treaty-ally, were carefully constructed on the basis of such political abstractions which in themselves might have seemed reasonable enough in their legal
contexts. But this was a deliberate piece of mystification, and the impact of
the publication of the Pentagon Papers was precisely that they revealed the
deception and its explicit motivations in concrete detail.

Now it was not political philosophy as such which was doing the mystifying here. But suppose the just-war debate in philosophical terms were to go
on in the absence of anything other than the *formal* definitions of, e.g.,
aggression, treaty-obligations, *and* the official account of where these stood?
Would not such a philosophical exercise be the effective analogue to the
deception practiced by the government in this case? Let's suppose, instead, a
'legal' argument cutting the other way: Massive U.S. military intervention and
bombing in force in Viet-Nam was based on an incident, (since revealed as
itself a deception), namely the alleged attack on U.S. warships by North Viet-
namese military craft, in the Bay of Tonkin. The Tonkin Resolution was
taken to be the enabling action by Congress for President Johnson's rapid
escalation of the war. Yet, it came to be argued that since the war-making
powers of the President require a declaration of war to be made by the Congress, under the powers granted it under Article I, Section 8 of the Constitution, and since no such declaration had been made, the war was in effect

unconstitutional. On these grounds, one could argue that it was an unjust war, in that it was being conducted illegally. Now such a narrow construction of 'just and unjust war' certainly seems to violate the common intuitions of what the terms connote, and to have regarded the war as unjust for such reasons alone would be to fall prey to the narrowness of a particular abstract definition of justice. For then, it would follow that every war following upon a legitimate declaration of war is, *ipso facto* 'just'.

I do not imagine that in this case, such patent 'mystification', mistaking the form for the content of the concept of justice, is either typical or common in political philosophy. The Viet-Nam war was itself too actual an event, too much present in its details, to permit one to overlook the concrete circumstances, and live only with the abstractions. Yet, at one remove, even such 'issue-oriented' themes in political philosophy as racism, violence and revolution *do* remain within the realm of such abstraction, even when the appearances are that they are being dealt with concretely. When the sources of racism come to be explained in such psychological terms as 'prejudice', or its victims are described in such euphemistic terms as 'disadvantaged', or racism is seen to be based on 'cultural differences', or is accounted for by the more openly blatant genetic arguments for differential abilities along the scale of 'conceptual, abstract skills' and 'affective, concrete skills', — then the abstractions used do indeed 'mystify' precisely in skewing the phenomena so that a certain appearance — i.e., a certain 'understanding' of racism will be maintained, and an alternative one denied. How useful was the myth of the 'Fatherless Black family structure' or that of 'Prenatal brain damage' in 'mystifying', (ostensibly in the interests of 'realism' and goodwill), just what the real sources of inequality were?

'Violence' has also had its share of mystification, of being presented either as the manifestation of an innate aggression characteristic of our species, or as the redeeming mystical-psychoanalytic confirmation of manhood, or as the requisite for self-esteem, for the 'wretched of the earth'. In each case, the mystification derives from a one-sided abstraction in which a rich and complex phenomenon is understood *not* in its full social, human and political context; but rather as an aspect of the phenomenon hypostatized as the whole of it.

Perhaps we are forever condemned to a succession of hypostatizations, so that every appearance-as-understood will be revealed in its one-sidedness, by a deeper understanding; and that, in its turn. That still leaves us with the injunction to bring to bear upon our abstractions the fullest range of *extra*-philosophical, *extra*-conceptual political contexts, to test our abstractive and theoretical analysis for what it leaves out, or for what it hides from our view.

Finally, as to the mystification which proceeds from the substitution of philosophical for political resolutions of political questions: first let me deal with its converse. The illusion that one can resolve a philosophical issue politically; that somehow, by sheer political practice, there will be generated 'right thoughts,' smells of the practicalism which sometimes masquerades as Marxism, sometimes as Calvinism. It is analogous to the 'cold shower' resolution for sexual frustration. It may make you feel better, but it sure isn't going to resolve the sexual problem! No more is 'political practice' in itself going to resolve any philosophical problems. Philosophical problems are resolved by philosophical practice, (to which, as the preceding section argued, political practice may very well be relevant.)

On the second sort of mystification: it occurs in political philosophy when the resolution of a philosophical problem is taken as the end of the matter. Having determined what the nature of the State is in theory, or what Justice is, politics is left only with the task of embodying the philosopher's ideal adequately. Politics becomes mere technology for philosophy, and 'technology' in a degraded sense: the sheer passive instrument for carrying out in practice solutions already arrived at in thought. This division of labor, between theory and practice, reflects the long history of class society, in which, at least on the ruling-class view, practice was the passive instrumentality to be directed by 'those who knew', i.e., the rulers who ruled in virtue of their knowledge. Thus, it is not simply a matter of somehow confusing a philosophical with a political resolution, as one might distractedly think one has answered a letter because one has thought of answering it and composed the letter in one's head. Theory here provides only one component of the process — the 'half' which figures in the proverb: "Well-begun is half-done". But political practice is not the mere 'carrying-out' of philosophical programs, completed in thought. And to the extent that political philosophy eschews the domain of political practice, it lends itself to an intellectual *hubris*, to illusions of potency and political importance in which great political enterprises are carried out in thought, vast critiques are levelled, and it is expected that the victims will fall, overwhelmed by philosophical argument. This is simply that mystification which is Utopianism in political philosophy. What political victories occur there! What deaths are suffered by the iniquitous! What futures arise before our eyes, and what fools there are who refuse simply to adopt the Word as Law!

This mystification of political philosophy is, of course, the most serious, because it is the *self*-mystification of philosophy, taking itself for politics proper, and taking politics proper as no more than its epiphenomenon, or its after-image. Lest this be taken as an argument for the self-isolation of philosophy from politics, or for a political philosophy which preserves its autonomy by refusing to sully itself with politics, I should add that it is not the relation of political philosophy to politics which is at issue here, but the illusion that political philosophy *is* politics. This is in effect the reduction of politics to political philosophy, the mystical identity of philosophical practice with political practice. Its result, where it has been successfully achieved, is the degradation of politics in two ways: in the first, the political philosophers play-act at politics. The consequences, we know, are disastrous. The gap between illusion and reality becomes unbridgeable, and the political philosophy itself becomes empty, fatuous and a distorted image of its once legitimate philosophical insights. In the second way, politics is degraded because it is left to the errand-boys, to the venal and the self-seeking, to the passive instruments of policy, to the hoods who will serve any master for the delegated power without responsibility which it affords them. It is not power which corrupts, but power without responsibility; that is, power simply transmitted, like imparted motion in classical physics, to inert bodies. Passivity corrupts, then; and a technological politics left to the 'doers', because the 'thinkers' have already finished figuring out what is to be done, leaves the thinkers passive in the realm of practice, and the doers passive in the realm of theory, and thereby corrupts both.

Unfortunately, the university as a setting, divorcing as it does theory from practice, tends to foster self-deceiving political philosophy, and the illusion of political power and importance where there is none. Fortunately, with occasional lapses, such self-important utopianizing political philosophy very rarely gets a crack at real political power.

In summary then, the 'mystification' or 'deformation' which political philosophy — (or more broadly conceived, political theory) — has been prone to take two forms: (a) The substitution of philosophical practice for the practice of politics in the larger sense, (in which philosophical or theoretical critique is simply one component); (b) the divorce of the practice of philosophy from the contexts and content of political life. Now it would seem that to overcome this divorce, philosophy should become political; or certainly, that political philosophy should. But then, from the resolution of (b), we seem to land in (a), i.e., philosophy itself, in becoming 'politicized,' becomes politics. Were one to take a simple-minded view of the theory-practice distinction, then a practically-oriented political philosophy would itself seem to be the unity of theory and practice longed for by politically responsible philosophers. But that is the delusion I have been arguing against here. A political philosophy which does achieve, in its *philosophical* practice, that unity of concrete political content with philosophical analysis, critique and systematization, is one which has overcome the abstraction of theory from practice *within* philosophy. Its achievement is an achievement within the politics of philosophy. But to construe this as the transformation of philosophy into politics itself, in the larger sense, and to think of resolution of the theory-practice dichotomy *within* philosophy as if the political questions at issue had themselves been resolved is to confuse the politics of philosophy with the larger politics which is its context. To be sure, political philosophy is itself a moment in political life, whether it is done poorly or well. Its sins of omission and distraction are constituents of and influences upon the larger political life; so too are its virtues of clarification and critique. But philosophical practice, as a theoretical practice, is not yet political practice as such, in the large sense; nor is this larger political practice *as such* theoretical. *That* unity goes beyond philosophy, and certainly beyond the precincts of the University and the library (even beyond the reading room of the British Museum). It is not that 'real' politics in the larger sense is 'more real' than the politics of philosophy; it is simply something more. But then, it may be charged, doesn't this reify the 'larger politics' itself, and make of it an abstraction? Doesn't it, in turn, become a Platonic form, exemplified, in this one case, in political philosophy's 'practice'? I think not. I haven't discussed the 'reality' (better, the 'realities' or 'actualities') of politics in the larger sense, nor *its* forms of mystification, except incidentally. I have instead relied upon an intuitive understanding of the term 'politics in the larger sense,' as involving all those historical and social modes of practice which organize human action either to change the present society, or to preserve it from change. My point is that the practice of philosophy, while it is *one* of these modes — the theoretical mode — is not yet *all* of them. Thus, to be 'political' in the fullest sense, philosophers need to become more than philosophers, and politics has to be more than the politics of philosophy. Yet, *as* philosophers, and specifically, as political philosophers, they are responsible not to mystify it; or indeed are responsible for demystifying it; to distinguish a proper formal analysis from a fetishized formalism; and to distinguish the practice of philosophy from a fetishized political practicalism. 'Super'-theory and 'Super'-practice represent the split which, in fact, exists, both in philosophy and in political life, and which finds its expressions in the politics of philosophy.

Thus does the politics of philosophy reflect, in complex ways indeed, the larger human politics, and nowhere more complexly than in political philosophy itself.

*Boston University*

KAI NIELSEN


# ON THE CHOICE BETWEEN REFORM AND REVOLUTION*


I

Given the history of this century it is understandable that there should be
both an extensive fear of revolution and a distrust of the efficacy of reform.
Yet when one considers such countries as the United States, Rhodesia, and
South Africa (not to mention the poorer and savagely exploited parts of the
world), it is also becoming increasingly obvious to any tolerably well informed
person who is also humane that a fundamental social transformation of these
societies is humanly speaking imperative. And, this, of course, thrusts one
back on the suspect ideas of revolution and far-reaching social reform. This is
turn raises questions about what one is committed to in believing in the moral
necessity of radical social transformation. Is one committed to revolution or
only to some form of very fundamental social reform? And this in turn
naturally provokes the question: What exactly is the difference between them
and what is one asking for when one advocates a progressive fundamental or
radical social transformation?

Such questions were debated by Kautsky, Bernstein, Lenin, and Luxemburg in another context, but, without even remotely suggesting that what
they had to say is irrelevant for us today, I want to look at this cluster of
questions afresh. Is the assumed distinction between revolution and fundamental or radical reform only a distinction concerning the means, the instrumentalities, of social change, or does it refer to what is aimed at as well, e.g.,
*the kind* of change and the extent of change? Is the putative distinction between fundamental or radical reform and revolution a spurious one? And if
the distinction is a genuine one, are they on a continuum? And more fundamentally still, if one is committed to seeking and advocating a fundamental
social transformation, is one necessarily for revolution? Or, contrariwise, is
the working for reform the only reasonable alternative for a humane human
being? This cluster of questions in turn raises a bevy of more specific questions
including such overtly conceptual questions as what is meant by 'revolution'
and 'reform'.

To gain some purchase on these issues, it is well to begin by asking: What

* Reprinted from *Inquiry*, Vol. XIV (1971).

*H. J. Johnson, J. J. Leach, and R. G. Muehlmann (eds.), Revolutions, Systems, and
Theories, 155–176. All Rights Reserved.*
*Copyright © 1971 by Universitets Forlaget, Oslo, Norway.*

are we asking for when we ask for a fundamental social transformation or a transformation of society?

If we are committed to a progressive transformation, we are surely asking for an end to human oppression and exploitation. Even if this is only a heuristic ideal and in fact we can only realistically hope to diminish the extent and severity of oppression and human degradation, it still remains a fundamental guiding ideal: it tells us to what we are aiming as far as possible to approximate in any progressive transformation of society. To achieve this transformation all forms of racism, ethnocentrism, chauvinism and rigid social stratification with its built-in privileges would have to come to an end. Class divisions and alienated labor would have to disappear. This would involve the abolition of the bourgeoisie; that is to say, there could no longer be a capitalist or any other kind of corporate ruling class, a bureaucratic or technocratic élite or establishment. The modes of production in the society would have to be thoroughly socialized so that their underlying rationale is to serve the interests of everyone alike. To be morally acceptable, specific privileges, when they are necessary at all, must be such that they further (typically in an indirect way) this underlying ideal.

The above characterization of what is involved in a progressive transformation of society is for the most part negative. Positively, our characterization will be vaguer. As we know from Dante, evil is much easier to characterize than positive good. It is difficult, in talking about such a transformation, to say anything general which is not vague or platitudinous or (what is more likely) both. A progressively transformed society would give men a fuller and more human life. This quasi-tautology unpacks into the claim that people in such a transformed society would attain a liberation in which their full human powers and their creative capacities would be developed in a many-sided way. They would not be one-sided, emotionally or intellectually stunted men or academic *Fachidioten*, but would be men capable of managing their affairs, helping in the management of society in the interests of everyone alike and capable of a wide range of enjoyments and creative activities. And they would not only have these capabilities, they would also be anxious to exercise them. In addition, there would be an end to possessive individualism and a commodity accumulation which goes beyond what humans need and would want when their wants are not artificially stimulated to enhance capitalist enterprise. Rather, there would be a commitment to social equality and to a fair and nearly equal distribution of the available goods and services. In different concrete situations these different notions, positive and negative, would of course take different specifications and amplifications. But the elasticity of these specifications is not endless since they are bounded by these general but non-formal conceptions. In transforming society our aim should be human freedom (the liberation of human creativity), equality and the enhancement of human happiness and the avoidance of misery. In our present historical circumstances this is best achieved in (a) a society founded upon common ownership of the means of production and (b) a society in which all men participate in the running of their society. To fully exercise our human agency, we need a common culture with a maximum of human participation. Here we have the leitmotive for a progressive transformation of society.

For societies to be transformed so that this would be a reality, we would need, even in the most progressive societies, a very considerable institutional change, and in such powerful advanced industrial societies as the United States and Western Germany, the changes would have to be structural and very profound indeed. Could such a transformation be achieved without a revolution? Before trying to answer this we need to gain some clarification about what we mean by 'revolution' and how it contrasts with 'reform' and what the conceptual links are between revolution and violence, for on *some* employments of 'revolution' our question would be nearly as silly as "Are all emerald things green?" That is to say, on some readings of 'revolution' it may be analytically (or at least in some sense necessarily) true that to be committed to seeking and advocating a fundamental progressive social transformation is to be for revolution.

## II

So let us first get some purchase on what is meant by 'revolution' and 'reform'. In doing this it is important to keep in mind that it is only against the background of a belief in progress that it makes sense to speak either of revolution or of reform. To reform is to convert into another and better form; it is, as the O.E.D. puts it, "to free from previous faults or imperfections". We speak of reforming institutions and social arrangements and by this we mean correcting them or improving them by amending or altering them through removing faults, abuses, malpractices, and the like. This implies that one social arrangement or set of social arrangements, or a practice or institution or set of practices or institutions, can be an advance or an improvement over another. But to believe in this is to believe that progress is possible within a limited time span at least, though this is not sufficient to commit one to the fullfledged conceptions of progress found in Condorcet, Hegel or Marx. A belief in the viability of revolutionary activity, as is well known and frequently remarked on, is even more obviously linked to a belief in progress. And if a belief in progress was one of the great and persistent illusions of the nineteenth century, then belief in either reform or revolution is belief in an illusion.[1]

One further preliminary. If the usage recorded in current dictionaries is focused on, it is evident enough that 'revolution,' or 'revolutionary', has a negative emotive force while 'reform', or 'reformer', has a positive emotive force. Given the conventional criteria for 'synonym' and 'near synonym', 'correct', 'improve', 'restore', and 'better' all, in certain types of sentence, count as synonyms or near synonyms for 'reform' when 'reform' is a verb; when 'reform' is a noun 'correction', 'progress', 'reconstruction', and 'reformation' count as synonyms. Here we clearly see that by definition 'to reform' is to do something which at least the reformer takes to be desirable, and, more generally, in many (perhaps most) contexts 'reform' is so employed that something would not as a rule be said within a society to be a reform unless it was thought to be desirable, though 'stupid and undesirable reforms' is not a contradiction in terms. The latter are reforms which have somehow misfired and misfired *as reforms*. Furthermore, if the word 'reform' is to continue to have a use, reforms regarded as stupid or undesirable must be exceptions and not the rule. If I assert that I have made a reform, I give you to understand that I have done something good. There is, in short, a pronounced positive emotive force to 'reform'. Only on some uses of 'reform', conspicuously where a reformer is equated with a zealot, crusader, or do-gooder, does the term acquire a negative emotive force. By contrast, given the usages assembled in dictionaries, it is evident enough that 'revolution' and 'revolutionary' typically have a negative emotive force. I approach this in an indirect way.

We are interested in revolution as a socio-political concept, but the word 'revolution' has other uses too and in attempting a very general characterization of 'revolution', one dictionary tells us that we are talking about 'a complete or drastic change of any kind'. And when we keep in mind that 'revolution' has this wide range of uses, it is worth noting that sometimes 'revolution' is equated with 'spasm', 'convulsion', 'revulsion', and 'cataclysm'. Here we have words which have negative emotive force. This emotive force is evident again in those contexts where 'revolution' is equated with 'rebellion', 'insurrection', 'subvention', 'destruction', or 'disruption', and we have adjectives such as 'radical', 'extreme', 'catastrophic', and 'intransigent' linked with revolution and revolutionary. And while it is true that the meanings of 'revolution' and 'reform' are not yoked to their emotive force, their emotive force is such that, unless one takes pains to account for it and neutralize it in arguments about the justification of revolution, one is at an initial disadvantage in defending revolution.

In order to know what the actual substantive claims of the reformers are, we must consider what their criteria for improvement, bettering, and the like are. Political reform involves legal, educational, economic, and generally institutional correction or improvements. Faults and abuses are corrected. Here what is crucial is to gain some clarity about the actual criteria for improvement, correction, amendment, or making better. In speaking of reforming West Germany's archaic university system, for example, are we talking about altering it to respond more efficiently to the needs of a modern industrial state, or do we primarily have in mind altering it so as to extend, sharpen, and systematize critical awareness among the Western German population, or do we mean something else again? What in such a situation is the amplification of 'reform'? But whatever we mean, we are also saying, when we defend educational reform, that we are for improvement in the existing educational structures and not for sweeping them away and replacing them by utterly new structures of a radically different nature. In talking more generally of socio-political reform, which typically would include as one of its crucial components educational reform, we are talking of amending or improving the fundamental institutions, practices, and social arrangements of a society so as to correct and remove, as far as possible, its faults, abuses, or malpractices.

Very typically, in speaking of reform we have in mind changes which apply to specific amendments or alterations of existing social arrangements. They are the type of reforms, aimed, as they are, only at the elimination of specific ills, that Karl Popper regards as the sole admissible reforms. They can be handled by intelligent picemeal social engineering without a challenge to the basic ideology of a culture, and they do not require argument about fundamental human ends or Utopian blueprints for the improvement of man's lot. Commitment to reform here makes a ready contrast with revolution. But when we speak, as we do, of 'far-reaching political reforms', 'fundamental reforms', 'sweeping reforms', or 'radical reforms', the contrast with revolutionary change is not so clear. I shall return to this point after I have characterized revolution.

Political theorists have given us typologies of revolution and many have stressed that there is a single type of socio-political revolution which is of the greatest critical interest when we ask about revolution and reform and about the justification of revolution.[2] This conception of a socio-political revolution is a more specific characterization and specification than the related characterization given in the dictionaries. In the dictionaries the characterization of

the relevant sense of 'revolution' is that a revolution is a complete overthrow
of a government or social system by those previously subject to it, and the
substitution of a new government or social system. Paradigms of revolutions
are the expulsion of the Stuart dynasty and the transfer of sovereignty to
William and Mary, the overthrow of the French monarchy and the establishment of republican government during the French revolution, the American,
the Russian, the Chinese, and the Cuban revolutions. But it is of some consequence to see that these are a mixed bag of examples. In particular, the
French, Russian, Chinese, and Cuban revolutions are very different — and
indeed particularly different in at least one important respect — from the
American revolution and the English revolution of 1688. The former revolutions — indeed the revolutions sometimes called 'the Great Revolutions' —
are distinguished from the others in that they *Altered in a profound sense the
social structure of the societies in which the revolution occurred*. When these
revolutions were consolidated, the social structure of the societies which were
so revolutionized (and sometimes some others as well) were radically altered.
But this was not so when the Stuart dynasty was overthrown and William and
Mary became the English sovereigns, and it was not true of the American
revolution. In the last example there was an overthrow of a government and
of colonial rule, but the rebellious colonists only established a government of
a slightly different sort. There was no change in basic social structure. The
change was quite unlike that from Batista's Cuba to present-day Cuba. With
so-called great revolutions there is what has been called a 'shock to the
foundations of society".[3] Such revolutions, as Karl Kautsky has pointed out,
do not come from nowhere. They are like births, sudden in occurring but
only possible after a complex development. When they occur there is "a
sharp, sudden change in the social location of power", but this change is not
one that can occur without certain tolerably determinate conditions obtaining.[4] For there to be a revolution, it is often claimed, there must be widespread misery, deprivation, and exploitation followed by a brief period of
rising expectations which, after some minor improvements in the oppressed
people's condition, are in turn dashed by a turn of events for the worse.
Where there is a despair over the system coupled with a sense that things
could be better, the ground of revolutionary activity is being broken; where
there is a widespread despairing dissatisfaction with the present social order
linked with a conception — often nebulous — of a new social order, where in
Fanon's phrase, we 'set afoot a new man', we have conditions — though indeed not sufficient conditions — for revolution.

Where under these conditions a revolution is actually sustained so that a government topples and a new social order is brought into being, we have the type of revolution − a social and political revolution − that is relevant to our discussions of revolution and reform. This sense of 'revolution' is properly caught by two political theorists on the Left: C. B. Macpherson and Herbert Marcuse. Macpherson characterizes revolution as

a transfer of state power by means involving the use of threat of organized unauthorized force, and the subsequent consolidation of that transferred power, with a view to bringing about a fundamental change in social, economic and political institutions.[5]

In a similar vein Marcuse writes that a revolution is

the overthrow of a legal established government and constitution by a social class or movement with the aim of altering the social as well as the political structure.[6]

If we mark the distinction between violent and non-violent radical activity around the refusal of the non-violent radical to injure or (where he can help it) tolerate injury to his antagonists, we can see that there is no *conceptual* reason why a revolution must be violent, though there may very well be substantial empirical justification for believing that all revolutions of the type characterized above by Macpherson and Marcuse will *in fact* be violent. (It is important to remember here that there are degrees of violence. Revolutions can and do vary here.) Thus on these terms it is a mistake to characterize a social and political revolution in such a way as to make 'a non-violent revolution' a contradiction in terms, and thus it is a mistake the define 'revolution', as Carl Friedrich does, as "a sudden and violent overthrow of an established political order".[7]

In the extant typologies, the kind of revolution Macpherson and Marcuse have characterized is contrasted with (1) *private palace revolutions*, e.g., the murder of Duncan by Macbeth followed by Macbeth's succession to the throne, (2) *public palace revolutions*, e.g., a *coup d'état* such as the typical South American revolution, (3) *systemic revolutions*, i.e., a change usually through a series of civil wars in the system of state organization (e.g., a city-state system) effecting a wide-ranging cultural community. (Examples are the change in the state system at the time of Pericles to that of the time of Augustus and the fall of the Roman Empire.), (4) *colonial revolutions* (rebellions) against rule by the government of another country. (The American revolution is a good example. But when, as in the Algerian revolution, there is also a considerable alteration of social structure, we have not only a colonial revolution, but also a socio-political revolution.) It is this latter kind of revolution − the socio-political revolution − that I am interested in when I ask about the contrast between reform and revolution. It clearly marks off revolutions from military *coups*, palace revolutions, colonial rebellions, and preventative counterrevolutions. It in effect limits 'true revolutions' by a reasonable *persuasive* definition to the great social upheavals which bring about lasting and extensive socio-political change.

## III

Given this construal, what exactly is the difference between revolution and radical reform? Typical reforms seek to amend, correct, and improve what we already have; they do not seek to destroy it and replace it with something new. In the United States, redistricting, lowering the voting age, guaranteeing an annual income, and a weakening of the filibuster rule would be reforms, though certainly not sweeping reforms. What would count as radical reform? Suppose — to take a fanciful but instructive example — the constitution of the United States was, through the normal channels, so changed that (1) the United States like England and Canada adopted a parliamentary system, (2) the division between federal and state government was abolished and newly drawn federally administrated districts were created, (3) capitalism was abolished and all the major means of production came to be socially owned, and, finally, (4) the new government, together with the educational apparatus of the State, officially declared its support for atheism and socialism. Would such a set of changes in the United States constitute a radical reform or a peaceful revolution?

Surely such a change would be like a reform in that it was accomplished by 'going through channels' and by using the legal and political apparatus of the State which was subsequently to be radically transformed. But it is unlike a reform in that, rather than simply improving or correcting the extant institutions and social arrangements, something quite new and different would be brought into being. Moreover, it is like a revolution in that there would have resulted a "radical transformation of the process of government, of the official foundations of sovereignty or legitimacy and of the conception of social order".[8] Yet here we have something which admits of degrees, for in the hypothesized change in the form of the government of the United States we still have a parliamentary system with political parties and the like. *From a certain point of view*, the change could be said to be not very deep — certainly not deep enough to constitute a radical transformation of the official foundations of sovereignty or legitimacy. At this point we have something which is so essentially contested that there is no objectively correct thing to say here.

There are paradigms of revolutions and revolutionary acts which could not properly be called 'radical reforms', e.g., the Chinese revolution and the Cuban revolution. But, as with so many quite useful concepts, there is no exact cut-off point. There is no exact point where we can show that here there is an end to reformist activity and here the beginning of revolutionary activity. As Wittgenstein in effect points out, we could by stipulation *set up* such a conceptual boundary, but this would settle nothing, for others with equal legitimacy could set up boundaries at other points.

Someone might resist at this juncture and assert that my above example is plainly only an example of radical reform, because there is in it no use or threat of organized unauthorized force, and the use of threatened use of such force is a necessary condition for revolutionary change. There is — it might be claimed — a natural boundary; we need not just draw one. But so to argue is in effect to emasculate the concept of radical reform, for surely what it would be natural to characterize as a radical reform would typically — in actual fact perhaps always — involve, through strikes (illegal or otherwise), demonstrations, disruptions, the seizure of factories, or riots, some form of unauthorized pressure to bring about the change in question. The radical reform would come about at least under the threat of the use of unauthorized force, and such deep structural changes as characterized in my example never in fact occur without the threat of force or extreme social disruption. It could, logically speaking, be otherwise, but it isn't. So it still remains true that my hypothesized change in the State apparatus and social structure of the United States could with equal legitimacy be called 'a radical or fundamental reform' or 'a revolution' or both. We have a *continuum* here and not a clearly demarcated boundary.

In turn it might be replied that actually a qualitative and important difference does reveal itself in my example, namely that with revolution in contrast to radical reform there is and indeed must be an overthrow of a legally established government. And since this cannot be so with a radical reform, it is a mistake to claim that there is no principled difference between radical reform and revolution. But I should reply that where there is extensive breakdown in the functioning of institutions and established ways of doing things, and where a government under the dire threat of violence and total chaos radically *alters itself*, so that we have a radically different government and set of social arrangements, it is hardly a deviation from a linguistic regularity to say that the legally established government has been overthrown. With Nixon out under such extreme pressures, the power of state governments and (consequently) of the South broken, and a self-consciously atheistic and socialist group of leaders firmly in control, with federal administrative districts rather than States, it would not be unnatural to speak of 'the overthrow of the United States government'. At the very least, the distinction between 'an orderly but radical change in government' and an 'overthrow of the government' would not in such circumstances be a clear one.

## IV

What I have been concerned to establish so far is that reform and revolution are on a continuum and that, while there is an evident difference between typical reformist activities and revolutionary activities, there is no principled difference between a commitment to a set of radical reforms and a commitment to a socio-political revolution. (I say nothing here of the weaker notion of 'a systemic revolution', the difference between it and at least some types of radical reform is even less pronounced.)

It is the rather pervasive but mistaken assumption that 'a violent revolution' is a pleonasm, that is the principal cause of the belief that there is a principled difference between radical reform and revolution and that if one is committed to one, one cannot consistently also be committed to the other. Moreover, to maintain that a 'violent revolution' is not a redundancy is not to use 'revolution' — as indeed it often is used in current political discussions — loosely.

Having said this, I do not mean to leave the impression that I believe that the question "Revolution or Reform?" is a pseudo-question. What is sensibly at issue when such a question is raised is whether it is more reasonable to adopt the moderate and piecemeal reformist tactics of liberal reformers or whether a commitment to a more radical political stance is in order. Among present-day political theorists — to amplify this question by giving it a local habitation and name — is the more reasonable course to adopt the general strategies of a Karl Popper, Ralf Dahrendorf, or Isaiah Berlin, or are the more radical positions of a Herbert Marcuse, Jürgen Habermas, or Alasdair MacIntyre more plausible? Note that within this liberal/radical division there is considerable room for technical philosophical differences yoked together with practical and theoretical political affinities. Surely MacIntyre is closer to Berlin philosophically than he is to Marcuse, but in political orientation he is closer to Marcuse. What I want now to do is to compare and assess some arguments of Popper and Marcuse which, I believe, sharply and paradigmatically, bring out many of the core substantive issues that should be argued out when we ask about the justification of an allegiance to either revolution or reform. Both Popper and Marcuse have a considerable corpus of influential theory and they have both been widely commented upon. But I want to focus on a single short but typical essay by each which, particularly when they are juxtaposed, dramatically and succinctly bring out what I take to be some of the central issues in the sometimes choice: reform or revolution. The essays in question are Popper's 'Utopia and Violence' and Marcuse's 'Ethics and Revolution'.[9]

Popper stresses that besides disagreements in factual belief – in opinion about what is the case – people also disagree because 'their interests differ'. Where interests clash there is, Popper maintains, no way – where the clash is a fundamental one – of proving or establishing that one interest or set of interests is right and the other or others mistaken. Where there is such a clash an agent must either seek a reasonable compromise or attempt to destroy or at least undermine the opposing interest (p. 357). Popper is convinced we should always resort to compromise here rather than to violence. Over questions of fact, by contrast, we must be guided by the weight of empirical evidence, and where there is a divergence concerning the assessment of that evidence, we must all be open-minded fallibilists prepared to listen to argument and prepared to be convinced by an argument that goes contrary to our beliefs. We must eschew all intellectual imperialism and dogmatism. Violence in human affairs can be avoided if people develop and practice an attitude of reasonableness in human affairs. That is to say, in coming to decisions, we must be willing to hear both sides, to realize and take into consideration that one is not likely to make a good judge if one is party to the case, to avoid claims of self-evidence, and to be willing, where interests conflict, to make reasonable compromises.

In adopting this attitude of reasonableness, we must give up all Utopianism, which Popper takes to be a persistent and disastrous rationalistic attitude which is found again and again in political theory from Plato to Marx.

We should not forget that Popper means something rather special by 'a Utopian'. A Utopian believes that an action is rational if it takes the best means available to achieve a certain end, and that we can only judge an action to be rational relative to some given end. Thus to determine whether a political action is rational, we.must ascertain the final ends of the political change the actor intends to bring about. His political actions will be rational only relative to his ruling ideas of what the State ought to be like. For this reason, as a preliminary to any rational political action "we must (the Utopian believes) first attempt to become as clear as possible about our ultimate political ends ..." (p. 358). The Utopian then plausibly but (on Popper's view) mistakenly concludes that to act reasonably we need first to determine the State or society we consider the best and then determine the means by which we can most efficiently realize or at least approximate that situation. The rationally mandatory thing to do is first to get clear about our fundamental political ideals. Only in this way, the Utopian believes, can we be reasonable about political actions. We must have, if we would act rationally, "a more or less clear and detailed description or blueprint of our ideal state" as well as "a plan or blueprint of the historical path that leads towards this goal" (p. 358). But it is Popper's belief that it is this political rationalism of Utopianism that we must decisively reject, if we would avoid irrationality and violence in human affairs.

We must reject it because we have, Popper would have us believe, no way of rationally ascertaining which set of these focal ends is the most reasonable, or even which to choose reasonably, "for it is impossible to determine ends scientifically" (pp. 358—9). This means, according to Popper, that there is no rational way of choosing between Utopian blueprints for a truly human society. Because of this, a reasonable man will abandon all forms of Utopianism and will avoid 'choosing ideal ends of this kind'. He will not have any Utopian blueprint — any conception of a truly human society — at all. It is not that he is criticizing the kind of political theorizing and organization that would lead to the holding of any ideals of this type at all. They are to be avoided (1) because they cannot be decided on rationally and (2) because the holding of them leads to violence and tyranny and not, as their proponents believe, to human happiness. Thus Popper in effect argues for an end to all ideology and Utopianism. And he counterposes against this a reformism which takes as its procedural rationale: "Work for the elimination of concrete evils rather than for the realization of abstract goods. Do not aim at establishing happiness by political means. Rather aim at the elimination of concrete miseries" (p. 361). Do not try to construct systematic normative blueprints for human liberation, but engage instead, without articulating ultimate social and political ideals, in practical piecemeal social engineering. "Choose what you consider the most urgent evil of the society in which you live, and try patiently to convince people that we can get rid of it". This means that we should fight for the elimination of hunger, disease, racism, and the like by direct means, e.g., by improved distribution of farm produce, by establishing medicare, by voter registration in the South, and by establishing non-discriminatory practices in housing and employment. We should work at these problems directly and forget about trying "to realize these aims indirectly be designing and working for a distant ideal of a society which is wholly good" (p. 361). We can reach agreement "on what are the most intolerable evils of our society and on what are the most urgent social reforms", but we cannot reach agreement about Utopian ideals for the radical transformation of our society (p. 361). We must steadfastly recognize and take to heart the poignant fact that "we cannot make heaven on earth", though we can, if we put aside Utopianism and reason realistically, reasonably hope "to make life a little less terrible and a little less unjust in each generation" (p. 362). We must accept man as he is and not try to set a new man afoot.

Marcuse is, in Popper's terms, an arch-Utopian. Unlike Popper, Marcuse believes that objective moral assessments can be made of what Popper calls Utopian blueprints for society, and he argues for an overall normative conception of society. Marcuse believes that the governing criteria here are whether or not a given set of social arrangements make for the greatest possible freedom and greatest possible happiness for man. And it is important to note, *vis-à-vis* Popper, that in talking of happiness in political contexts, Marcuse has in mind primarily the task of the avoidance of misery. He takes it to be the case that the role of government in the advancement of human welfare and happiness should primarily be to insure "a life without fear and misery, and a life in peace" (p. 134). So here, in terms of what should be aimed at, the difference between Popper and Marcuse is verbal rather than substantive. Marcuse is also one with Popper in believing that such a radical change as would be involved in a socio-political revolution would bring with it violence, but Popper denies that this revolutionary violence is ever justified, while Marcuse argues that it is *sometimes* justified and asks about the conditions under which it is justified. In this context, it should first be noted, so as not to raise spurious issues, that Marcuse, like any sane and humane man, shares Popper's detestation of violence and with him takes it as one of the foremost human tasks to work for "its reduction and, if possible, for its elimination from human life" (p. 335). This attitude toward violence is, or at least ought to be, a commonplace in the moral life. Radicals and liberals, revolutionaries and reformers, are not divided on this issue. They are not always or even typically divided over the use of violence in the settling of social issues, for Popper sanctions the use of counterviolence against the threat of revolutionary violence. What does divide them is the issue of whether violence is ever justified "as a means for establishing or promoting human freedom and happiness". Popper denies that it is, while Marcuse argues that it is justified when and if certain conditions prevail. (He also argues that as a matter of fact they sometimes prevail.)

What is likely to be forgotten here is that while socio-political revolutions of the type we have been describing have almost invariably involved violence, and that while they permit and, as Marcuse puts it, sometimes even demand "deception, cunning, suppression, destruction of life and property and so on", if there is a demand *prior* to a revolution for fundamental reforms which will substantially increase equality and alleviate misery and degradation through a substantial redistribution of wealth and privileges, then this peaceful demand for fundamental reforms, if it shows promise of gaining momentum, will be met by the privileged classes with violence and attempted suppression. But without persistent advocacy and pressure for such basic reforms, we still have the day-to-day and year-to-year rather unspectacular yet extensive and persistent violence of any exploitative and repressive society. It does not make headlines, as do terrorist bombings, but it is usually more persistent, threatening, destructive, and pernicious. We surely should join with Popper in his detestation of violence, but the issue he fails to face, and one Marcuse squarely faces, is that in such situations violence cannot be avoided. The central relevant question is whether the use of revolutionary violence will, rather than the available alternatives, make for less misery and human degradation all round. The alternatives to violent revolution are (1) pressure for radical reforms or even revolution — since it is not a conceptual truth that a socio-political revolution must be violent — which deliberately always stops short of using violence as a policy, (2) trying to preserve the *status quo*, or (3) advocating and seeking to implement the type of mild, small-scale reforms that are not likely to offend or threaten the bureaucratic establishment sufficiently to provoke counter-revolutionary violence.[10] We certainly, at least on the general ground he appeals to, cannot rightly claim, as Popper in effect does, that revolutionary violence is never justified, or indeed never something that reasonable and moral men ought to advocate and defend. We must go case by case and look at each situation as it comes before us. It may very well be that in some situations the use of violence as a political instrument will minimize misery and injustice and thus be morally mandatory or at least morally in order.

A standard argument here is that while sometimes revolutionary violence is justified, it is never justified in a democracy, because in a democracy we have fair procedural means for making the needed social transformation through elections, lobbying, uncoerced public advocacy, and the like. But such a response reflects an extraordinarily idealized and naive picture of how bourgeois democracies work. The realistic, and indeed the most reasonable, moral stance is again to keep (1) to the above principle, i.e., that the underlying rationale for political action is to seek a society which will most likely enable all men to achieve the fullest "possible satisfaction of needs under the priority of vital needs and with a minimum of toil, misery and injustice", and (2) to go case by case (p. 145). We need to ask whether, in the long run, less misery, degradation, and injustice will result by going through channels, by playing the game according to the rules the bourgeois democracy sets, rather than by using revolutionary violence. If the answer is yes or even probably yes, then revolutionary violence should not be used, but if resort to revolutionary violence will lessen the total misery, degradation, and injustice, then revolutionary violence is justified and ought to be advocated. There are, as far as I can see, no conceptual barriers or moral barriers which turn this last *prima facie* possibility into either a conceptual or a moral impossibility. And it might very well actually be something which we are morally required to do. Much would depend on the particular bourgeois democracy. What should be said about Sweden might very well not hold for the United States. Much depends on the present level of social equality and justice, on corruption in the society, on ruling class intransigence, and on the extent to which the democratic procedures actually work or can, by reasonable effort on the part of the oppressed, be made to work, so as to enhance social equality, help achieve liberation for everyone, and lessen misery and injustice.

It is fairly obvious that in capitalist countries such as the United States and West Germany the outlook for such a transformation by going through channels and working within the system is very bleak indeed. But it is also true, loud alarms to the contrary notwithstanding, that these countries are hardly in a revolutionary situation, though there has with some segments of the population been an increase in class consciousness. What the outlook for change here is can hardly be settled in a philosopher's armchair, but once this is recognized, and if my above arguments are sound, it should also be recognized that it is equally arbitrary to rule out on general and aprioristic grounds, as Popper and many others do, the use of revolutionary violence as something which cannot be justified.

Marcuse wishes to show not only that in certain circumstances revolutionary violence is justified, but also that in certain of the great revolutions in the past it was justified. He believes, as Popper does not, that "there are rational criteria for determining the possibilities of human freedom and happiness available to a society in a specific historical situation" (p. 135). Marcuse argues that what constitutes human freedom and the possibilities of human freedom and happiness varies with the historical epoch. "Obviously", Marcuse remarks, "the possibilities of human freedom and happiness in advanced industrial society today are in no way comparable with those available, even theoretically available, at preceding stages of history" (p. 139). But, given this partial historical relativity of what the particular fettering and degrading conditions are from which man needs liberation, it remains the case, according to Marcuse, that the great revolutions have, everything considered, reduced toil, misery, and injustice, and so, since none of the historically possible alternatives could match this, these revolutions are on the whole justified.

In thinking about the justification of revolution, we are forced here into admittedly rough historical calculations. On the one hand, we must take into account both the likelihood of Bonapartism or Stalinism in the successor State after a successful revolution and the likelihood that this State, whether Stalinist or not, will be brutal and authoritarian and actually harm more than it helps human liberation. On the other hand, we must "take into account the sacrifices exacted from the living generations on behalf of the established society, the established law and order, the number of victims made in defense of this society in war and peace, in the struggle for existence individual and national" (p. 140). In addition, we need to ask questions about the intellectual and material resources available to the society and the chances of the revolutionary group being able to utilize them in reducing the sacrifices and the number of victims. Finally, we must keep in mind the very value of the professed values originating in revolutions, e.g., the conception of the inalienable rights of man coming out of the American and French revolutions and the conception of the value of tolerance emerging from the English revolutions.

Popper makes utilitarian calculations too, but he limits them to the more immediate and palpable sources of misery and injustice and deliberately resists taking into account more distant and less easily calculable phenomena. This surely has the advantage of giving us more manageable materials, but it also cuts off morally relevant data which, to the extent that they are determinable at all, should be taken into consideration. In our calculations concerning what we ought to do, we should take it as a relevant consideration that some phenomena are less readily determinable than others, but this does not justify our ignoring the less easily assessable data. By skewing what we will take as relevant material in the way he does, Popper cuts off the very possibility of discovering (1) systematic interconnections between human ills and (2) any (if indeed there are such) deeper causal conditions of the ills he would alleviate. Thus his theory unwittingly plays into the hands of conservative defenders of the *status quo* with which he would not wish to align himself. Marcuse's wider ranging utilitarian calculations are perfectly capable of taking into account and giving due stress to the phenomena Popper would account for, but they also hold out promise for attaining a more complete, and thus more adequate, account of the relative harm and relative human advantages accruing to different social arrangements.

For Marcuse, and for the revolutionary tradition generally, when violence is justified it is justified by reason in accordance with the overriding end of revolutionary activity, namely "greater freedom for the greater number of people". Popper, too, in spite of his distaste for Utopian blueprints, holds this as a guiding rationale, but he never establishes that violence can never be the means to its attainment or that the great revolutions did not extend and enhance human freedom.

It should not be forgotten that the English and French revolutions attained "a demonstrable enlargement of the range of human freedom". There is, as Marcuse points out, a general agreement among historians that the English and French revolutions brought about an extensive redistribution of social wealth, "so that previously less privileged or unprivileged classes were the beneficiaries of this change, economically and/or politically" (p. 143). Even when we take the subsequent periods of reaction and restoration into the reckoning, it remains true that these revolutions brought about "more liberal governments, a gradual democratization of society and technical progress". When the extent and permanency of this are taken into consideration in our historical calculations, it outweighs the terror and the excesses of these revolutions, though to say this is not to condone all the actions carried out in their name, for it is a correct grammatical remark with moral overtones to say, as Marcuse does, that "arbitrary violence and cruelty and indiscriminate terror" cannot possibly be justified by any revolutionary situation (pp. 140–1).

To the argument that the same changes would have come about more gradually but without terror and violence, it should be replied that while this is an empirical *possibility*, it is also only an unfounded speculation. We do not have comparable situations in which the ruling élite of an *Ancien Régime* voluntarily gave up its privileges and desisted from exploitation and repression where it was not true that there were no previous successful revolutions in similarly situated countries to serve as a warning prod that extensive reforms must be made. What we can say with confidence is this: there is the fact of the moral advance of mankind brought on by these great revolutions, and no adequate grounds have been given for believing that in those circumstances — those great turning points of history — advances would have occurred in anything like a comparable way without the use of force against the old order.

## V

What we can conclude from our discussion so far is that there have been circumstances in the past and there will no doubt be circumstances in the future in which violence is a morally legitimate instrument for promoting radical transformations in society toward a greater degree of human freedom and happiness. It is toward this conclusion that a critical comparison of Popper and Marcuse leads us.

If what I have argued in the previous section has been for the most part sound, Popper could only defend himself by laying very considerable stress on, and indeed by establishing the soundness of, what I shall call, 'the sceptical side' of his thought. Marcuse assumes, and I do too, the correctness of what should be the morally important truisms that human freedom and human happiness are very great goods and that misery and injustice are plain evils. Popper indeed makes the same assumptions himself; his very passionate rejection of Utopianism is fueled by emotions rooted in these assumptions. But he does not believe that such value judgments are rationally supportable since they are not scientific claims. (This note is perfectly general: it applies to any fundamental value judgment simply by virtue of its being a fundamental value judgment.) Thus, on Popper's view, if someone has a Utopian blueprint in which the above moral truisms are not held (respectively) to be very great goods or manifest evils, there is no way of showing that that Utopian blueprint is mistaken or unreasonable and that a blueprint in which these truistic moral considerations have the weight Marcuse, Popper, and I give them is right in this regard, or at least is a more reasonable moral point of view than a moral point of view which rejects or ignores them.

This is hardly the place to argue the general question of moral scepticism and/or some kind of radical non-cognitivism in meta-ethics. Suffice it to say for this occasion that the main developments in analytic ethics since World War II have put such conceptions very much on the defensive. Popper, pulling against the stream of contemporary ethical theory, writes as if moral scepticism and non-cognitivism were plainly true, though he does not provide any extended argument for them.

Moreover, as MacIntyre has pointed out, *in practice* Popper assumes the objectivity and rationality of certain ideals — general moral ideals very close to Marcuse's and my own — which, if he would consistently apply them, would hardly allow him to shun all ideology in the way he does.[11] That is to say, for Popper the importance of relieving misery and developing the reasonable attitudes of human give and take, the stress on freedom and on the equal right of "every man . . . to arrange his life himself so far as this is compatible with the equal rights of others", are all leading moral ideas which inform many of his political judgments, and together they commit him to a general set of political and moral ideals in accordance with which particular practices, institutions, governments, and societies can and indeed should, if these principles are to mean anything, be appraised. But this is precisely to utilize a Utopian blueprint, and it is this Popper would avoid. Moreover, if he continues to apply this blueprint, the Marcusean arguments for the rational justification of revolution seem at least to be inescapable; and if he rejects reasoning in accordance with these general moral principles and holds steadfastly to an 'end of ideology approach', he gets himself into the position where he could have no grounds for rejecting as barbarous and irrational ideologies which he indeed rightly believes to be barbarous and irrational, namely Nazi and other Fascist ideologies.

Surely this is a conclusion that Popper does not wish to embrace, and his grounds for not accepting such ideologies turn on some commitment to something very like a form of negative utilitarianism. But this saddles him with a set of abstract moral principles which he should, in consistency, regard with distaste as Utopian.

Some tougher 'end of ideology' political theorist may really take this 'moral-scepticism-side' to heart and argue that even if avoidance of misery and attainment of happiness are great goods, he sees no rational grounds for adopting some principle of equality or fairness and extending such teleological considerations to all men. Whether, he reasons, we should opt for such a universalistic ethic as underlies both Marcuse's and Popper's thinking, is an utterly non-rational matter resting on human preference.

If such a moral scepticism is rationally mandatory, then the very assumptions of progress essential for even Popper's commitment to mild reform are undermined. There can be no justification of reform or revolution, or any other normative principles. It may indeed not be easy to defend any system of overall normative principles, but if it is not possible to do so, the whole program of moderate reform and a commitment to reasonableness is undermined. It is only because Popper himself has an unacknowledged but reasonable set of general political moral principles that his 'end of ideology approach' does not appear immediately to be an abandonment of any kind of reasoned defense of a set of normative standards or even of the taking of any principled stand at all.

Popper aside, what can we conclude about reform or revolution? There is plainly much injustice and unnecessary misery in the world and the level of human liberation is hardly what is could be. Without even remotely assuming that we can make a kingdom of heaven on earth, a perfectly good society, or anything of that fanciful Utopian order, it is not Quixotic to hope, and rationally work, for a transformation of society in which these ills are greatly lessened and perhaps some of them even altogether eliminated. Such a social order may never come into being, but there is nothing unreasonable about struggling for its achievement.

I have suggested that there can be no reasonable, unequivocal, non-contextual answer to the question. In struggling for a better social order should we be reformers or revolutionaries? In the Scandinavian countries the needed transformation might very well come about gradually through a cluster of small reforms which, taken together, might add up in time to a considerable transformation. In Brazil, the United States, and Argentina, to take some striking examples, this hope would seem to be unrealistic. And while there is a moral need, and a considerable material base, for revolution in Brazil, the United States — the linchpin imperialist power in the Western social system — is at present at any rate hardly a country in which there is a material base for revolution. Morally speaking, however, the United States is surely in dire need of radical transformation; whether this should be by radical reform or revolution is, if my earlier arguements are sound, an empty question, more a matter of political rhetoric than anything else. What is evident, particularly when one considers the United States in relation to the rest of the world, is that it becomes increasingly obvious the closer one looks, that very deep structural changes need to be made. It is surely better, everything else being equal, if they can be attained without a violent revolution. But if one considers Vietnam, the Blacks, and America's imperialist politicies in the poorer parts of the world, the level of violence is already very high. It is also true, however, that actions which would trigger off or even risk a nuclear war are insane. And to work to bring about in a decade or so a revolution in America which would involve something comparable to the Russian or Spanish civil wars is also something morally equivocal (to understate it); but, as we have seen, there are revolutions and revolutions, and there are various levels of violence. What Marcuse has given us are general criteria in accordance with which we can reasonably answer when, humanly speaking, revolutionary violence of a certain kind and at a certain level is justified and when it is not. In many situations it is difficult to tell, though in others (present-day Iran, Zaire, South Africa, and South Korea, for example) it is quite evident that, when revolution has a reasonable chance of success, it is morally justified.

We have also seen that reform and revolutions are on a continuum and that there are contexts in which the choice of labels for description of the transformation in question is — ideology and expediency aside — quite immaterial. Moreover, it is important to see, as Rosa Luxemburg did and stressed in the opening paragraphs of her *Reform or Revolution*, that a revolutionary should not oppose piecemeal reforms, though he should seek to give them a direction which will lead to a socialist transformation of society. But a vital means for the attainment of a socialist revolution is the attainment of reforms. It is true that reforms have bought off the working class, but they have also raised their level of expectation, given people of working class and peasant origins the education and consciousness to escape the bondage of prejudice and ignorance, and, with the rising new working class, reforms together with the transformation of the working force through technology have gradually given this new white collar working class the capacity to govern themselves.[12] Moreover, since I lack the orthodox faith that history is necessarily on the side of socialism, it seems to me that where it is evident that certain reforms will appreciably improve human conditions, they should be worked for. They are at least small gains in an uncertain world, though this should not freeze us into being satisfied with them. Apocalyptic and quasi-apocalyptic moves are dramatic but rarely politically or morally sound. That is to say, use of the *nach-Hilter-wir* slogan is to be avoided. Working for Hitler's victory over the Social Democrats, even granting they were ersatz socialists, was a suicidal way of attempting to build socialism and a truly human society. Similarly rationalized tactics in working for the victory of Reagan — to turn to a much lesser villain — while not suicidal, were counterproductive for progressive forces. Our ability to make long range social predictions is so slight that it is irrational to develop any long range confidence about how things must be, and thus it is irrational and indeed morally irresponsible to accept, where we can avoid them, extensive human ills in the hope of realizing long range social achievements. Noam Chomsky was realistic and responsible when he remarked: "Surely our understanding of the nature of man or of the range of workable social forms is so rudimentary that any far-reaching doctrine must be treated with great scepticism."[13] This does not mean that revolutionary hopes should be abandoned as an opiate of intellectuals, but it should warn a reasonable and humane person away from the dangerous game of hoping for reaction to help produce revolution. Sometimes extremism on the Left paves the way for moderation, but victories for reaction seldom pave the way for socialist revolution. The thing to be done is to work persistently for a socialist transformation of society. Day by day this means supporting all genuinely progressive reforms, even in those contexts in which this will strengthen liberals against conservatives, while working for a broader structural transformation of society by radical peaceful reforms where possible, and by violent revolution where necessary and where the cure is not likely to produce worse ills than the disease. The rub, of course, is to tell in a particular historical situation whether the cure is worse than the disease. This surely takes more than just philosophical sophistication and moral sensitivity; it requires historical, sociological, and economic understanding in depth of the situation that confronts us.

*University of Calgary*

## NOTES

[1] I have tried to give a kind of minimal and de-mythologized defense of the idea of progress in my 'Progress', *The Lock Haven Review*, No. 7 (1965).

[2] Eugen Rosenstock-Hüssy, *Out of Revolution* (1938); Crane Brinton, *The Anatomy of Revolution*, Vintage Books, New York, 1952; George S. Pettee, *The Process of Revolution*, Harper & Row, New York, 1938, and 'Revolution-Typology and Process', in Carl J. Friedrich (ed.), *Revolution*, Atherton Press, New York, 1966. See also C. B. Macpherson, 'Revolution and Ideology in the Late Twentieth Century'; Eugene Kamenka, 'The Concept of a Political Revolution'; and Richard A. Falk, 'World Revolution and International Order'; all in Carl J. Friedrich, *op. cit.* See also Peter A. R. Calvert, 'Revolution: The Politics of Violence', *Political Studies* 15 (1967), No. 1.

[3] Paul Schrecker, 'Revolution as a Problem in the Philosophy of History', in Carl J. Friedrich, *op. cit.* p. 35.

[4] Eugene Kamenka, *op. cit.*, p. 124.

[5] C. B. Macpherson, *op. cit.*, p. 140.

[6] Herbert Marcuse, 'Ethics and Revolution', in Richard T. De George (ed.), *Ethics and Society*, Anchor Books, Garden City, New York, 1966.

[7] Carl J. Friedrich, 'An Introductory Note on Revolution', in Carl J. Friedrich, *op. cit.*

[8] Eugene Kamenka, *op. cit.*, p. 124.

[9] Karl Popper, *Conjectures and Refutations*, Routledge & Kegan Paul, London (3rd ed.) 1969, pp. 355–63 and Herbert Marcuse, *op. cit.*, pp. 133–47. Subsequent references to these two works are made in the text.

[10] For a defense of a revolutionary but principled non-violent stand see Barbara Deming, 'Revolution and Equilibrium', in Eleanor Kuykendall (ed.), *Philosophy in the Age of Crisis*, Harper & Row, New York, 1970.

[11] Alisdair MacIntyre, 'Breaking the Chains of Reason', in E. P. Thompson (ed.), *Out of Apathy*, London 1960.

[12] Serge Mallet, *La nouvelle classe ouvrière*, Seuil, Paris 1962; and Norman Birnbaum, 'Is there a Post-Industrial Revolution?', *Social Policy* 1, No. 2 (July/August 1970).

[13] Noam Chomsky, 'Notes on Anarchism', *The New York Review of Books* 14, No. 10 (21 May 1970), p. 32.

JEAN ROY

# COMMENTARY ON PROFESSOR KAI NIELSEN'S PAPER

Before tackling the practical problem of choosing between reform and revolution, I would like initially to comment on the conceptual series of terms used by Professor Nielsen: "liberal reformism", "radical reformism", "revolution".

We find, in fact, in this text two definitions of 'revolution', each of which poses some difficulties. The first is *a priori* ("set up by stipulation", p. 163); it undoubtedly implies a passage to the opposite, but not necessarily violence. In scholastic terms, we would say that violence is not a 'constitutive note' in the concept of revolution. The advantage of this abstract convention is to get a precise and sharp definition which purges the language of its applications, overly diluted by political mythology, fashion, advertising, etc. The shortcoming of this approach rests in the arbitrary margin left to the author of the definition.

This arbitrariness becomes clear when one compares it with the two empirical definitions, deemed authoritative, and both embodying, implicitly or explicitly, the element of violence. Similarly the references to the Chinese and Cuban revolutions, taken to be paradigmatic (p. 160), also connote a certain violence, at least in so far as we are well-informed regarding them. According to this view, violence would be an adventitious stain without conceptual basis, even though practically unavoidable.

The emphasis is put on the idea of a radical transormation in such spheres as the constitutional, ideological, institutional or moral. The violent mode of the passage to the new regime is accidental and contingent, although the accident almost always occurs.

The uncoupling of the connection between the pure concept of revolution and its empirical actualization is nonetheless suspect. The hiatus perhaps accentuates the mythical character of the concept, which cannot be determined without being negated. If partial, the revolution would more aptly be called 'reform'; if total, it could only be thought of as imaginary. The accomplished revolution soon becomes a 'revolution betrayed'. . . .

It is true that spectacular violence — of riots, of barricades thrown up in a few minutes, of occupations of premises, of seizure of employers, of general strike — is likely to be deemed revolutionary. But so little is it so that when

*H. J. Johnson, J. J. Leach, and R. G. Muehlmann (eds.), Revolutions, Systems, and Theories, 177–194. All Rights Reserved.*

sudden and violent troubles do not lead towards a profound and durable re-
organization of the human condition, one looks in vain for a revolution.
Rather 'events', 'crises', 'movements', or 'revolts' are then spoken of. And R.
Aron writes *La révolution introuvable* . . . . (Cf. *The Elusive Revolution*, New
York 1969).

Not all violence is revolutionary, far from it, but the socio-political revolutions with which we are familiar link a fundamental change of this kind to a
good deal of violence. One cannot well imagine a revolution without a phase
of turmoil and confusion, but this is only its most acute moment. Violence,
under one form or another, accompanies the revolutionary process, in its
phase of attack as well as in the final phase of consolidation of the new
regime. (The distinctive feature of the over-all change of scene produced by
the Third Reich and of its violence comes from the fact that it *followed* the
regular accession of Hitler to supreme power.) "Revolutions wipe out weakness and give birth to force," say Bertrand de Jouvenel.[1] It is not Henry the
Eighth who is beheaded, but Charles the First; it is not Louis XIV who falls,
but Louis XVI; it is not Peter the Great who is overthrown, but Nicolas II.
And by whom are these unfortunate sovereigns replaced? By Cromwell, by
Robespierre and Bonaparte, by Lenin and Stalin. History does not offer us
any revolutionary power that was not tyrannical. Only in the long run and
through the cunning of reason can past violence serve a present good order,
but this retrospective consideration cannot serve as a basis for the project of
a rational politics. It can only sustain historical hope.

Even the most sane and rational state still bears within itself an invincible
element of arbitrariness and of violence, be it only the residual violence of
legal restraint and *jus belli*. By what miracle could violence be absent from
those moments of political creation which revolutions are? What sense does
it make to contend that violence is not logically implied in their essence
and to accept at the same time that is it practically unavoidable? Would
it not be better to recognize frankly that violence is not the entire revolution, but that a revolution cannot avoid violence for the simple reason that
the sudden replacement of one constitution or of one regime, by another
embodying a completely different principle of legitimacy, cannot be instituted legally without contradiction. (A process of constitutional reform
is something quite different.) On the contrary, power tends naturally to
preserve and to extend itself. The legitimacy of insurrection cannot but be
ethico-political, or meta-juridical in any case, if in fact law and violence are
opposed. To be sure, one finds in article 35 of the *Declaration of the Rights
of Man and of the Citizen* (1793) the following proposition: "When the

government violates the rights of the people, insurrection is, for the people and for each portion of the people, the most sacred of rights and the most indispensable of duties."[2]

But this proclamation remains as vague as it is solemn, devoid of any effective sanction. It in no way prevents the governments issuing from such a revolution from providing, just as the others do, a more humble and more exact code which calls for the most severe punishments against those who threaten the security of the State.

Professor Nielsen himself agrees with that; it is highly improbable that a fundamental innovation would come about in the socio-political sphere, within a short period of time, without violence (if the complete metamorphosis of a regime extends over a long period one would speak of a 'progressive transformation' or of a 'reform' but not of a 'revolution'). Historians have not failed to note the contrast between the clashing and jerky rhythm of political evolution and the slowness and continuity of economic progress.

According to Julien Freund, the distinctive mark of a revolution consists precisely in joining together an idea and violence:

Revolution is a war in the name of a universal idea (freedom or equality, liberation of the world proletariat and establishment of communism), and therefore it is led to battle the enemies of this idea, wherever they may be found. The worst of illusions would be to believe that revolution, in the modern meaning of the word, could dispense with war and violence and come to the same result by 'democratic' means. That would be 'the revolution without revolution' that Robespierre derides.[3]

This political lucidity does not exclude the moral right to resist and the legitimate will to rebel against an authority judged to be tyrannical, but it leads logically to posing the problem of revolution in a truer light and to resolving it prudently. It is easier to start to escalate to extremes than to de-escalate. Are not the great revolutions one of those areas of human existence where the ethical vision of the world is toppled into tragic theatre? Are not the actors of the drama in reality trapped in the gearwheels of events which they initiated, poor jumping-jacks of a History which no one in particular wanted, and which takes on the features of a hostile Destiny?

The second point I wish to raise concerns the ambiguity of the intermediate concept of 'radical reformism,' which participates in typical, i.e., 'liberal' reformism (p. 162) in that it appropriates the legal ways of innovation, but also those of revolution through the depth of the intended change. Within the relative continuity of this conceptual gamut, Professor Nielsen places the cesura between the liberal approach and the radical attitude, and further

affirms the proximity of radicalism to revolutionary action by pointing out
the practically necessary role of violence in radical reformism ["through
strikes (illegal or otherwise), demonstrations, disruptions, the seizure of
factories, or riots, some form of unauthorized pressure to bring about the
change in question" (cf. p. 163)].

According to this view revolution retains its attractiveness and its prestige
(the idea of a break in the evil genius of history and of the coming of a totally
new regime in accord with the humanistic aims of politics) since violence no
longer appears as a necessary ingredient of the concept itself: revolution is, in
principle, dissociated from its dramatic images, stripped of its emotional and
negative resonances. On the other hand, radicalism is provided with a stock of
illegal acts with a view to qualitative change. Now, reformist strategy has been
characterized by the decision to use the normal channels ("through normal
channels", p. 162), in order to amend the system from within.

At the level of definition, the theoretical status of radical reformism
appears to me inconsistent. The violence, more or less extensive, which is
carried along by radicalism and revolution falls outside these concepts into
the empirical contingency of particular circumstances. "It could, logically
speaking, be otherwise, but it isn't", it is said (p. 163). But to what logic is
reference here being made? If it is a matter of the logic of the political, that
embodies arbitrariness and violence in its very essence. Power is precisely that
area where a certain rationality coincides with a certain violence in such a
way that it essentially leaves itself open to a radical challenge which is arbitrary and violent as well. Because the order of preference maintained by a
society cannot impose itself on all with the force of pure evidence; because
the principles of legitimacy are likewise multiple and none of them possesses
an intrinsic and indisputable superiority over the others; because, finally,
politics goes on in the chiaroscuro of human opinions, one does not see how a
trial by force can be avoided if there is an insistence on a clear-cut decision
among the possibilities. The reasonable alternative to a violent outcome lies in
the consent to an authority which persuades its subjects to consider its decision as the expression of reason. Legitimate authority normally lasts as long
as it enjoys the support of a favourable public opinion. The liberal West is
distinguished in this connection by its remarkable tolerance towards the
plurality of values. But that is an unstable equilibrium, always threatened.

For my part, I would substitute for the static and spatial metaphor of a
*continuum* the dynamic one of a *dialectic* between reform and revolution.
Furthermore, within that dialectic I would place the dividing point between
reformism and revolutionary strategy. In fact, the determination of the

degree of radicality of reform lends itself to some very disputable estimations: for every radical, radical-and-a-half can always be found. In contrast, the distinction reform/revolution is much easier: one can establish that the change is produced by relying on the legal resources of the socio-political system, or, on the contrary, violently assails the system as such. Between liberal reformism and radical reformism the difference is one of degrees; between reform and revolution it is essential. Of course, the realm of violence is more vast than that of illegality, but it is still the case that legal forms constitute one of the principal mediations through which the volume of violence can be reduced. In principle "Right is [therefore] the sum total of those conditions within which the will of one person can be reconciled with the will of another in accordance with a universal law of freedom".[4] Now this objective itself cannot be realized without the help of a certain violence. It is Hobbes who has given this idea its striking formulation: "Laws without swords are but words". Even more, a juridical institution can also become the objective support for tyranny or abuse of power. In that case, the denunciation of the violence of power can only proceed from a meta-juridical, ethical, point of view: the radical basis for the invocation is of an ethical order. The problem is then to know whether it is better to endure an order morally unjust on certain points, rather than to risk engendering an even more terrible disorder than the violence imbedded in the legal system. There is no general answer to this problem: as Aristotle would say, it is a matter of prudence.

The determination of the degree of radicality sufficient to situate a reformism in ideological continuity with a revolutionary project, is, as we were saying, very much open to dispute. Let us take the hypothesis sketched by Professor Nielsen (pp. 162—64). I believe that the revolutionary authenticity of such measures can reasonably be put in doubt at this closing of the twentieth century. After 1789 and 1917, in the West as in the East, the revolutionary avant-grade aspires to a revolution which is no longer primarily socio-political but frankly cultural.

1. The passage from a presidential regime to a parliamentary (or vice-versa) does not seem to me particularly 'radical' since both regimes remain within the constitutional and pluralist frame of reference which characterizes liberal democracy. It would be quite otherwise if a dictatorship replaced these regimes.

It should be noted that the idea of reform, like the modern idea of revolution which was transposed from astronomy and mechanics to politics, does not itself determine any precise content. The bitterness with which the

concrete implications of a revolutionary praxis are debated in the name of a
'true' revolution is well-known, for what one deems to be the way to the
most human future, another declares to be defeat, treason, return to what is
most odious in the past. Is the advent of socialism in Russia (if socialism is
something besides the surrogate term for the myth of the perfect society)
essentially revolutionary, or does it mark the restoration of despotism? Certainly today, Revolution and Progress tend to be taken for the same thing,
but that is an amalgamation connected with the contemporary revolutionary
trend. "The word 'revolution' is always used in a favourable sense; when it is
no longer so used, we will have changed epoch", observed J. Monnerot.[5]

2. The redistribution of power between a federal state and its different
component states still maintains a federal structure. Now it is well known
how federalism has a bad reputation, in the mind of Quebec 'radicals' and
'revolutionaries' for instance, in spite of the fact that it passes for being a
'progressive' project in Europe.

3. Here the radical avant-grade rather brings us back to a type of pre-
Marxist socialism which short-circuits both authoritarian socialism and the
economic liberalism of capitalist regimes. The practice of self-management
aims to go beyond the authoritarian structure of industry in the East as in
the West. But we well know that, in both instances, some men still work in
factories and are commanded by others, without participating in the administration of the enterprise. The personnel and the formula for the ruling class
change; the class itself remains. The juridical status of property is no longer
invested with the same importance today as previously.

4. As for atheism, I doubt that the believers are today sufficiently numerous and sufficiently convinced to defend their faith by submitting to a test of
force. Few among them would be ready to redescend into the catacombs or
to revive the wars of religion. Atheism, institutionalized and made official,
would not add much to the practical atheism of the masses. The dissolving of
transcendental religion into secular religions, which today are constituted by
the great political ideologies, relativizes institutional atheism as a possible
element of a socio-political radicalism. Since Bayle (and perhaps Hobbes), we
know that a community of atheists can form a good State. Moreover, it alone
can be truly autonomous. But it is hard to see how radical reformism would
pass muster as a sort of Constantinism-in-reverse.

How do things now stand regarding the *choice* between reform and revolution? Professor Nielsen remarks at the beginning of his paper that this problem has been actively discussed within the socialist movement since Kautsky,

Bernstein, and Lenin. Is it possible to reflect critically upon the history which has taken place since and draw some instruction on our subject?

I venture to say that history has, in a certain way, decided in favour of Bernstein: the big industrial countries have been spared revolution. Besides the success of reformism was not the direct fruit of socialist parties, nor of revolutionary or reformist unionism, but rather of the managerial classes who have gradually assimilated what is essential in the socialist critique and taken the initiative in its applications. Interventionism has become reformist. That was enough for it to take on a counter-revolutionary meaning. Today a series of measures, embodied in the tissue of political democracy, have notably drawn together the condition of workers of countries which have chosen these different roads: social security system providing for medical care and the protection of the unemployed, institution of strong unions having a juridical status (the law protects or tries to protect union delegates), easing of access to schooling for disadvantaged classes, rise of the standard of living, etc. In fact "the spread of salaries is more narrow in the U.S.A. than in France and in France than in the U.S.S.R., which is rather unexpected by doctrinaires".[6] In this matter the 'bourgeois democracies' bear comparison with the 'popular democracies' rather well. This is an element to add to the dossier of the choice between reform and revolution: we are no longer at the beginning of a radically new, unpublicized problem. The swelling of the middle class inclines us rather to believe that we are in the phase of dissolution of the problem in the advanced industrial societies; the problem of the communist or capitalist form of 'civil society' gives way to a new question, that of aims: "Affluence, to what end?" What, finally, do we want? To speak with Eric Weil, now that modern society has surmounted the violence of external nature, that is, the pressure of need and the fear of barbarians, now that slave or serf is no longer necessary, that war between big states becomes improbable (except by way of small nations interposed between them), it is collectively that we come to the question of direction. We, who have avoided the socio-economic revolution through reforms, without having completely satisfied the indignation which could trigger it, have already entered upon the cultural revolution.

The aims mentioned by Professor Nielsen include certain aspects of this transformation of aspirations which are themselves here intended by the term 'cultural revolution'. However this formulation, which approximates that of Marcuse, does not emphasize enough, for my taste, the first requirement of a reasonable and meaningful freedom as compared with the growth of happiness and the elimination of suffering. It is Kant who warns us of the dangers of excessive politicization of the aspirations to happiness understood in a hedonistic sense: "The sovereign wants to make the people happy as he thinks best, and thus becomes a despot, while the people are unwilling to give up their universal human desire to seek happiness in their own way, and thus become rebels".[7] We well know with what force Dostoyevski has depicted the proud solicitude of the Grand Inquisitor ready to strip man of the aristocratic torment of freedom in order to deliver him into the happy servitude of democratic pastures. With what readiness the masses would unburden themselves of the weight of autonomy and responsibility in order to sink into a happiness without content! We also well know Nietzsche's execration of the 'last man', captive of his need for security and his little happiness . . .

To realize these aims the dogma of the collective ownership of the means of production, advanced as the best means to realize the objectives of the radical transformation of society, seems to me disputable. The analyses of Michels, Burnham, and Aron in the West and of Djilas in the East lead us to relativize the importance of the juridical status of property. Capitalism in the primitive and barbarous form with which Marx was acquainted has been changed and not been replaced by socialism, if by that term one should understand the institution of a free and classless international society. Thus the direct exploitation of the worker has been succeeded by a psycho-political and psycho-cultural alienation ushered in by the tightening of the decisional process in big industry and in global society. The upper levels of the oligarchies — technocratic, financial, political, cultural, *etc.* — reduce the multitude to mere objects of decision. In modern society, the owners of the means of production are no longer the managers: the apparatus of production and consumption is handled by the 'technostructure'. This is why the experts, servants and/or judges of the 'system', have the role of an *avant-garde* in the enlightened and constructive confrontations of modern society, as pointed out by Professor Nielsen at the end of his paper. Furthermore, the philosopher, conversant with socio-political reality, should also intervene in the debate, disentangling the ethical dimension of apparently technical choices offered to the community.

But again, what about the *dialectic* reform-revolution' considered in its greatest generality and with respect to the present situation?

The position which I adopt here on this problem is inspired by various articles that Professor Paul Ricoeur has devoted to this subject as well as to some related themes. The particular interest of these texts lies in the intimate conjunction of the strictest philosophical reflection with the most burning issues of our day.

Seen in the light of this thought, the general problem of *choice* between reform *or* revolution appears as a pseudo-problem, or, if you will, as an exclusive disjunction to be dissolved and a dynamic dialectic to be kept always alive. This is a position of principle to be inscribed in the fundamental dialectic of action, drawn towards the infinite, but rooted in the finite. Indeed, taken in its original upsurge, the revolutionary impetus carries the aspiration for a total transformation of society, a complete regeneration of humanity. That is why it is not surprising that the modern revolutionary spirit can be treated as a secularized prophetism or a metamorphosis of medieval millennialisms. But this noble aspiration cannot be totally achieved, even less be achieved all at once. To believe it would be precisely to surrender to eschatological illusion; to hold, on the contrary, that revolutions change nothing is the skeptical illusion. There can be but an approximate realization of this aspiration through the multiplicity of its acts and its works. Philosophical 'praxeology' must frankly assume the incurable ambiguity of finite objectification, at once expression and concealment, realization and alienation, of the absolute aspiration inherent in our most profound desire. At the same time that it embodies the intention of its total accomplishment, the deed veils its full splendour. The deed bears witness to the absoluteness of the will, but at the same time that it verifies its authenticity, it contracts it into a finite concretion. It is in the deed that the unlimitedness of consciousness and the limitation of the world are mediated.

In order not to remain abstract, the task of liberation must be actualized in deeds and institutions which give it an objective reality. But the absoluteness of the idea already begins to become alienated with the very movement by which it historically comes to be. The revolution crumbles into concrete reforms. Surrounding itself with the precarious harshness of a new order of things, the Revolution loses its ideal splendour. What a deadly staleness is exhaled from the new order when it has left behind the absolute of the dream ... But also, on the other hand, the necessity of finite mediations becomes a trap where revolutionary dynamism risks being stifled and perhaps lost entirely, if it is not supported and always re-launched by the inexhaustible project of total change. Unless magic and historical actions are to be confused, the fatal antitheses between reform and revolution must be short-circuited in favour of a dialectic of concrete action which displays the logical opposition of concepts as a process of contradictions overcome. In other words, one must be revolutionary in the long run, and reformist in the short.

The revolutionary utopia gives to human effort its greatest, its most long-range, scope; on the other hand reformist action embodies the total objective in determinate institutions which, without it, would wander in a dream. The intimate articulation of the short-term achievement on the long-run project breathes life and meaning into a reformism which tends to be short-sighted and asthmatic when left to itself. Revolutionary fervour goads on the reformer's prudent and precise action; but the latter sifts out the incoherencies of global and sudden change and disciplines revolutionary fury. Not everything can change at once, that is all too evident. One must approach installation of a new society from a certain angle and follow through in a certain way according to a definite strategy. The instantaneous passage from one type of society to another is, properly speaking, impossible. After all, to change individually and even collectively means to remain the same in certain aspects; otherwise there would be no substratum for such a change, and we would be face-to-face with an absolute creation. But in splitting into an indefinite series of reforms, the revolutionary ideal is already virtually pinned down, reconquered by the global force of 'the system'. Following the bent of reformism, the radical dissident takes the groove which leads him back within the 'social mechanism'. Reformism thus participates in the fundamental ambiguity of concrete action since it is at once the intelligent way to be conservative and the real way to be revolutionary. That finite objectification be twisted into a deadly alienation, that is the permanent risk of an action which would be effective in the world as it is.

In our 'bourgeois democracies', to take up again Professor Nielsen's expression, and what I would call, as Aron does, 'constitutional-pluralist democracies' (just as one speaks of either 'popular democracy', or 'totalitarian democracy', according to his point of view): Is revolution morally and politically justified? On the other hand, can liberal democracy defend itself by resorting to 'forces of order' without contradicting itself?

It is commonplace in the justification of revolutionary violence to oppose to the arbitrariness and violence of the legal order the salutary and purifying violence of revolution. In fact, serious and prolonged tyrannical situations may develop with regard to which it is hard to see how a remedy could be found which dispensed with violence. Political rationality, particularly open to degeneration, more often then we generally admit fences us into some limit-situation where we must choose in the most risky uncertainty. Normally the sane State embodies a certain reason marching through history, a rationality which enlists into its service a certain violence, the regulated violence of legal constraints and defensive war (which may go as far as preventive aggression). But if this State becomes crazy, i.e., violent, what is to be done? In such a conjuncture, the recourse to a liberating violence is legitimate. Even more, passivity may be culpable to the extent that I make myself an accomplice of unfettered power. Professor Ricoeur then speaks of an 'ethics of distress' [éthique de détresse]. Today, notably in the Third World, such situations do exist. Yesterday, the German resistance movement had to answer to the question. It is known how Dietrich Bonhoeffer, in particular, answered it, taking upon himself the meaning and the consequences of the tyrannicide. At what exact point is such and such a form of violent resistance justified? There is no totally comprehensive and determinate casuistry which would allow me, personally, to come to an indisputable conclusion — in the sense of such and such an option, here and now. I respect both Gandhian non-violence, morally the most costly struggle, and Simone Weil's confession to G. Thibon in 1941: "I shall never expiate sufficiently the criminal error of pacifism".[8] I bow to C. Torres's commitment and to Helder Camara's declaration: "As for myself, I prefer a thousand times more to be killed than to kill". One should not despise too quickly the particular effectiveness of pure and prophetic testimony, apparently without historical implications but acting upon the conscience; these gestures belong to history now in the making (or which will be made) as an anticipated incarnation, untimely and without compromise, of the humanistic ends of politics, which the man of action pursues by other means, ordinarily less pure; they light the road by symbolizing the approximation of the final objective: a fraternal and reconciled humanity. It is not granted to all to imitate these exceptional destinies. As for us, especially if we are in a position to attract a great number of persons to follow us into action, it is no doubt prudent to evaluate as well as possible the consequences of our acts; to lead one's followers to heroic catastrophe does not seem to me to be a reasonable policy. To be sure, an 'ethics of responsibility' does not exclude the use of force with the same intransigence as does as 'ethics of conviction', but it does require the conciliation of the greatest effectiveness possible with the minimum of violence if violence is necessary.

In our 'advanced industrial societies', are we in a situation such that revolutionary action could be justified? On the other hand, does the actual relation of forces within society provide a sufficient political justification for a reasonable commitment to that course? In other words, has the revolution some chance to succeed? An affirmative answer to the first question does not necessarily imply an identical answer to the second. On the other hand, it is improbable that the revolution will succeed if it does not develop out of a revolutionary situation.

The prophet of the angry students, Herbert Marcuse, answers yes to the first question; he remains skeptical concerning the second, conscious as he is that, no matter what has been said, a revolution without the working class is difficult to conceive. However his pessimism regarding the 'new historical subject' seems to have become more profound recently: he now turns towards the peasants. "The peasants alone", he declares, "are capable of changing radically today's world. The students are only the directing minorities of the revolution. I do not believe in the workers as a revolutionary factor since, especially in the heavily developed countries, they are integrated and merged with the bourgeoisie. Nor, if it really does exist, do I have any more confidence in the intellectual class as an active factor of revolutions, because this 'class' has only an intellectual and political preparation; it is not active, it is not turned towards action".[9]

According to Marcuse, within this uni-dimensional society of ours, alienation is total: "I believe that nobody is free in this society. Nobody".[10] Now, this alienation is so much the more unjustifiable "in that never in the history of the humanity have the resources necessary for creating a free society existed to such a degree".[11] Technical rationality now serves the productivist system, the manipulation of individuals by advertising and the mass-media, repression and even over-repression, the conditioning of the masses in leisure as well as in work, etc. But it could as well serve the advent of a society, free, happy, diversified, qualitatively new in its needs and its aspirations. In that society, "Eros redefines reason in its own terms. Reasonable is that which sustains the order of gratification".[12] However the majority, well integrated and relatively satisfied with its lot, is not conscious of its own alienation. Besides there exists an elite of intellectuals who, like Marcuse, are conscious of the unhappiness and are ready to lead this society towards a new culture under the double sign, of Orpheus and Narcissus:

> Là, tout n'est qu'ordre et beauté,
> Luxe, calme et volupté.

[There all is order and beauty,/Luxury, calm and sensuousness.]

Citing these verses of Baudelaire, Marcuse adds: "This is perhaps the only context in which the word *order* loses its repressive connotation: here, it is the order of gratification which the free Eros creates".[13] With its very superior degree of lucidity and of human responsibility, why would this elite not have the moral right to take the leadership of the movement of liberation (with its inevitable element of intolerance and violence)? Given that capitalist society is fundamentally unjust and rests in the final analysis on an indefensible 'repressive tolerance', namely upon an appearance of freedom linked to the reality of an institutionalized violence, by what right would one oppose the *diktat* of this enlightened and generous minority?[14] Is it not its task to proceed with the re-education of the needs of the people, now far too vulgar? In the short run, the sole liberating tolerance, then, would mean "intolerance against movements from the Right and toleration of movements from the Left".[15] As a consequence of the absence of the concrete conditions capable of making universal tolerance workable, it is necessary to practice in the meantime a partisan tolerance and a counter-indoctrination in order to restore an equilibrium between Left and Right: "Withdrawal of tolerance from regressive movements before they can become active; intolerance even towards thought, opinion and word are finally intolerance in the opposite direction that is, toward the self-styled conservatives, and to the political Right — these anti-democratic notions respond to the actual development of the democratic society which has destroyed the basis for universal tolerance. The conditions under which tolerance will again become a liberating and humanizing force have still to be created."[16] Such is the teaching of the little black book.

For these leaders, self-designated in the circumstances, there must be troops and a strategy. Marcuse recognizes that the working class is now integrated, at least in the United States, and that it wishes to be so. The revolutionary potential has emigrated towards other marginal groups: students, hippies, intellectuals, leftist groups immigrant workers and — last but not least — the American Blacks. By their grouping on huge campuses, by their relative material independence, by their knowledge, by the idealism and ardour proper to their age, by their politicization, students constitute a critical mass, eminently flammable, predestined to serve as an ignition device. Moreover, 'student power' is concentrated in a strategic place of the advance society, in fact at its control-center, the University, which is, in the bargain, the most critical and the most liberal and consequently the most vulnerable institution of society. The new revolutionary strategy passes by way of the University as the old strategy rested on the industrial proletariat. It is through students that the liberating conflagration may come by communicating their revolt to "the substratum of the outcasts and outsiders, the exploited and persecuted of other races and other colors, the unemployed and the unemployable. They exist outside the democratic process; their life is the most immediate and the most real need for ending intolerable conditions and institutions. Thus their opposition is revolutionary, even if their consciousness is not".[17] As to the role of violence within revolution, Marcuse is without illusion:

> L'Express: In order to destroy this society, guilty of violence, you consider that
> violence is at once legitimate and desirable. Do you then judge it impos-
> sible to evolve peacefully and within the democratic framework towards
> a non-repressive and more free society?
> Marcuse:   The students have said it: a revolution is always as violent as the violence
> which it fights. I think they are right".[18]

For his part R. Aron, recently asked him: "In short, your philosophy is
violence to arrive at a completely pacified society?" "That is exactly so," he
answered. Aron comments: "Answer enough for judging that philosophy;
there is no example of violence leading to total pacification (which I do not
believe compatible with human nature in any case)."[19]

This contradiction between the means and the end to be reached betrays,
in our opinion, the incoherence of this impassioned thinking. In a general
way, Marcuse under-estimates the weight and the constraints inherent in the
vast and complex organizations which provide the structure of 'technodemocracy'. On the other hand, he over-estimates the attractive force of the liber-
tarian utopia and the creative value of spontaneity. Certainly the utopian
imagination fills an eminently positive social function, that of opening to the
fullest the field of possibilities offered to our collective freedom and thus of
giving a long term direction to our effort. This aspect is lacking, it seems to
me, in Popper's article. On the other hand, I join with Popper to say that any
utopia which does not recognize itself as such is pregnant with tyranny. One
does not bend the complexity of 'social nature' to the simplicity of an idea
without some violence. The structure of modern society is far too complex
and too sensitive to evolve in a progressive direction as a result of improvised
and brutal actions. These gestures, immediate and without any result, are
more like shouts to be interpreted than energetic remedies for the 'malaise of
civilization'. Sometimes inevitable, and salutary in shaking up an indifferent
public opinion and the inertia of certain responsible authorities, the recourse
to 'direct action' first of all sharpens the antagonism within society. The
conservative undertow we are now in tends to demonstrate that, in the short
term at least, violent and global challenging of the System reinforces the
'structure of power' that it would strike down. Today the coherent and
responsible revolutionary ought undoubtedly to start by revolutionizing the
models of action inherited from the past (the flamboyant and theatrical style
of the modern revolutions with their barricades, their solemn public executions, their conspiracies, etc.) and to invent original forms of struggle which
preserve the positive accomplishments of modernity, and particularly a certain political liberalism. In our eyes the 'formal liberties' which many leftist

intellectuals despise, assured as they are of enjoying them, constitute a part of the quality of life from now on. Not every crisis of growth is necessarily cathartic; it can also be regressive. Among those who challenge the prevailing society, some place themselves short of modern society, owing to their incapacity to play its rational game, while others are drawn towards a specifically political synthesis beyond the effective but formal rationality of technique, beyond the particular holies of the historical community, beyond the individual's lack of fulfillment, but yet starting with the individual, his community, and his society. One cannot place on the same footing the romantic *lamento* of empirical particulars, and the demand for *meaning*. It will be understood that it is a dialectical conception of revolution that is in question here, a conception which encompasses the old reformism while going beyond it, which yields to the law of long and complex mediations with a view to a synthesis that will be reasonable even though also imperfect. I deplore the anarchist, and even nihilist, twist given by the professionals of the violent left to their action. But in this only-too-uneven and long-winded struggle with Power, I fear repression even more, the slide towards a sort of larval fascism. I share this uneasiness with a number of moderate socialists and liberals — of the right and left, to use common language of politics — who are hardly suspected of complacency towards 'bourgeois democracy'. I think of J. Habermas who did not hesitate to call the SDS a "fascism of the left".[20] Furthermore, I recall having heard Paul Ricoeur[21] speak of "red facism" with reference to certain tactics of confrontation, (raids, occupations, kidnappings. sabotage of meetings set up by 'the Right' . . . or of other leftist sects, *etc.*). Maurice Cranston has sharply criticized Marcuse's theses on "repressive tolerance".[22] Alasdair McIntyre judges these no more favourably: "The majority was, in the Soviet Union, the passive object of a re-education in the interest of their own liberation. What Marcuse invites us to repeat is part of the experience of Stalinism . . . Marcuse underrates most men as they are; the false contempt for the majority into which his theory leads him underpins policies that would in fact produce just that passivity and that irrationalism with which he charges contemporary society. The philosophy of the young Hegelians, fragments of Marxism and revised chunks of Freud's meta-psychology: out of these materials Marcuse produced a theory that, like so many of its predecessors, invokes the great names of freedom and reason while betraying their substance at every important point."[23] Z. Brzezinski fears a long-lasting hardening of the reactionary and conservative elements of American society.[24] In his most recent book, M. Duverger, analysing the conservative effects of confrontation, warns us: "If the economic structure of technodemocracy is very strong, its political structure is less so. Any liberal system which rests upon the tacit agreement of citizens to apply a set of rules necessary for the social life by themselves remains fragile. Without self-discipline and without respect for others, democratic institutions can no longer function and capitalism turns towards dictatorship in order to survive."[25]

If the problem is now envisaged from the viewpoint of the liberal state, I share, and I believe without contradiction, the attitude at once firm and open, of Raymond Aron formulated at the *Rencontres internationales de Genève*, in September 1969:

The principle of a liberal society is not to accept the violation of its own legality, this legality being the condition of the security of each and of the institutionalization of conflicts. That having been said, I am ready to admit that in some historical circumstances, the liberal society would be wrong to maintain in all its rigour the principle of respect for legality. It is better sometimes that the opponents resort to more or less illegal methods in order that the satisfied society become conscious of the dissatisfaction of certain groups and that the violence of the threat force it to make reforms. I know that I am on a tight rope. There is a certain consent to illegality which carries with it the death of institutions; but there is also a juridical rigidity which prevents the transformation of institutions .... In each precise case, I believe I can say where the limit is located. But if it is asked of me in the abstract how a liberal society maintains its liberal structure during a phase of acute conflicts, I answer that each case must be studied individually. As to what touches the contemporary period, the danger is that the resource to symbolic illegality or to violence, even verbal, within institutions grounded in civility would lead to the ruin of these institutions .... The struggle is, in the face of absurd or impossible demands, to denounce them as such; in the face of illegality, to maintain legality; but if the illegal protest carries in itself the will for necessary reform, we will not answer simply by the maintenance of existing institutions; we will try to suppress the basic causes of this protest, even of a violent protest.[26]

So we see that whatever the aspect under which one attacks the question, one comes more and more to the shifting grounds of reason vs. violence, which P. Ricoeur calls "the political paradox". From whatever quarter they come, is it not appropriate to distrust those who act with too much assurance within this terrible contradiction? In trying to enlighten the unlikely marriage of equity and force, of freedom and constraint, the philosopher, like a tightrope walker, moves forward under threat. This suggestion intrigues me. I venture to believe that after having tried to a few steps on the tight rope, I can count on the net of your kindly remarks!

*Université de Montréal*

## NOTES

[1] "Les révolutions liquident la faiblesse et accouchent la force". Bertrand de Jouvenel, *Du pouvoir*. Genève, 1945 (*On power*, Boston, 1962).

[2] *Les constitutions de la France depuis 1789*. Garnier, p. 83.

[3] Julien Freund, *L'essence du politique*, Sirey, 1965, p. 579.

[4] E. Kant, 'Metaphysics, of Morals,' in *Kant's Political Writings*, translated by H. B. Nisbet (Cambridge 1971), p. 133.

[5] J. Monnerot, *Sociologie de la révolution*, Fayard, 1969, p. 8.

[6] J. Fourastié, *Les 400,000 heures*, Laffont, 1965, p. 143.

[7] E. Kant, 'Theory and Practice' in *Kant's Political Writings*, p. 83.

[8] Quoted by G. Thibon in *La violence*, Recherches et débats, DDB, 1967, p. 121.

[9] Interview published from the daily Mexican newspaper *Excelsior* in *La Presse*, 29 March 1972.

[10] Interview in *L'express*, 23–29 September 1968, p. 126.

[11] *Ibid.*, p. 125.

[12] H. Marcuse, *Eros and Civilisation* (Vintage, New York, 1963), p. 205.

[13] *Ibid.*, p. 149.

[14] On this idea of an educating dictatorship applied by an intellectual elite, cf. *Eros and Civilization*, p. 206; *One-Dimensional Man* (Beacon, 1964) pp. 251–257; *A Critique of Pure Tolerance* (Beacon, 1969), pp. 81–123, esp. 117–123; 'Le vieillissement de la psychoanalyse' in *Partisans*, October-November, 1966, p. 19; *L'express*, 23–29 September, 1968, pp. 126–127; *Essay on Liberation* (Beacon) p. 89.

[15] H. Marcuse, 'Repressive Tolerance' in *A Critique of Pure Tolerance*, p. 109.

[16] *Ibid.*, p. 110–111.

[17] H. Marcuse, *One-Dimensional Man*, Beacon, p. 256.

[18] *L'express*, 23–29, September 1968, p. 125. Since that interview some years have passed. With the benefit of that distancing, Marcuse has himself proceeded to the critical revision of his positions on this point. His self-criticism has developed precisely in the direction of the apprehensions formulated hereafter. To the question of S. Keen, Marcuse replies: "Yes, I must say about myself that I have probably emphasized unduly the most extreme and radical goals of the revolution-to-be. And I did not see to what extent we are already in the midst of what I call a preventive counterrevolution in which the established society is using all possible mental and physical means to suppress the radical opposition. So the heroic period of the militant student opposition is over. You see the heroic period was that of the hippies and Yippies. They did their thing. They did an indispensable job. They were heroes. They probably still are, but we have moved into a different period, a higher period in terms of historical sequence. We are now in the midst of the organized counter-revolution. You cannot have fun with fascism. What is required is a wholesale re-examination of the strategy of the movement." (*Psychology Today*, February, 1971, p. 66). See also the discussion with Hans Magnus Enzensberger Kurbuch 22, 15 December 1971, reproduced in *C'est demain la veille*. Seuil, 1973; *Forces*, no. 22, 1973, p. 56.

Marcuse concludes that interview in tossing back to the students themselves the task of elaborating and putting into practice a new strategy.

[19] R. Aron, *La révolution introuvable* (Fayard), p. 119; cf. *The Elusive Revolution*, (New York 1969).

[20] Quoted in *La fin de l'utopie*, Seuil, 1968, p. 139, note 6.

[21] See particularly his forward to J. Debelle, *Conceptions de l'Université*, Editions universitaire; *Le Monde*, 10, 11, 12 June, 1968, reprinted in *Esprit*; 'Le philosophe et le politique devant la question de la liberté' in *La liberté et l'ordre social*, Genève, 1969; 'L'avenir de l'Université' in *L'enseignement supérieur: bilans et prospective*, Les Presses de l'Université de Montréal, 1971. Cf. *Political and Social Essays*, coll. and ed. D. Stewart and J. Bien (Athens, Ohio, 1974).

[22] M. Cranston, *The New Left*, The Bodley Head, London, 1970.

[23] A. McIntyre, *Marcuse*, 'Fontana Modern Masters', London, 1970, p. 92.

[24] Z. Brzezinski, *Between Two Ages*, The Viking Press, 1970, pp. 236–256. See also: M. Crozier, *La société bloquée*, (Seuil, 1970; cf. *The stalled society* (New York 1973).

[25] M. Duverger, *Janus*, Fayard, 1972, p. 240.

[26] 'Liberté libérale ou liberté libertaire' in *La liberté et l'ordre social* (Genève 1969), pp. 216–217.

# INDEX

195

# THEORY AND DECISION LIBRARY

An International Series in the Philosophy and Methodology
of the Social and Behavioral Sciences

*Editors:*

Gerald Eberlein, *University of Technology, Munich*
Werner Leinfellner, *University of Nebraska*

1. Günther Menges (ed.), *Information, Inference, and Decision.* 1974, viii + 195 pp.
2. Anatol Rapoport (ed.), *Game Theory as a Theory of Conflict Resolution.* 1974, v + 283 pp.
3. Mario Bunge (ed.), *The Methodological Unity of Science.* 1973, viii + 264 pp.
4. Colin Cherry (ed.), *Pragmatic Aspects of Human Communication.* 1974, ix + 178 pp.
5. Friedrich Rapp (ed.), *Contributions to a Philosophy of Technology. Studies in the Structure of Thinking in the Technological Sciences.* 1974, xv + 228 pp.
6. Werner Leinfellner and Eckehart Köhler (eds.), *Developments in the Methodology of Social Science.* 1974, x + 430 pp.
7. Jacob Marschak, *Economic Information, Decision and Prediction. Selected Essays.* 1974, three volumes, xviii + 389 pp.; xii + 362 pp.; x + 399 pp.
8. Carl-Axel S. Staël von Holstein (ed.), *The Concept of Probability in Psychological Experiments.* 1974, xi + 153 pp.
9. Heinz J. Skala, *Non-Archimedean Utility Theory.* 1975, xii + 138 pp.
10. Karin D. Knorr, Hermann Strasser, and Hans Georg Zilian (eds.), *Determinants and Controls of Scientific Developments.* 1975, ix + 460 pp.
11. Dirk Wendt, and Charles Vlek (eds.), *Utility, Probability, and Human Decision Making. Selected Proceedings of an Interdisciplinary Research Conference, Rome, 3–6 September, 1973.* 1975, viii + 418 pp.
12. John C. Harsanyi, *Essays on Ethics, Social Behavior, and Scientific Explanation.* 1976, xvi + 262 pp.
13. Gerhard Schwödiauer (ed.), *Equilibrium and Disequilibrium in Economic Theory. Proceedings of a Conference Organized by the Institute for Advanced Studies, Vienna, Austria, July 3–5, 1974.* 1978, l + 736 pp.
14. V. V. Kolbin, *Stochastic Programming.* 1977, xii + 195 pp.
15. R. Mattessich, *Instrumental Reasoning and Systems Methodology.* 1978, xxii + 396 pp.
16. H. Jungermann and G. de Zeeuw (eds.), *Decision Making and Change in Human Affairs.* 1977, xv + 526 pp.
18. A. Rapoport, W. E. Stein, and G. J. Burkheimer, *Response Models for Detection of Change.* 1978 (forthcoming)
19. H. J. Johnson, J. J. Leach, and R. G. Mühlmann (eds.), *Revolutions, Systems, and Theories; Essays in Political Philosophy.* 1978
20. S. Gale and G. Olsson (eds.), *Philosophy in Geography.* 1978 (forthcoming).